A CULTURAL HISTORY OF WESTERN EMPIRES IN THE AGE OF ENLIGHTENMENT

A Cultural History of Western Empires
General Editor: Antoinette Burton

Volume 1
A Cultural History of Western Empires in Antiquity
Edited by Carlos Noreña

Volume 2
A Cultural History of Western Empires in the Middle Ages
Edited by Matthew Gabriele

Volume 3
A Cultural History of Western Empires in the Renaissance
Edited by Ania Loomba

Volume 4
A Cultural History of Western Empires in the Age of Enlightenment
Edited by Ian Coller

Volume 5
A Cultural History of Western Empires in the Age of Empire
Edited by Kirsten McKenzie

Volume 6
A Cultural History of Western Empires in the Modern Age
Edited by Patricia Lorcin

A CULTURAL HISTORY OF WESTERN EMPIRES IN THE AGE OF ENLIGHTENMENT

Edited by Ian Coller

BLOOMSBURY ACADEMIC
LONDON • NEW YORK • OXFORD • NEW DELHI • SYDNEY

BLOOMSBURY ACADEMIC
Bloomsbury Publishing Plc
50 Bedford Square, London, WC1B 3DP, UK
1385 Broadway, New York, NY 10018, USA
29 Earlsfort Terrace, Dublin 2, Ireland

BLOOMSBURY, BLOOMSBURY ACADEMIC and the Diana logo are trademarks of Bloomsbury Publishing Plc

First published in Great Britain 2018
Paperback edition published 2023

Copyright © Ian Coller and Contributors, 2018

Ian Coller and Contributors have asserted their right under the Copyright, Designs and Patents Act, 1988, to be identified as Author of this work.

Cover design: Raven Design
Cover image: Dido Elizabeth Belle © ART Collection/Alamy Stock Photo

All rights reserved. No part of this publication may be reproduced or transmitted in any form or by any means, electronic or mechanical, including photocopying, recording, or any information storage or retrieval system, without prior permission in writing from the publishers.

Bloomsbury Publishing Plc does not have any control over, or responsibility for, any third-party websites referred to or in this book. All internet addresses given in this book were correct at the time of going to press. The author and publisher regret any inconvenience caused if addresses have changed or sites have ceased to exist, but can accept no responsibility for any such changes.

A catalogue record for this book is available from the British Library.

A catalog record for this book is available from the Library of Congress

ISBN: HB: 978-1-4742-4262-2
PB: 978-1-3503-5824-9
ePDF: 978-1-3502-9039-6
eBook: 978-1-3502-9038-9

Series: The Cultural Histories Series

Typeset by RefineCatch Limited, Bungay, Suffolk
Printed and bound in Great Britain

To find out more about our authors and books visit www.bloomsbury.com and sign up for our newsletters.

CONTENTS

ILLUSTRATIONS vii
GENERAL EDITOR'S PREFACE xiii

   Introduction 1
   Ian Coller

1 War 23
   Christopher Tozzi

2 Trade 45
   Junko Thérèse Takeda

3 Natural Worlds 69
   Laura J. Mitchell

4 Labor 93
   Abigail Swingen

5 Mobility 117
   Michael H. Fisher

6 Sexuality 143
   Merry E. Wiesner-Hanks

7 Resistance 167
   Karwan Fatah-Black

8	Race *Vanita Seth*	185

FURTHER READING	209
NOTES ON CONTRIBUTORS	227
INDEX	229

ILLUSTRATIONS

INTRODUCTION

0.1 Four Chinese gods, 1728, by Bernard Picart. Found in the collection of Rijksmuseum, Amsterdam. Credit: Fine Art Images/Heritage Images/Getty Images.   10

0.2 *Candide; or Optimism*, 1759, illustration for the 1785 edition of the philosophical tale by Voltaire (1694–1778). Paris, Bibliothèque Nationale de France (Library). Credit: De Agostini Picture Library/Getty Images.   13

0.3 Nicolas Monsiau (1754–1837), French School. Decree of the National Convention Abolishing Slavery in the Colonies, February 4, 1794. Paris, Musée Carnavalet. Credit: Christophel Fine Art/UIG via Getty Images.   20

CHAPTER 1

1.1 Edouard Detaille (1848–1912), French School. The Battle of Fontenoy (1745), won by Maurice de Saxe. 1912. Oil on canvas, 2.10 × 3.20 m. Paris, Musée de l'Armée. Credit: Christophel Fine Art/UIG via Getty Images.   24

1.2 The Surrender of Breda, by Diego Velasquez (1599–1660). Madrid, Museo Del Prado. Credit: De Agostini Picture Library/Getty Images.   27

1.3 The north front of the Invalides: Mansart's dome above Bruant's pedimented central block. Credit: Daniel Vorndran/DXR. Licensed under the Creative Commons Attribution-Share Alike 3.0 Unported license: https://creativecommons.org/licenses/by-sa/3.0/deed.en. 27

1.4 Exercitiegenootschap Sneek by Hermanus van der Velde, 1786. Sneek, Netherlands, Fries Scheepvaart Museum. Public domain. 29

1.5 Opening of The Estates-General, Versailles, 1789 (1885). Credit: The Print Collector/Getty Images. 40

CHAPTER 2

2.1 City of Batavia, headquarters of the Dutch East India Company in south-east Asia (Indonesia), in 1619. Credit: Universal History Archive/UIG via Getty Images. 48

2.2 Shah Abbas I "The Great," fighting against the Turks. Fresco, seventeenth century. Sutun Chihil Palace, Isfahan, Iran. Credit: PHAS/UIG via Getty Images. 54

2.3 Brothers Wetter's Indian textile factory by Joseph Gabriel Rossetti, 1764. Municipal Museum, Orange. Credit: Leemage/Corbis via Getty Images. 55

2.4 December 16, 1773: A group of Bostonians dressed as Native Americans dump crates of imported British tea into Boston Harbor as a protest against the British Tea Act. Credit: MPI/Getty Images. 59

2.5 Turkish merchants, detail from The Port of Marseille, 1754, by Claude-Joseph Vernet (1714–89). Credit: De Agostini Picture Library/Getty Images. 64

CHAPTER 3

3.1 Jan Leeghwater, Dutch mill builder and hydraulic engineer, 1608. Print by W. Steelink, 1870. Credit: The Print Collector/Getty Images. 73

3.2 Harvesting of the almond crop at Kand-i Badam (Bhawani), sixteenth century. © The British Library Board. 75

ILLUSTRATIONS ix

3.3 The Vergenoegd Farm of Mr. Lochner (South Africa). Watercolor by Jan Brandes, 1778. Public domain: courtesy of the Rijksmuseum, the Netherlands. 79

3.4 Tuna preparation depicted in "Conil de la Frontera," from Civitates Orbis Terrarum. Georg Braun and Franz Hogenberg, sixteenth century. Credit: DEA/R. MERLO/De Agostini Picture Library/Getty Images. 82

3.5 Plantation in Surinam. Oil Painting by Dirk Valkenberg, 170. Public domain: courtesy of the Rijksmuseum, the Netherlands. 85

CHAPTER 4

4.1 Map of the Caribbean, antique Spanish atlas, eighteenth century. Credit: goldhafen/Getty Images. 95

4.2 Men rowing canoes through Amsterdam. Warehouse of the West India Company in Amsterdam, the Netherlands. Built in 1641. Credit: Bettmann/Getty Images. 97

4.3 Map of Martinique created by Matthieu Seutter. Details: Merchants and Native American Indian. Musée du Nouveau Monde. Credit: De Agostini Picture Library/Getty Images. 99

4.4 View of a sugar plantation in the West Indies. Public domain. 101

4.5 James II (1633–1701). © National Maritime Museum, Greenwich, London. 105

4.6 Central America, Jamaica, West Indies, 1721. Credit: Historic Map Works LLC/Osher Map Library. 107

4.7 "A New and Exact Map of the Coast, Countries and Islands within the Limits of the South Sea Company," Herman Moll. Public domain. 110

4.8 Cover of the English translation of the *Asiento* contract signed by Britain and Spain in 1713 as part of the Treaty of Utrecht that ended the War of Spanish Succession. Public domain. 112

CHAPTER 5

5.1	Dutch Fluyt (1642). Public domain. Courtesy of the Rijksmuseum, the Netherlands.	123
5.2	Catherine II Empress of Russia portrait, engraved for the Eclectic by Geo. E. Perine, N.Y. Public domain. Retrieved from the Library of Congress, https://www.loc.gov/item/96516267/.	126
5.3	Characters of the French Revolution. Musée de la Ville de Paris, Musée Carnavalet, Paris, France. Credit: Le Sueur Brothers.	128
5.4	William Penn. Held at the Los Angeles County Museum of Art, California. Public domain.	132
5.5	Stowage of the British slave ship *Brookes* under the regulated slave trade act of 1788. Public domain. Retrieved from the Library of Congress, http://www.loc.gov/pictures/item/98504459/.	136
5.6	Title page of *The Interesting Narrative of the Life of Olaudah Equiano*, 1794. Public domain.	141

CHAPTER 6

6.1	King Louis XIV of France and the royal family in the personae of classical deities, *c.* 1670. Living room of the Oeil-de-Boeuf of the Grand Trianon of Versailles. Credit: Roger Viollet/Getty Images.	144
6.2	Portrait of Mademoiselle Guimard, ballerina of the Paris Opera, by Frederic Schall (1752–1825). France, eighteenth century. Nantes, Musée des Beaux-Arts de Nantes. Credit: De Agostini Picture Library/Getty Images.	149
6.3	Female musicians lead a concubine of the sultan into a room, miniature from Turkish Memories, Arabic manuscript, Cicogna Codex, Turkey seventeenth century. Credit: De Agostini Picture Library/Getty Images.	150
6.4	Bailiffs arrest a woman for selling sex, from A Harlot's Progress, 1732. Engraving by William Hogarth. Credit: Culture Club/Getty Images.	154
6.5	A family group, with the patriarch smoking a pipe, early seventeenth century. Woodcut from the Roxburghe Ballads (early seventeenth century). Credit: Ann Ronan Pictures/Print Collector/Getty Images.	156

ILLUSTRATIONS xi

6.6 A casta painting showing a couple of differing ancestry and their child, 1774, by Andres de Islas (active *c*. 1753–75). Mexican painter. Museum of America, Madrid, Spain. Credit: PHAS/UIG via Getty Images. 158

6.7 A black woman and mixed-race woman of Santo Domingo, colour engraving from a drawing by Labrousse (active 1796), from Encyclopedia of voyages, by Jacques Grasset de Saint-Sauveur. Greater Antilles, eighteenth century. Paris, Bibliothèque des Arts Decoratifs (Library). Credit: DeAgostini/Getty Images. 162

CHAPTER 7

7.1 Engraving Print Depicting Scene of Surinam: The Slave Rebellion by D.K. Bonatti. Credit: Historical Picture Archive/CORBIS/Corbis via Getty Images. 169

7.2 Smugglers coming ashore, *c*. 1750. Credit: Rischgitz/Getty Images. 173

7.3 Dutch ships fight Portuguese carracks in long-running trade dispute. Credit: Richard Schlecht/National Geographic/Getty Images. 175

7.4 Toussaint Louverture, former black slave who went over to the French after the first proclamation of the abolition of slavery. Credit: Photo12/UIG/Getty Images. 178

7.5 The Bostonians Paying the Exciseman, or Tarring and Feathering, 1774. Lithograph by Snooks. Credit: The New York Historical Society/Getty Images. 182

CHAPTER 8

8.1 Antique colored illustrations: Ethnicities: American Indian, Mongolian, Caucasian, Ethiopian, Malay. Credit: ilbusca via Getty Images. 186

8.2 Explorers on the Shores of the Saint Lawrence River, seventeenth century. Credit: duncan1890 via Getty Images. 188

8.3 Point of No Return Monument detail, infamous gateway of slavery, Route of Slaves (Route des Esclaves), Ouidah, Benin. Credit: Gallo Images. 200

8.4   Vintage engraving of a Plantation Master with whip at the Slave market, while a man begs not to be separated from his son and daughter. From the antislavery story De planter brunel en zijne slaven asa en neno, by Henderikus Christophorus Schetsberg, Netherlands. 1858. Credit: duncan1890 via Getty Images.   201

Every effort has been made to trace copyright holders and to obtain their permission for the use of copyright material. The publisher apologizes for any errors or omissions and would be grateful if notified of any corrections that should be incorporated in future reprints or editions of this book.

GENERAL EDITOR'S PREFACE

Histories of empire have been transformed in the last three decades by a combination of new methods, new archives, and a new generation of scholars who have come of age in a postcolonial world. The impact of these historical forces on how imperialism is understood has been remarkable. For decades the province of geopolitics, diplomacy, and the "official mind," imperial history is now just as likely to be told from the bottom up as from the top down. The rise of cultural history has played a significant role in how we think about and narrate imperialism from the ancient world to the twentieth century. With an emphasis on evidence drawn from literature, the arts, life-writing, and a host of fragmentary sources, cultural historians think through patterns of representation and experience that shape the conditions in which histories of all kinds—economic, political, social—happen. They investigate often overlooked subjects and offer new angles of vision on familiar topics through a cultural lens. The ambition of *A Cultural History of Western Empires* is to advance conversations about the work of culture in shaping how empire took root, took shape, was maintained, and faced challenges whether its regimes were of long or short durée. Indeed, no thoroughgoing histories of the subject can afford to ignore the influence that culture has had on the shape of empires in local, regional, and global contexts.

The geographical remit of *A Cultural History of Western Empires* is indicated in its title. As compelling a topic as the wide variety of imperial formations is, and as interconnected as west and non-west have been along the axis of empire from Greece to Beijing and back again, the authors in this volume explore empire's cultural histories in a broadly western European setting. And while the differences between French and German and English imperial experiences are often notable, what is equally striking are the features that cultures of labor, trade, sexuality, race, war, mobility, natural worlds, and resistance share across imperial locales. Even allowing for specificities of time and place, there is a value to taking a very long view of the concept and practice of *imperium*—not simply to note commonalities or differences but to be able to discern through lines across such widely distinctive terrains as the Frankish kingdoms and the world of the post-Versailles settlement. In no small respect, attention to cultural forces, identities, rhetorics, tropes, relationships, and imaginaries make this kind of discernment possible. Reading for culture—which is to say, developing the capacity to plumb a variety of sources and archives for evidence of how meanings and forms were constantly made and struggled over across a range of domains—reveals the work of historical forces that have undergirded and, at times, have redirected or undone imperial power. Empire simply cannot be understood in all its limits and possibilities without an analysis of its cultural histories.

This is a work of scholarly synthesis rooted in the original scholarship and intellectual vision of the volume editors and their contributors. Its audience is students seeking a comparative, interdisciplinary, and evidence-based account of how empires worked at multiple scales. Readers will get a sense, then, of the cultural impact of large-scale territorial expansion and hegemony *and* of the meaning and experience of conquest and colonization in more intimate environments. Contributors have written their essays to make available a broad overview of their theme or topic. Each one draws on a range of materials and case studies to make a larger argument about the history of cultural formations and influences that pertain to their subject. The series is structured around six time periods: Antiquity, The Medieval Age, The Renaissance, The Enlightenment, The Age of Empire, and the Modern Age. These are conceptual and pedagogical, signaling a periodization that modern Western imperialism itself has played an important role in shaping and sustaining. Casting Rome as an imperial touchtone and colonized territories as "ancient" or "medieval" in temporal terms remains an important cultural resource for contemporary empire-building, and it draws on a long cultural legacy that contributors both address and challenge. Each volume takes up the chronological parameters assigned in critical conversation with the historical evidence, allowing readers to see the pros and cons of thinking about empire itself as a maker—and breaker—of time periods. Of equal significance, each volume is organized with the same chapter titles so that readers can either follow a theme across time frames—mobility in the Enlightenment as compared to the twentieth century, for example—or read through a single period by exploring the range of thematic lenses on offer. This combination of diachronic and synchronic affords us a unique opportunity to cultivate comparisons that are as deep as they are broad, and to appreciate the indispensability of cultural history to practically all aspects of imperial regime making and unmaking across this particular swath of the global past.

Such a purposeful focus on culture at this juncture in the history of the historiography of empire is worth remarking on. As an object of historical inquiry, culture is arguably the carrier of a number of historical forces that attention to politics or economics alone cannot capture. Though embedded in and constitutive of every aspect of imperial geopolitics, race, gender, and sexuality were long invisible to the historians' eye because they were considered trivial, or at best inconsequential, to the workings of real power. Cultural history practices, which bring new forms of seeing and reading as well as new subjects to our sightline, open up the imperial archive to aspects of the past, which, in turn, shed new light on old paradigms. Thinking with and through culture also reorients our gaze, pulling us toward sources—diaries, images, discursive motifs—in a diverse array of formations and spaces that illuminate dimensions of hegemony and power otherwise invisible: dismiss-able, even, as immaterial because they are ostensibly "only cultural." What the collective example of this series accomplishes is to suggest how, why, and under what conditions culture has been a maker of imperial history—indeed, that empires have been done and undone by the cultural forces they sought to control but which were not always completely in their grasp. As twenty-first-century forms of imperial power emerge, claiming historical newness and relying on past models of conquest and occupation all at once, we need narratives that insist on the power of histories attuned to the ideological and material work of culture more than ever.

Culture is at the dynamic heart of all imperial histories. It operates in spaces of high command and conjugal intimacy; in ceremony and in ordinary life; in military documents and botanists' texts; at court and on the plantation; through trade routes and refugee settlements; in the pronouncements of empresses and the movements of the lowly beetle; in the signing of treaties and the violence of the battlefield and the inner workings of the household. Thinking through cultures of empire, in turn, throws us back on the protocols and presumptions of the discipline by encouraging us to be ever vigilant about where—in what spaces and through what repertoires—history happens. Empire is not, perhaps, unique in this regard. The irony is that while imperial ambition and self-regard have often been steeped in convictions about the power of culture to conquer and colonize, imperial narratives on a grand scale are often the most impervious to the argument that culture matters. What follows is a wide-ranging and lively set of arguments about how and why that has been incontrovertibly so from antiquity to modern times.

Introduction

IAN COLLER

In the period between 1650 and 1800, European thought went through a great shift that has been characterized as both a leap forward and a crisis. Many of the fundamental structures of our world have been traced back to that period: the scientific world-view, the sovereign democratic nation-state, the ideals of liberty, equality, tolerance, and human universality. Men and women who later became household names were conscious even as they wrote of belonging to an "Age of Enlightenment," indeed to an imaginary "republic of letters" (Goodman 1994) stretching not only between cosmopolitan cities like Paris, Edinburgh, and Amsterdam, but among hundreds of small provincial academies in France, between cities in Italy, Scandinavia, colonial America and, as recent scholars have emphasized, as far afield as Istanbul, Quito, Manila, and the Cape Colony in South Africa (Withers 2007; Safier 2008; Johnson 2012; Erginbas 2013; Donahue-Wallace 2017). As those place names suggest, this was also an age of empires old and new.

This volume explores the cultural history of those empires, and must therefore engage with the question of Enlightenment itself, and the shifts and transformations that accompanied it. It does not, however, assume a simple or unidirectional relationship between Enlightenment and empire. Instead, it explores the ways in which these great changes taking place concurrently across this period shaped one another. Rather than treating Enlightenment as an intrinsically European intellectual development that reached the world through the spread of empire, the contributors to this volume consider it as a repertoire of practices born into, and deeply imprinted by, a world that was in rapid imperial transformation. Enlightenment was as much a product of an imperial world as a reflection upon it.

Cultural history here refers not to the limiting sense of "culture" as a distinct layer of symbolic representations, but rather to a much broader approach that invites ideas from a variety of disciplines and historical methodologies, from anthropology and art history to intellectual, political, and social history and the study of religion: as one recent volume has suggested, this new cultural history is situated "at the point of interaction between perceptions, values and ideas on the one hand, and social communication and agency on the other" (Calaresu *et al.* 2010: 11). This is of particular value in the study of a period so dense with the production of ideas, texts, and images, and at the same time the epoch of a great transformation in everyday life, often identified as the "birth of the modern world." In line with the words of Daniel Roche, the authors instinctively "avoid artificial distinctions between intellectual and political history ... or the history of ideas and the history of practice" (1998: 450). In the same way, older separations between the underlying economic dynamics of social relations and the cultural representations that served to legitimate or disguise the nature of those relations no longer hold. In their place we see the shifting relationship of ideas and social structures and their impact on economic behavior—conceived not only in terms of production, but equally as an activity of consumption. It is what Emma Rothschild (2011)—examining this period from the vantage-point of a single family—has called "the inner life of empires."

That inner life is evident in all of the chapters contained here: Merry Wiesner-Hanks demonstrates the key role of the family and sexuality from the highest to the lowest levels of imperial power, and the shifts in sexual regimes occasioned by the encounters that empire created. Junko Takeda follows the trade routes that spread out across the world during this period, linking the developing worlds of the Atlantic to the traditional trading spaces of the Mediterranean and the Indian Ocean, and penetrating into the vast Pacific space, while Abigail Swingen investigates the world of labor and work that the plantation complex reshaped, revealing the centrality of unfree labor but also its extent and diversity. Michael Fisher shows that people—both free and unfree—were increasingly in motion as advances in navigation made the journey between coasts easier than many difficult treks through the interior of continents. The impact of this mobility of both products and people is clear in Laura Mitchell's chapter on the environment: the humble potato, the tiny cochineal beetle, and the fields of sugarcane wrought great revolutions in spaces across the globe, even as the spread of empire was shaped by changes in climate, and also by new kinds of knowledge about nature. That poses the question, for Vanita Seth, of how racial ideas emerged as so powerful an organizing force by the end of this period. Was racial thought a preexisting condition for the enslavement of Africans that became crucial to the functioning of these new forms of empire, or an expedient discourse that served belatedly to legitimate this economic exploitation? Karwan Fatah-Black shows that even chattel slavery and violent racial hierarchy were never able to extinguish forms of resistance, which were inherent in the imperial system itself, both driving it onward and on occasions bringing it crashing to its knees.

All of the chapters reveal a period that is in the course of a profound reconsideration; in part because it is the moment of what Kenneth Pomeranz (2000) has called the "great divergence" between Europe and the rest of the world; a trajectory that appeared to the nineteenth and much of the twentieth century to be a manifest European or western destiny. That "special path" no longer appears self-evident. With the disintegration of a Eurocentric exceptionalist narrative, categories like Enlightenment, modernity, and empire that once seemed so self-evident are now in question, and with that more rigorous examination, their darker shadows come into view. Much of the historiography of empire in this period is shaped by later imperial trajectories, and particularly by a distinction between "first" and "second" colonial empires of which this period has been seen to be the tipping point. Part of the problem has been the tendency to write histories of individual empires—the British, French or Dutch, for example, and even the Ottoman and Russian—without recognizing that on the ground, these frames did not always exist, were rarely stable, and often shifted rapidly over time.

RETHINKING EMPIRES

Empire is not a single form: as Jane Burbank and Frederick Cooper have observed, empires employ different governing strategies—different "repertoires of imperial power"—to incorporate diverse territories and peoples into a single system (2010: 2). Empire is a complex conception with both an analytic and a historical usage: it is used to denote multiple systems across history, although many of these forms of rule did not themselves employ the term. Its use may distort local conceptions (Hui 2014: 30) as well as obscuring the understanding of the term when it was used. We must also be aware that the meaning of "empire" changed powerfully over time, as other competing conceptions emerged or faded.

The essays in this volume all in various ways rethink a top-down conception of empire, investigating empires as constituted by multiple actors and processes, coming from below as well as from above; in which both indigenous peoples and creole networks played a crucial role in shaping the nature of empire; and in which multiple empires were not simply governed from the imperial capitals as an extension of national or dynastic power, but rather intersected and overlapped in colonial spaces, which exerted constant influence back onto the metropole itself. Taking cues from the work of trans-oceanic historians, they draw a picture of "empires on the move": not simply spreading outward as frontier or oilstain, but jostling, reacting, retreating, and competing.

Most importantly, in line with the most recent work on empire, these essays recognize the part played by indigenous peoples: not simply as the passive object of colonial forces, or solely in terms of resistance—although as Karwan Fatah Black's chapter reveals, this resistance took much more complex forms than we may imagine. Rather than looking outward from European metropoles to their colonial possessions, they confront the multiplicity of empires functioning within these spaces: a perspective that Michael McDonnell has called "facing empire" (2012: 221). Empire, as McDonnell notes, has been reconceived in recent work not as a spoked wheel, or even as oceanic currents washing to and from the metropole, but rather—following Tony Ballantyne (2012)—as "webs" of relations, both fragile and dynamic, relational and interdependent. Such flexible ways of thinking about empire take us beyond the traditional barrier between colonial and contiguous empire and allow us to think of the Ottoman, Russian, and Habsburg empires alongside their British, French, Dutch, and Iberian counterparts.

The two great reference points Burbank and Cooper cite are Rome and China—neither the first, nor the only imperial models, but long-lasting, territorially vast, and influential longer after their collapse: they were repeatedly reimagined into the modern era. The comparison is instructive: when the Manchus conquered China from Mongolia in the mid-seventeenth century, they adopted Chinese culture along with a new dynastic name, the Qing. They sought, with considerable success, to maintain the integrity of the empire, and to expand its control deep into central Asia, while maintaining tributary relations with neighboring states, Confucian modes of government, and the imperial bureaucracy. Most importantly, they assumed the "mandate of heaven," a universalist ideal model of political legitimacy that was shared—and contested—by other states in the Chinese cultural sphere.

No successor of the Roman *imperium* was able successfully to assert its universal claims in the way that successive Chinese dynasties managed (with, of course, great difficulty) to do: this failure was confirmed by the religious wars of the Reformation. The Holy Roman Empire was unable to levy its claims over the French crown's special relationship to the Church, and even less over the breakaway kingdom of England, the rebellious Dutch provinces, and even its own German dependencies. Meanwhile, the Russian empire emerging under Peter the Great from 1672, and declared officially in 1721, was equally a pretender to the western *imperium*, claiming the mantle of orthodox Christianity, and the title of Tsar from the Roman Caesar (Sunderland 2007). The growing apprehension of Russia's imperial power and territorial expansion helped fuel the shift in trans-imperial politics: by the end of the eighteenth century a huge contiguous Russian empire extended from the Baltic to Alaska, and from the Arctic Circle to the Black Sea.

The ruler of the Ottoman empire, known under the Arabic title of Sultan, and claiming the succession to the Prophet Muhammad as caliph of the world's Muslims, seems an even less likely pretender to Roman *imperium*. Yet in the sixteenth century, Muslims appeared the most likely to realize that inheritance. The Sultan's empire extended across three continents, from eastern Europe through western Asia—or "Rum" (Rome) as the western part of the empire was known—and across North Africa, encircling the eastern Mediterranean and the Black Sea, ruled from Roman cities like Adrianople (Edirne) or Constantinople (Istanbul). The Ottomans were crucial to the shaping of empire in the Age of Enlightenment, at once as a model of long-lasting imperial rule, as a key stakeholder in the "balance of Europe," and as potential prey in the case of their long-anticipated collapse. In 1650, many in Europe still had reason to fear the Ottoman advance: others greeted it with apocalyptic fervor or with hope of greater religious tolerance. That offensive was halted in 1683 with the lifting of the Ottoman siege of Vienna, and confirmed by the humiliating treaties and wars of the following century. The Ottoman empire was not the declining "sick man" other imperial powers sometimes hoped it to be, but the perception of Ottoman weakness, like that of Russian strength, was grist to the mill of European imperial rivalry in the form of the much debated "Eastern question" (Aksan 2013). Ottoman strength helped to legitimate Christian conceptions of universal empire: Ottoman decline served to awaken competing and contradictory claims.

In a temporal sense, this broader attention to the diversity of empires and trans-imperial dynamics raises a challenge to the division between "first" and "second" colonial empires common across imperial historiographies. In the British and French cases, this division is a chronological one, where other empires are understood to have remained caught in a "first empire" dynamic (Spanish, Portuguese, Dutch) or to have remained outside of imperial competition until well into the second (or even third) phase (German, Italian, Belgian). The watershed is conventionally located in the "Age of Revolution" of the late eighteenth century, which began with the emancipation of Britain's American colonies, then passed through the creation of a nominally French empire stretching across most of Europe, and ended with France's almost total loss of its imperial possessions, and the establishment of a British preponderance of imperial force across the globe from Australia and India to Canada. Yet, as the essays in this volume suggest, the revolutionary era was not so much a *rupture* in the imperial story as a part of its fabric. Indeed, as recent historians have argued, the key revolutions of this period were inextricable from imperial webs (Klooster 2009; Polasky 2015).

By examining the empires of this period together and from a cultural angle, these essays accomplish a double shift of perspective away from conventional political histories of empire told from the metropole. The cultural terrain allows us to see changes taking place at different points across empires, not in a simple radiant or top-down process, but rather in a much more spatially diffuse and interactive fashion. If anything can be said to define empire, it is that it does not primarily seek to define and police its borders, or to regularize its realm—although, as Michael Fisher suggests in his chapter, empires both promote and control mobility in territories they control—but rather to maintain a differential and expanding system that allows for a multiplicity of forms of rule and organization. Empire is essentially a hybridizing process that creates a new synthesis of elements out of resistance, collaboration, competition, exchange, circulation: it is also a system prone—as the classical theory of empire maintained—to imperial overstretch, failures of intelligence, and sudden catastrophic reversals. What emerged across the period from 1650 to 1800, however, was the structure of an imperial system that would dominate the world for the subsequent century and a half—and perhaps may be said to continue in many of its elements today. Although we think of our world as a collection of sovereign nation-states, the relationships created by empire in the period of this volume continue to govern its key economic and social relationships.

Instead of considering this period as the "before and after" of a revolutionary break between phases of empire, the chapters in this volume examine it as a whole, and discover both significant continuities and important shifts in the structures of empire. The period begins in what has been called the "general crisis of the seventeenth century": a series of climatic disasters, rebellions, uprisings, and wars on a global scale. As Laura Mitchell observes, this was the heart of what has been called the "Little Ice Age," which made competition over resources in a colder Europe more intense, and created a climate that favored conflict and protest. The most well-known "revolts" of the period 1640–60 are the English Civil War (1642–60), the Irish rebellion (1641–9), the Fronde noble rebellion against the French crown (1648–53), the Catalan revolt (1640–53), the overthrow of the Ming dynasty by the Manchu (1644–59), Aurangzeb's rebellion against his father, the Mughal emperor Shah Jahan (1659), and the riot and murder of the Ottoman Sultan Ibrahim (1648); but revolts also took place in Portugal, Italy, Ukraine, and Mexico, as struggle raged between Dutch and Portuguese in Angola, Ceylon, Guinea, and Malacca.

Observers of the time were conscious of this global context: an English vicar wrote in his diary of concurrent events in France, Spain, Poland, Scandinavia, and Turkey. A Spanish pamphlet wrote of "all the North in commotion . . . England, Scotland and Ireland aflame with civil war . . . The Ottomans tearing each other to pieces . . . China invaded by the Tartars, Ethiopia by the Turks, and the Indian kings who live scattered through the region between the Ganges and the Indus all at each other's throats" (Parker and Smith 1997: 2). Eric Hobsbawm (1954) saw this crisis as a symptom of the emergence of capitalism and its destruction of feudal society. Other historians have located the crisis in a widespread destabilization of the structures of political legitimacy, or a more general degeneration of human living conditions based on a multiplicity of factors.

It is not for nothing that Thomas Hobbes depicted the "state of nature" in his *Leviathan* of 1651 as an anarchic "war of all against all." "In such condition," he wrote,

> there is no place for industry, because the fruit thereof is uncertain, and consequently no culture of the earth, no navigation nor the use of commodities that may be imported by sea, no commodious building, no instruments of moving and removing such things as require much force, no knowledge of the face of the earth, no account of time, no arts, no letters, no society, and which is worst of all, continual fear and danger of violent death, and the life of man, solitary, poor, nasty, brutish, and short ([1651] 2008: 84).

Hobbes argued that an ordered society must be assured by an inviolable state, meaning that its members must give up their rights to govern themselves.

The emergence of the strong state—whether absolutist or constitutional—is an inescapable dimension of the late seventeenth and early eighteenth centuries. The treaties of Westphalia (1648) and Utrecht (1713) formalized the existence of multiple states within the Christian polity. At the same time, the defeat of the Ottoman siege of Vienna in 1683, confirmed by the Treaty of Karlowitz in 1699, ended the expansion of the Ottoman empire in Europe—and with it Louis XIV's hopes of dividing Europe with the Sultan (Wolf 1968). In the century that followed, the Ottomans also accepted coexistence alongside other Muslim empires, the Safavid and the Mughal. In all of these empires, new forms of state control, taxation, and bureaucracy emerged alongside expanding trade both within and between states.

If Westphalia represented an agreement to the existence of multiple states against the claims of universal monarchy, this did not prevent ambitious rulers from pursuing imperial dreams in other ways. Louis XIV, rocked in his youth by the uprising of the Fronde, subjected the French nobility to absolute rule and distracted them with a new court culture that became the model for much of Europe: Versailles represented a spectacular form of power reminiscent of Istanbul's Topkapi or the Forbidden City in Beijing; styles of *turquerie* and *chinoiserie* were consciously adapted as elements of its decoration. The War of the Spanish Succession (1702–13) pitted Louis XIV against Leopold I, the Austrian ruler of the Holy Roman Empire, backed by the English and Dutch who hoped to resist the aggrandizement of the Sun King's power. The final result was the accession of Philip V, Louis's grandson, partitioning the Habsburg empire, but also preventing the unification of France and Spain that was so feared by the other European powers. Two years later, Louis was dead, and his only remaining great-grandson came to the French throne.

These wars and treaties increasingly drew in imperial possessions in the Americas and Asia, traded against cities in Europe, or on occasion (as in the case of Bombay) transferred as a marriage dowry. Neither the Dutch nor the English played the central roles in these European wars, but continued to expand their trading networks, displacing Arab traders with their more effective shipping, as Michael Fisher reveals in his chapter. But as Christopher Tozzi observes in this volume, the military revolution driven by this competitive warfare was transforming the state as well as expanding its power and effectiveness. Military shifts helped European states to expand their colonial empires, but the different kinds of warfare practiced by indigenous peoples also shaped the way wars were fought on the continent, above all in the Seven Years War of 1756–63—sometimes called the "First World War" of the eighteenth century—and the American War of Independence from 1776 to 1783. Yet, as Tozzi notes, until the end of the eighteenth century, these wars did not involve mass armies or extensive fighting that intruded directly on the lives of large numbers of civilians. War was just one element of a larger transformation that left the world of 1800 so different from that of 1650.

AN AGE OF ENLIGHTENMENT?

What is Enlightenment? The answer to this question is complex: in effect, it depends which Enlightenment we are talking about. As J.G.A Pocock has argued, the Enlightenment "occurred in too many forms to be comprised within a single definition and history, and we do better to think of a family of Enlightenments, displaying both family resemblances and family quarrels (some of them bitter and even bloody)" (1999: 9). Immanuel Kant, responding to the question in 1784, declared memorably that it represented man's exit from a self-imposed immaturity, a transition to adulthood crystallized in the motto *Sapere aude:* "Dare to know." There is, no doubt, something to this heroic conception, but for most Europeans of the eighteenth century, Enlightenment in practice meant better roads, new forms of sociability and subjectivity, challenges to traditional practices, and expanding awareness of a wider world. For those coming into contact with Europeans in colonies and trading posts, however, Enlightenment might mean compelling new forms of knowledge and practice, but equally new kinds of war, violence, and coercion. The parochial European conception of Enlightenment must be recast in its wider epoch.

What, then, do we mean by the "Age" of Enlightenment? Over the past decade, Dorinda Outram has noted "the traditional idea of the Enlightenment as confined to European nations and their colonies has given way to a new perception of Enlightenment as a world drama of cross-cultural contact, a drama with enormous consequences for both European and indigenous peoples" (2004: 551). At the same time, not only the boundaries and sources, but the very nature of the Enlightenment itself have come into question. As Outram has written elsewhere, "It might . . . seem that as our picture of the

Enlightenment became more complex, as we have begun to study ideas not as autonomous, discrete objects, but as deeply embedded in society, so the term Enlightenment itself might have become increasingly obscure or even meaningless" (1995: 12). Indeed, the term was not familiar in eighteenth-century English, and even up to the twentieth century, translators struggled to translate the German *Aufklärung* (Schmidt 2003). The French term *lumières* or "lights" was more current in the eighteenth century, describing a more pervasive form of social transformation not confined to a set of philosophical ideas.

In his seminal book, notably entitled *France in the Enlightenment* (*La France des lumières*) (1998)—and not *The Enlightenment in France*—the French historian Daniel Roche looked for the origins and processes of the eighteenth-century transformation in demography, urbanism, and consumption, a pragmatic rethinking cognate with the approach taken in this volume. But the contributors here rethink these Enlightenment changes in a world already structured by relations of imperial and colonial power. The great challenge in this period is to investigate how shifts in imperial power structured the emergence of the "new" and, conversely, how these new ideas, epistemologies, subjectivities, and practices shaped the conditions of the imperial system of the nineteenth century.

In his 1935 work *The Crisis of the European Mind*, Paul Hazard remarked on the apparent suddenness of the shift from a world in which tradition, stability, and received ideas formed the substrate of everyday life to a world in which newness, originality, and the challenge to received ideas had moved from the periphery to the center of social experience. Looking at that period from 1680 to 1715 from the perspective of Europeans, he saw at the center of that shift not an autochthonous process in the heart of Europe, but a "startling influx of new ideas" from the world beyond ([1935] 2013: 9). The travels of François Bernier into Persia and India during the 1660s inspired Bayle, Montesquieu, Rousseau, and other influential writers of the Enlightenment, most notably in the *Persian Letters* that used fictional foreigners traveling to Paris as mouthpieces for a challenge to social customs (Dew 2009). A ten-volume work of Bernard Picart in the 1720s brought together the "Religious Ceremonies and Customs of the World" in both text and images, concentrating in one place the destabilizing impact of discovering the vast variety of human beliefs and traditions (Hunt and Jacob 2010) (Figure 0.1).

In 1769, Denis Diderot, one of the organizers of the great project of the *Encyclopédie*, could write humorously of the devastating effect of a handsome "new" scarlet dressing-gown—an adaptation of an Asian banyan robe in a color made possible by the importation of cochineal from Mexico (Diderot [1979] 2016). At the same moment, Captain James Cook was in Tahiti viewing the transit of Venus, and continuing on a voyage that would reveal the outlines of the last unknown continents on the earth's surface, and give rise to the first

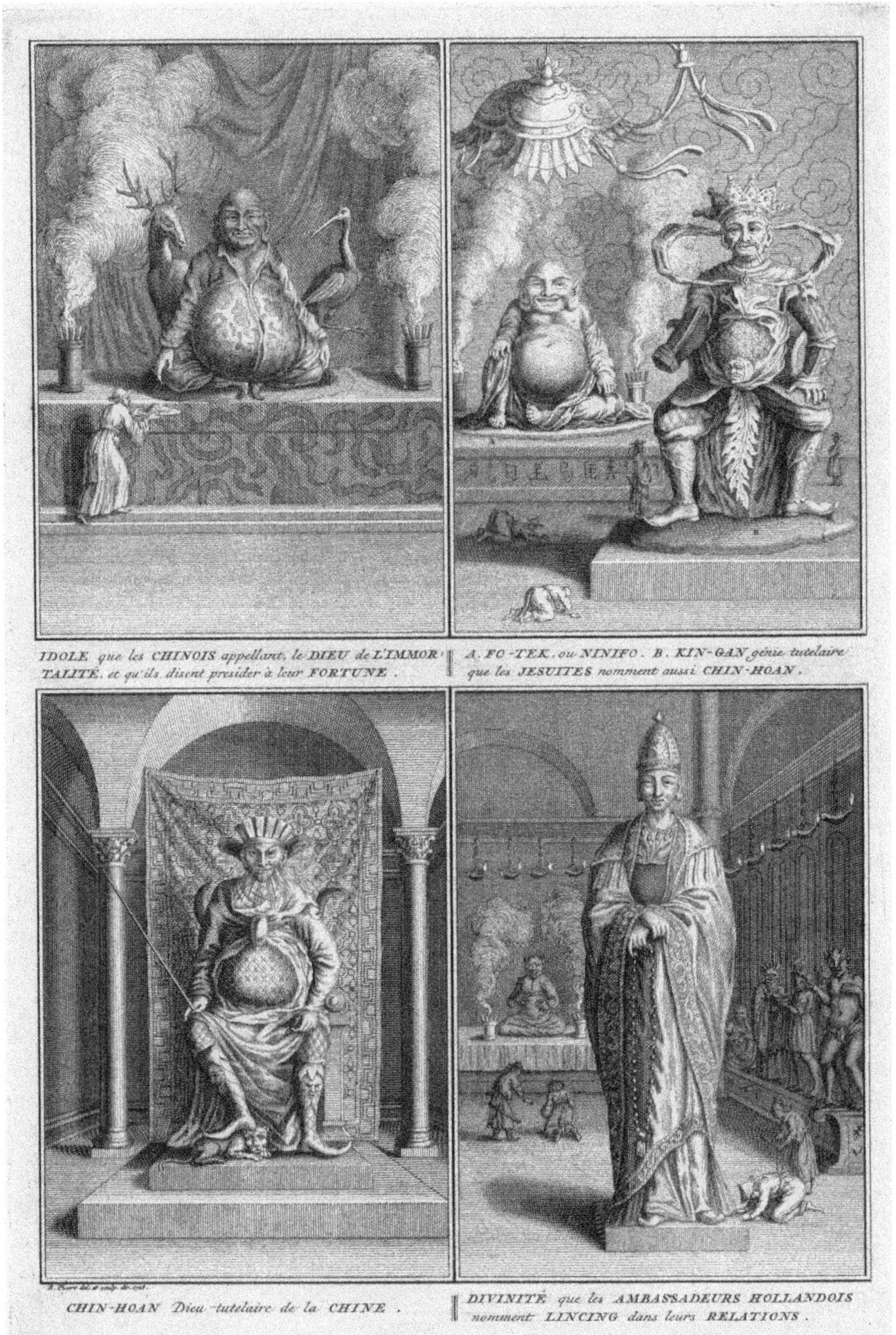

FIGURE 0.1: Four Chinese gods, 1728, by Bernard Picart. Found in the collection of Rijksmuseum, Amsterdam. Credit: Fine Art Images/Heritage Images/Getty Images.

globalizing geographical, ethnological, and botanical knowledges. Women, too, were part of the Enlightenment, in the world of the literary salons, and as writers and thinkers in their own right (Hesse 2001).

Yet with astonishing rapidity, in the wake of the fall of the Bastille in July 1789, this new and exciting world of change would appear as a stodgy, backward, tradition-choked world of inequality and violence: an *"ancien régime"* whose traces should be forever erased. Granted, the heroes of the Enlightenment were dug up and reburied in the neoclassical grandeur of the Pantheon (a repurposed convent), but those luminaries would hardly have recognized the world through which their remains were paraded. This period of 1650–1800 must be considered *both* as Enlightenment and *ancien régime*, punctuated at its end by a revolutionary shift. All of these worldly relations that helped to fuel the shifts of Enlightenment Europe were deeply embedded in relationships of power and violence that were not simply peripheral but central.

In recognizing that the world of the Enlightenment was a hybrid of old and new, we must recalibrate our notions about religion and secularism. The choice to think about the eighteenth century through the matrix of Enlightenment has tended to sideline the persistence and importance of religion in favor of those trends understood to be leading inexorably toward the separation of religion from politics as a secondary and private matter of conscience. But religion remained central throughout this period, a key domain of struggle rather than a vanishing remnant. The Enlightenment was not a struggle *against* religion, but in multiple ways a struggle *over* religion and its place both in the state and in the lives of ordinary people. Religion and Enlightenment no longer appear as contradictory terms. Not only have historians identified distinctive Protestant, Catholic, and Jewish Enlightenments (Bradley and Van Kley 2001; Sutcliffe 2003; Lehner 2016) but David Sorkin (2011) has argued that this religious Enlightenment crossed religious and national borders to encompass all three major European religions. This notion of religious Enlightenment not only opens up the transformations of this period to a wider range of actors and agents, but breaks down some of the intellectual barriers that have prevented historians from seeing cognate shifts taking place in other societies, in the Muslim world for example (Schulze 1996).

Although the story of the Enlightenment was conventionally told within European limits, it was always implicitly an imperial story: Enlightenment could only achieve its universal, humanity-wide vocation through the extension of empire. In this sense, the conventional story of "the" Enlightenment was itself a colonial one that dovetails with that of the European civilizing mission, the duty to assist (or indeed to coerce) other peoples to emerge from their adolescence (or senescence) and achieve this new form of vigorous adulthood under European tutelage. In this way, other peoples were consigned, in the words of Dipesh Chakrabarty, to the "imaginary waiting room of history" (2000: 7). The project of "decolonizing" Enlightenment is a necessary development of the critiques waged for the last seventy years.

After 1945, the philosophers of the Frankfurt School and French thinker Michel Foucault challenged in different ways the story of reason and progress in the Enlightenment, tracing the uses of technical rationality as a means of power and control, the repression of "unreason," the confinement of the mad, the exclusion of women. However, in his essay on Kant's "What is Enlightenment?", Foucault rejected the "blackmail" implicit in the conception that one should be "for" or "against" the Enlightenment, rather than investigating the "set of political, economic, social, institutional, and cultural events on which we still depend in large part" (Foucault 1984: 42). This position heralded a shift in historical practice that moved from charting a singular and monolithic "Enlightenment" to one that questioned both its substance and its boundaries. Scholars of intellectual history have diversified that lineage by positing a wider range of approaches within the same broad trend, distinguishing "radical" from more moderate versions of Enlightenment thought and practice (Jacob 1981; Israel 2001) or through a "counter-Enlightenment" that employed the same philosophical tools (McMahon 2001).

Some scholars have insisted on the geographical distinctiveness of different Enlightenment traditions—Scottish, French, Ibero-American, Lithuanian (Aldridge 1971; Butterwick *et al.* 2008), while others have challenged this trend by insisting on the common concerns of thinkers as far apart as Scotland and Naples (Robertson 2005). New digital projects are mapping networks of correspondence, publication, and travel that linked individual writers and thinkers across great distances (*Mapping the Republic of Letters*).

The new scholarship on the Enlightenment does not simply place in question our traditional assumptions about center and periphery, metropole and colony. It opens up new ways of thinking about how imperial shifts both reflected and shaped the emergence of new ways of thinking and living, and with them the new ideas that circulated across a much larger space than the western cape of Eurasia known as Europe.

ENLIGHTENMENT AND EMPIRE

For a snapshot of these complex dynamics of Enlightenment and empire we may glance at Voltaire's novel *Candide*, perhaps the most popularly known Enlightenment text (Figure 0.2). It offered a satirical rejoinder to the theodicy of Gottfried von Leibniz (recast as Dr Pangloss), who insisted that since the universe we inhabit was created by God, it must be "the best of all possible worlds." Leibniz, among his many scientific accomplishments, was also closely engaged in geopolitical questions, and in 1671 offered Louis XIV a memorandum exhorting him to invade Egypt, couched explicitly in the

FIGURE 0.2: *Candide; or Optimism*, 1759, illustration for the 1785 edition of the philosophical tale by Voltaire (1694–1778). Paris, Bibliothèque Nationale de France (Library). Credit: De Agostini Picture Library/Getty Images.

language of holy war. Leibniz argued that a crusade against the Muslims in Egypt would serve to unite the Christian world, divided by war and heresy. If he had moved ahead in mathematics, the German philosopher remained deeply rooted in older religious conceptions of universal empire. At the same time, he was powerfully influenced in his thought by new ideas about China (Perkins 2004).

As Junko Takeda points out in this volume, "the notion that European exploration and colonization was characterized solely by impositions of 'western' supremacy is a mischaracterization." As Europeans came into closer contact with immense and powerful Asian states, they began to conceive of their own power differently: indeed, they discovered that Muslim and Chinese rulers—even the emperor of Morocco—often considered European pretensions to sovereignty and civilization to be null or hardly worthy of consideration. But the exposure to new belief systems also helped to shake older certainties, not only for philosophers, but for the merchants and traders who traveled increasingly out into other parts of the world.

Leibniz's "ideal" world was caught uneasily between the unity of Christendom and the (often threatening) diversity of a wider world. Voltaire had his hero Candide face these contradictions squarely, traveling to South America and Surinam to witness the brutality of European conquest, the horrors of slavery in the sugar islands, and end his weary travels "tending his own garden" in the Ottoman capital of Constantinople. Voltaire expressed strong opposition to slavery and conquest elsewhere in his work, but this did not prevent him investing much of his wealth in the *Compagnie des Indes* (Miller 2008: 428–9), and sycophantically praising the conquests of Catherine the Great. The point here is not to determine whether Voltaire, or the Enlightenment as a whole, was "for" or "against" empire (Muthu 2003) but rather to observe the ways in which these new forms of thought were already embedded in the political, social, and economic processes of empire and shaped by the transitions from one form of power to another.

The "crisis of the European mind" can be seen to emerge in the context of the breakdown of universal monarchy. In the mid-sixteenth century, the House of Habsburg, uniting Spain and its conquests in the Americas with the Holy Roman Empire, appeared poised to seize ascendancy in the figure of Charles V. Yet the struggle with France on one side and the Ottoman empire on the other, combined with the violence ushered in by the Protestant reformation, shattered the dream of universal monarchy. After the Thirty Years' War demonstrated the failure of any state to win supremacy and reestablish the Roman/Christian *imperium*, European powers were compelled to accept an uneasy truce that recognized multiple states, and opening the way for imperial power to spread at a "molecular" level through the action of traders and companies, even as these local connections on the ground remained in dynamic relationship to large-scale planning from imperial hubs.

These currents were best represented in the early seventeenth century by the spread of the Dutch empire, a new kind of merchant empire driven by the first great multinational corporation. In 1602, the Dutch East India Company, known as the VOC, came into being to challenge the Portuguese crown's monopoly on the pepper trade, and was awarded monopoly privileges by the

States General of the Dutch Republic (Jacobs 1991: 15). In 1751, Malachy Postlethwayt wrote that the reason for the Dutch company's success "is its being absolute, and invested with a kind of authority and dominion . . . [it] makes peace and war at pleasure, and by its own authority; administers justice to all; . . . settles colonies, builds fortifications, levies troops, maintains numerous armies and garrisons, fits out fleets, and coins money" (Neal 1993: 196). The material innovation of this scheme was the development of a joint-stock company in which trading of shares provided permanent capital that funded constant expansion. A century later, the company was netting its shareholders a dazzling return of 22.5 percent. In the process, it functioned to transform places as far distant as Java and the Cape of Good Hope, and even Nagasaki in Japan, not as territorial empire, but, as Kerry Ward has argued, in a complex, mobile and flexible imperial network (Ward 2009). As Laura Mitchell notes in her chapter, in the wake of the "Little Ice Age", societies with "access to long-distance trade networks and diversified agriculture tended to cope better with the consequences of climate change." The forces thus unleashed would not only build but also shatter empires: British attempts to force their American colonies to buy only from their own East India Company would spark the famous dumping of tea into Boston Harbor, and the first colonial war of independence.

The English East India Company, chartered two years earlier, was slower in gaining traction in the spice trade, but eventually outpaced its competitor by the end of the eighteenth century due to its even greater territorial acquisitions. Its "company men" returning home to England were lampooned as "nabobs" (from the Indian princely title *nawab*) because of their rapidly acquired wealth and their arriviste manners (Nechtman 2010). The French Compagnie des Indes was chartered in 1660, but was embroiled in a series of scandals and failures that betrayed its rigid dependence on a powerful state. The Swedes, Danes, Austrians, Portuguese, all attempted with varying degrees of success to imitate the VOC model, and chartered companies competed on every inhabited continent. These molecular forces of empire were crucial in the forging of a capitalist world system. Where conventional narratives of world history dated the decisive shift to modernity in the "industrial revolution" of the late eighteenth century, recent historians have identified an "industrious revolution" earlier, and placed its heart in Asia (de Vries 2008). The companies both profited from and helped drive this revolution.

The trajectory of empire across this period lies in the welding together of these molecular forces with the growing power of states. It was a powerful but uneasy match. Ward has called the VOC "an empire within a state" (2009: 57), and Philip Stern has noted how the growth of corporate sovereignty threatened the internal balance between Parliament and monarchy in Britain, giving rise to "an unprecedentedly concerted if diffuse battle in print, via petitions, pamphlets, books, and broadsides" in the 1690s (2012: 145). That fight was largely won by the company, which continued to expand its power for another century and a half. In contrast, French state control proved a liability for the companies it sought to foster, with the exception of the Compagnie d'Afrique, which remained based in Marseille. Several of the essays in this volume show how Dutch traders, whether in the VOC or outside of it, proved an uncontrollable irritant to the larger empires, including their own. As Junko Takeda observes, we must look below the state level to see the "local angles and pirate activities" that created and sustained empire on the ground.

The predominance of imperial trading networks in this period should certainly not blind us to the territorial expansion taking place. Great swathes of the vast American inlands came under the control of Britain, France, and Spain. Russia spread inexorably across Siberia, a region larger than all of Europe. With that spread, indigenous peoples became newly the subjects of empire and the objects of enlightened knowledge. In 1783, Catherine II unilaterally annexed the Crimea from its Ottoman suzerain, and might have pushed the resulting war as far as Istanbul itself if the French Revolution had not intervened. But these vast expanses were ultimately secondary: indeed, the overstretch that resulted often threatened imperial possession. Britain lost its key American colonies in the 1770s, and almost all of Central and South America became independent over the next fifty years.

This was not primarily an era of conquest: its significance lies in the shift from dispersed trading empires to a new form of plantation economy. It was no longer gold and silver that colonizers sought. The most profitable of all colonial implantations were those that produced the new commodities of an age in which the "middling sort" could aspire to the kinds of food, stimulants, and clothing that had once been the jealously guarded preserve of the noble elite: tea and coffee, silk and cotton, tobacco and above all sugar. These luxury goods would become the fuel of empire in the Age of Enlightenment. Tiny sugar islands in the Caribbean became the most concentrated wealth-producing places on the planet.

Producing these precious commodities demanded human power: incessant labor under a blazing sun in humid tropical conditions. The indigenous Caribs had been devastated by the impact of Spanish colonization: now, these islands passed into British and French hands, along with the *asiento*, the license to conduct the slave trade out of Africa, which Abigail Swingen has made a central dimension of her study of labor in this volume. Between 1650 and 1800, around six million men, women, and children were taken by force from their homelands in Africa and carried across the Atlantic (Manning *et al.* 2015). Those who survived the journey in cramped and filthy conditions were forced to perform back-breaking labor as the property of plantation owners: their children born into slavery were equally chattels to be disposed of at the pleasure of their owners.

SLAVERY AND ENLIGHTENMENT

The question of slavery emerges without fail as a key dimension in every chapter in this volume. Whether through the environmental and economic impact of the triangular trade and the plantation complex, the new military strategies needed to seize or defend these extraordinarily lucrative colonies, the mass forced mobility and labor of humans, their sexual exploitation both for pleasure and for the increase of slave populations, or the complex forms of resistance that emerged among enslaved people, slavery is impossible to ignore in considering the enlightenment forms of empire. Debates have long raged regarding Enlightenment attitudes toward slavery, and why the chief proponents of enlightened thought did not view enslavement and trade in humans as the most flagrant contradiction to freedom and equality.

The image that appears on the cover of this volume speaks to the tensions of that essential condition of empire in the Age of Enlightenment. The ostensible subject of the portrait, Lady Elizabeth Murray—portrayed according to Enlightenment fashion with an open book in her hand—remained for two centuries the portrait's sole titular subject, with little attention paid to the "servant" in the background, who was in fact her cousin, Dido Belle, the "natural" daughter of Admiral Sir John Lindsay and a slave of African origins, Maria Belle. Dido wears a turban, traditional Muslim attire that was frequently used for the livery of "exotic" servants, but the clothing and jewelry of an aristocrat. Elizabeth's gesture to catch Dido's arm subtly reveals the familial ties of the two women. Dido, carrying a platter of fruits reminiscent of the cornucopic symbols of African "plenty", points coquettishly upward to her face, in a way that appears to draw attention to her dark skin, creating a contrast that played an explicit role in the vogue for black servants. The two women were raised in the household of William Murray, 1st Earl of Mansfield, the Lord Chief Justice of England, who was called upon to deliver decisions on the legality of the slave trade, and notably in the famous case of the slave ship *Zong* whose crew threw hundreds of captives overboard in order to collect the insurance money.

The portrait speaks to many of the themes of this volume, and the ways in which slavery runs through them all. It reminds us that empire was a question of home and not just abroad, and that the family played a central role in the reproduction of empires. It speaks to the revolution in world mobility that empire catalyzed in this period, transforming the populations of metropole as well as colony; the trade in silk, pearls, lace, and ostrich feathers that created the sumptuary elegance of these women, and the fascination with taming nature that united the sweeping grounds of the English mansion with the distant plantation complex; the military power that armed this sea-borne trade and the forced labor (including unfree sexual labor) that gave birth to the simmering racial tensions animating the painting. But it also points to the complexities of this period. Empire could offer opportunity as well as exploitation, among an array of characters far wider than colonizer and colonized. It raises the question of where resistance might lie in the spectrum of responses to empire, from outright rejection to active collaboration, when we zoom in from the macro to the micro level of history. As Vanita Seth observes in her chapter, the color binary of "black and white" was overlaid with religious distinctions of Christian and heathen, and equally by the distinctions of free and unfree. As Abigail Swingen notes, unfree laborers came in many colors and forms: slaves, serfs, indentured servants, *engagés*.

Debate long raged over the relationship of slavery to the emergence of capitalism in the early modern period. Eric Williams (1944) argued that it was the unfree labor of millions of Africans that formed the backbone of the capitalist system and financed the industrial revolution: abolition came only when slavery was no longer profitable. Subsequent historians challenged Williams's case, insisting that abolition came at the point of the maximum flourishing of the trade and adversely affected the British economy (Drescher 1977). Others argued that he had overstated the degree to which capital accrued through slavery was the driving force of industrial development in Britain (Eltis and Engerman 2000). Williams equally argued that capitalism was the driving force behind the emergence of racism associated with slavery, something that Vanita Seth interrogates here in her chapter on race, emphasizing the multiplicity of factors that were at work alongside the economic in the process of "inventing" race. In particular, she demonstrates the importance of preexisting Iberian ways of classifying color and status as they came into contact with other emergent imperial systems on the ground, leading to the codification and regulation of bodies previously imagined as mutable and not fixed. As Abigail Swingen notes, the British resistance to "behaving as the Spanish had in the New World" led them to reject indigenous slavery, even as they competed for control of the contract to provide African slaves to Spanish colonies.

If commerce was the "blood" of the new empires, as Jeremy Adelman (2006: 14) suggests, that relationship was literalized in the body of the slave, whose blood remained theoretically enslaved forever by passing from generation to generation through sexual reproduction, regardless of the color and status of the father. Merry Wiesner-Hanks observes that this "sexual regime" was as important as economics in the reproduction of the slave complex. But blood also flowed in other directions: the mobility of Africans, although massively controlled by European traders, also began to flow across the "black Atlantic" into Europe, launching the racial diversity that is a key dimension of European societies today. In 1685, the *Code Noir* for the first time offered a legislative framework for the practice of slavery in the islands. By 1777, French authorities had become so anxious about the presence of people of color in the metropole that they issued draconian restrictions on their rights (Cohen 1980: 111).

As Michael Fisher observes, a freed slave like Olaudah Equiano could write a memoir against the slave trade, while himself participating in an imperial experiment to create a black colony in Sierra Leone. Tozzi reveals the presence of black and Asian troops in European armies, and Wiesner-Hanks the consequences of marriage and illicit sexuality across colonial, religious, and racial boundaries. The pressure of new groups—not only the classical bourgeoisie—excluded from political participation under the *ancien régime*, but equipped with powerful new ideas shaped by the expansion of print culture and the public sphere, helped to shape the conditions for an age of revolution at the end of the eighteenth century.

THE DAWN OF THE REVOLUTIONARY AGE

From the perspective of empires, none of the contributors here sees a rupture or break in the period conventionally associated with the American and French revolutions. There is little doubt that the spectacular push for independence of Britain's American colonies had a powerful resonance in the world, yet as Fatah-Black shows, resistance of all kinds had been a feature of empires throughout the period. The American model of settler independence built on the preservation of slavery and perpetuation of indigenous dispossession did not translate immediately into other colonial contexts. Indeed, the effects of the American Revolution could most immediately be felt in Europe, where the revolutionary catchwords of liberty and equality circulated widely, particularly in France, whose monarchy had further undermined its critical financial state by offering aid to the American rebels against their hated English enemy.

When the French Revolution broke out in 1789, France too was a complex imperial web, with parts of its own metropole still remnants of treaty negotiations: Alsace and Lorraine were interlaced fabrics of French and German prerogatives; Corsica was still officially contracted to Genoa; Avignon and the Comtat Venaissin belonged to the pope. Concurrent revolutions broke out across the border in Liège and Brabant; Poles, Irish, Italians, and Swiss all looked to the model of revolution. France's most productive region was across the Atlantic in the Caribbean possessions of Martinique, Guadeloupe, and above all Saint Domingue, and France had a South American landfall in the form of French Guiana. Despite the losses of the Seven Years War, the French retained five *comptoirs* in India, the Indian Ocean islands of Bourbon (Réunion) and Ile-de-France (Mauritius), and the Seychelles. In Senegal, the settlement of Saint-Louis was also part of France, while throughout the Mediterranean, a pattern of French and allied communities in Ottoman port cities (the échelles of the Levant and Barbary) also formed an important layer of French commerce.

Thus, the French Revolution was by necessity, and from the first, an imperial revolution. The French decision to enter the American War of Independence was provoked by the anger over France's colonial losses in the Seven Years War: by contrast, the king's failure to intervene to assist the Dutch Patriots in their revolt against Austria, and to protect the Ottomans, allied with France, from a dual invasion by Russia and Austria combined, proved powerful mobilizing factors in the heady political contention of 1788. At first, the powerful colonial planter lobby embraced the new regime after the fall of the Bastille in 1789, but soon sought to influence the direction of revolutionary politics to ensure the maintenance of their privileges and the blocking of claims to citizenship by free people of color. The National Assembly's refusal to legislate in their favor led the white planters to secede, and to a failed uprising by the *gens de couleur* in Saint Domingue. This was but the first act in a build-up to a full-blown slave uprising that ultimately led the revolutionary regime in France to declare slavery abolished in all parts of their empire on February 4, 1794 (Figure 0.3). Yet in the turbulent years that followed, the imperial system would reassert itself in the French invasion of Egypt (1798), intended as the spearhead of an attack on British India: a failed enterprise that marked the end of French

FIGURE 0.3: Nicolas Monsiau (1754–1837), French School. Decree of the National Convention Abolishing Slavery in the Colonies, February 4, 1794. Paris, Musée Carnavalet. Credit: Christophel Fine Art/UIG via Getty Images.

revolutionary expansion. The fall of Tipu Sultan's resistance in India in 1799 marked a highpoint of the East India Company's imperial expansion in the subcontinent, as the accession of Napoleon Bonaparte in France launched the beginning of a new kind of "universal empire" in Europe under the sign of enlightened progress. In a crucial reversal, Bonaparte reinstated slavery in 1802, but the inhabitants of Saint Domingue fought back and won their independence as the state of Haiti in 1804.

If the American Revolution sent shockwaves across the world, the Haitian Revolution marked an epoch that lies beyond the end of this work, a far precursor of the decolonization movements of the mid-twentieth century, and a key driver of the racial reaction that characterized the nineteenth century. These three revolutions, straddling the end of the century, were crucial in bringing this period to an end, but they were also the product of the processes and contradictions of the Age of Enlightenment: not just its ideas, but also its practices, from printing to slavery, and from acceleration of mobility to colonial expansion. Moreover, they were part of a much larger world in the process of rapid, transformational change. That they were the epicenters of this diffuse and complex shift does not mean that they were its point of genesis any more than the epicenter of an earthquake is a marker of its subterranean origins. That they should have emerged in a European imperial metropole, a settler colony, and a slave plantation society aligns very clearly with what this volume demonstrates, that the Age of Enlightenment and revolution was also fully an age of empire.

CHAPTER ONE

War

CHRISTOPHER TOZZI

Messieurs les Anglais, tirez les premiers! ("English gentlemen, fire first!"). With these words, or something approximating them, a French aristocrat famously offered his British enemies the honor of delivering the first volley of musket fire at the battle of Fontenoy, in present-day Belgium, in 1745 (Bell 2007: 45) (Figure 1.1). The scene suggests a culture of warfare during the Age of Enlightenment that was defined by chivalrous officers, disciplined and regimented soldiers, and martial politesse.

In reality, the waging of war during the Enlightenment only occasionally conformed to this neat model. Armies and their activities varied widely between different time periods, geographical and national contexts, and social and political circumstances. The Enlightenment era was one of constant change and extremes in the military realm. Its opening in the seventeenth century was marked by profound transformations in the way states recruited and administered military forces. Its conclusion during the age of Atlantic World revolutions witnessed the eruption of radically new types of conflicts, in which nations rather than kings waged war on an unprecedented, massive scale. Military operations varied widely in form, purpose, and outcome on colonial frontiers as well as in European metropoles. While colonial warfare tended eventually to mimic the modes of combat that predominated in Europe itself, this was not the case during the earlier stages of European settlement overseas.

This chapter explains the nature and evolution of warfare during the Enlightenment era. The first half deals primarily with the organization and composition of armies. It discusses the changes to recruitment and tactics that arose out of what scholars call the "military revolution," as well as the cultural norms that predominated in European armies during the Age of Absolutism. It

FIGURE 1.1: Edouard Detaille (1848–1912), French School. The Battle of Fontenoy (1745), won by Maurice de Saxe. 1912. Oil on canvas, 2.10 × 3.20 m. Paris, Musée de l'Armée. Credit: Christophel Fine Art/UIG via Getty Images.

also highlights the rich religious, racial, linguistic, and cultural diversity that imperial networks introduced to European armies, both in the metropole and on overseas frontiers.

The second half of the chapter focuses on warfare itself and its impact on European imperial societies and cultures during the Age of Enlightenment. It explores the rationale behind warfare during the period, as well as attitudes toward war—both within European courts and among the population at large. It concludes by highlighting the significance of warfare in driving political change as the Age of Enlightenment came to a close at the end of the eighteenth century and in inaugurating practices of "total war" during the revolutionary age.

THE MILITARY REVOLUTION AND THE FOUNDATIONS OF ENLIGHTENMENT WARFARE

At the outset of the Enlightenment era, an officer standing before disciplined, uniformed troops and inviting the enemy to fire first, as one did during the scene from Fontenay described earlier, would have been virtually inconceivable to most Europeans. That was because military forces until the early seventeenth century consisted mostly of irregularly equipped, loosely organized troops that formed what historians have called "aggregate contract armies" (Lynn 1997: 7–8). Soldiers in these forces were recruited and paid by military entrepreneurs rather than by the state itself. Governments contracted with these entrepreneurs to field the large number of troops they needed to wage war. This approach to military recruitment and organization was financially expedient because it obviated the need for the state to pay and supply large standing armies on a permanent basis. The contract system constituted the only way that most European states at the dawn of the Age of Absolutism could afford to marshal troops.

Yet if aggregate contract armies saved money for early modern governments with weak financial and bureaucratic structures, the trade-offs were reliability and standardization. Because aggregate contract armies did not receive constant funding from governments, they were not permanent. They typically disbanded at the end of each campaigning season, requiring the state to contract again with military entrepreneurs in order to raise new forces for the following year's battles. Soldiers also tended to be unreliable; they answered to the particular officer who paid them rather than to the sovereign of the state for which they fought. They did not hesitate to desert or switch sides if more lucrative opportunities presented themselves elsewhere. With government-issued uniforms and armaments almost non-existent, troops dressed in and fought with whatever materials they could procure for themselves, making standardization impossible. Lacking centralized supply systems or anything approaching barracks, armies generally acquired provisions and housing for themselves at the expense of local populations (Roberts 1995).

By the middle of the seventeenth century, aggregate contract armies had given way in most European states to commission armies, which were commanded by officers who were directly commissioned by the state and swore fealty to its monarch. This transition, which constituted the process that scholars call the military revolution, was hallmarked by reforms such as those of Maurice of Nassau, the stadtholder of the Dutch Republic from 1585 to 1625, who introduced new standards of drill and training to his armies in order to bring troops more directly under the control of the state (Roberts 1995: 14–15). In France, Henri IV (r. 1589–1610) had expanded the royal army from a mere four permanent regiments to seventeen by the end of his reign, drastically reducing his state's reliance on contract troops (Thion 2008: 38).

Although the military revolution had its roots in changes that stretched back to the late Middle Ages in some parts of Europe, the military revolution was not fully underway across most European societies until the middle decades of the 1600s. On Europe's margins the military revolution took longer to arrive; for example, it was not until the reign of Selim III (r. 1789–1807) that the Ottoman army underwent reforms modeled on those that the military revolution had brought to other powers (Aksan 2015: 253–4).

The Thirty Years' War (1618–48) accelerated the process of military standardization and state control in most parts of Europe by highlighting the effectiveness of more reliable, better-supplied armies. The Swedish armies commanded by Gustavus Adolphus turned the tide of the war by forgoing the massive *tercio* formations of poorly trained pikemen, which formed the cornerstone of Spanish armies of the time, in favor of troops who fought in line formations. The latter required more careful training and drilling in order to be effective on the battlefield, but the investment paid off as Swedish troops routed their Hapsburg enemies throughout Germany (Roberts 1995: 13–14). The war also drove home the importance of military reform for the French, whose recurring attempts to invade the German states starting in 1635 proved futile until the state assumed a greater role in organizing and funding forces late in the war (Jones 1995: 150–1). The French monarchy continued the rapid pace of military reform through the reign of Louis XIV, who oversaw a massive standing army of 400,000 men—a figure unprecedented in Europe at the time—along with a system of royal intendants who traveled with the armies and enforced the king's control over his forces (Jones 1995: 157–8; Roberts 1995: 18–19).

Louis XIV also established most of France's first permanent army regiments, which remained mobilized both in peacetime and wartime (Corvisier 1964; Lynn 1997: 7). This was a significant change because previously, the majority of units with which the French monarchy waged war were raised at the beginning of a conflict and disbanded upon its conclusion. The establishment of permanent regiments not only augmented the military power that the Sun King was able to exert abroad, but also reinforced his absolute political power inside France by ensuring that royal troops would always be available to respond to domestic challenges to royal authority. By the early decades of the eighteenth century, armies in Europe generally looked and operated very differently than they had a hundred years before (Figure 1.2).

The military revolution's consequences extended beyond the realm of warfare. Because state commission armies cost much more to raise and maintain on a permanent basis, they encouraged the growth of stronger royal bureaucracies throughout Europe, which were better equipped to extract taxes from the king's subjects. At the same time, mercantilists advocated stronger armies as an important resource for protecting favorable trade networks as overseas empires expanded (Roberts 1995: 26).

Military reform was intertwined as well with the cultural and intellectual changes that emerged from the Enlightenment. For example, new modes of drill and discipline reflected efforts to reconstitute the moral and political status of soldiers in ways that were consistent with Enlightenment thought (Guinier 2014). They also resulted from advances in science and mathematics, which theorists such as Sébastien Le Prestre de Vauban leveraged to model troop movements, fortress designs, and artillery barrages (Figure 1.3).

FIGURE 1.2: The Surrender of Breda, by Diego Velasquez (1599–1660). Madrid, Museo Del Prado. Credit: De Agostini Picture Library/Getty Images.

FIGURE 1.3: The north front of the Invalides: Mansart's dome above Bruant's pedimented central block. Credit: Daniel Vorndran/DXR. Licensed under the Creative Commons Attribution-Share Alike 3.0 Unported license: https://creativecommons.org/licenses/by-sa/3.0/deed.en.

The military revolution also reconfigured the relationship between the army and the rest of society. The introduction of barracks, which replaced the unpopular practice of billeting troops inside private homes, engendered a starker separation between civilian society and the army. It was with this isolation in mind that the historian André Corvisier wrote that soldiers in the Age of the Enlightenment "no longer belonged to the Third Estate, but to another milieu," in which they were subject to special restrictions, such as prohibitions against marrying without the permission of senior officers (Corvisier 1964: 1:119). In a similar fashion, the introduction of stricter military discipline and the state's assumption of responsibility for supplying troops reduced the extent to which warfare impinged upon civilians, whose homes and fields were less likely to be plundered by marauding, poorly disciplined soldiers. By the early decades of the eighteenth century, armies in Europe generally looked and operated very differently than they had a hundred years before.

MILITARY REFORM AND THE COLONIAL FRONTIER

The same was not necessarily true in European colonies, however. The administrative, political, and cultural practices that emerged from the military revolution in European metropoles tended to arrive later on the colonial frontier than they did in Europe itself. In some cases, they never arrived at all.

For English speakers weaned on the Anglo-American historical tradition, this fact may be difficult to appreciate fully. The major battles of the colonial conflicts that involved British troops during the Enlightenment—the Seven Years' War of 1757–63 (of which the French and Indian War of 1754–63 was a part) and the American Revolutionary War (1775–83)—were fought in large part by forces that exemplified the state commission armies introduced to Europe during the military revolution. For example, the pivotal battle for Quebec on the Plains of Abraham in 1759 pitted the regimented British troops of General James Wolfe against the Marquis de Montcalm's equally well-trained French regulars. During the American Revolution, the rebel Continental army scored its first major victory at Saratoga in 1777 by deploying disciplined forces in pitched battle against their British and Hessian enemies. The Franco-American triumph at the battle of Yorktown four years later was made possible by French regulars and warships imported from Europe. In places closer to the frontier, cultures and practices of warfare looked quite different than they did in Europe during the Enlightenment era (Figure 1.4).

Yet the extent to which any war on colonial frontiers during the Enlightenment boiled down to a "European conflict in a New World setting," as one historian characterized colonial warfare during this period, was clearly limited (Brumwell 2002: 192). The battles cited in the preceding paragraphs were the exceptions, not the norm. They occurred centuries after Europeans had first arrived in the

FIGURE 1.4: Exercitiegenootschap Sneek by Hermanus van der Velde, 1786. Sneek, Netherlands, Fries Scheepvaart Museum. Public domain.

Americas, and they were fought in the regions of North America where European settlement was most dense. In earlier times, and in places closer to the frontier, cultures and practices of warfare looked quite different during the Enlightenment era.

One key difference was the involvement of native peoples and the indigenous military cultures they embraced in conflicts in the colonial world. While Native Americans played relatively little role in the battles of Quebec, Saratoga, or Yorktown, they proved profoundly important to colonial warfare elsewhere. For example, the "massacre" of British troops who had surrendered to the French by Montcalm's Native American allies after the siege of Fort William Henry in 1757 flew in the face of European norms of warfare. Indeed, as Christian Crouch (2014) has shown, the deep divide between the ideal of European-style "noble" warfare and the reality of irregular military practices shaped by Native American cultures during the Seven Years' War in North America was an important motivation for French ministers in Paris to decide to abandon their empire in Canada at the end of the war. In south Asia, the British East India Company relied primarily on local Indian recruits commanded by European officers to conduct warfare (Bryant 1978).

Even in cases where Native Americans were not themselves involved in fighting, the limited impact of the military revolution on colonial frontiers was clear. Troops from the British metropole who served in North America during the eighteenth century may have ridiculed local colonial militia when they arrived, but they discovered soon enough that the European-style tactics and organization on which they prided themselves were of little use in most parts of the Americas. The tactics of *petite guerre*, or wars and ambushes, came to dominate the strategy of British metropolitan troops who served in the New World. These practices not only allowed European soldiers to cope with the demands of campaigning and combat on rough terrain, but also helped European armies to develop tactics, such as amphibious assault and light infantry skirmishing, that they eventually imported back to Europe as the Age of Enlightenment came to a close (Brumwell 2002: 227).

RACE, RELIGION, AND CULTURE IN EUROPEAN ARMIES

If practices of warfare and military organization were diverse during the Enlightenment era, the racial, religious, linguistic, and political identities of the men who served in armies of the period were even more so, in both the metropole and colonial settings. In many cases, the ways in which soldiers looked, worshiped, spoke, or understood their political allegiances had little in common with the values of the monarchs for whom they nominally fought.

This reality may seem surprising. As noted earlier, the state assumed a much more prominent role during the Enlightenment in recruiting troops. There might therefore appear to have been no reason for the presence within a European state's armies of large numbers of soldiers who were born outside its borders. Nor was religious toleration for troops who adhered to creeds other than those associated with the state an obvious proposition in an era when absolute monarchs often bound their political legitimacy to the defense of whichever faith they endorsed. Differences of language within the ranks, as well as shifting political loyalties of troops when they fought in the name of foreign sovereigns, may have appeared to undercut the military effectiveness of armies.

Yet demographic diversity was commonplace in Enlightenment-era armies of Europe and European empires. It stemmed in large part from the reliance of most armies on foreign populations to supply significant portions of their troops. Eighteenth-century states not only tolerated but encouraged foreign recruitment for several reasons. One was that, by enlisting men from abroad, they hoped to spare some of their own subjects from service in the army. This strategy reflected the mercantilist economic theories of the time, which linked a society's prosperity to the number of subjects available to work. It was for this reason that Maurice de Saxe, a German aristocrat who fought for France in the mid-eighteenth century, quipped that each foreigner in the army "serves us as three men: he spares one in France, he deprives our enemies of one and he serves us as one" (Corvisier 1964: 1:260).

In addition, foreign recruits served as symbols of royal prestige and international influence for absolute monarchs of the Enlightenment era by highlighting the king or queen's ability to attract the subjects of foreign sovereigns to his army. Recruiters from throughout Europe also sought foreigners from certain regions, especially Germany and Switzerland, because they believed that men from these locales were among the most physically fit and well-disciplined of the continent.

For most large states, foreign recruitment was a formal, standardized process, which was oriented around specially designated foreign units that governments levied for the express purpose of enlisting men born abroad. To take the French army as an example, on the eve of the French Revolution in 1789, the monarchy officially designated thirty-two of the royal army's 168 regular regiments as "foreign" regiments (Rapport 2000: 149). In theory, these units drew their personnel from six distinct foreign groups—Swiss, Irish, Italians, Germans, Liégeois, and Hungarians—but in practice their ranks were much more diverse. They included men from nearly every corner of Europe. They also occasionally enlisted soldiers from as far away as Madagascar, India, and New York (Tozzi 2016: 25–6). French natives enlisted in the foreign regiments as well, despite recurring efforts by the state throughout the eighteenth century to prohibit or limit this practice by, for example, issuing decrees that ordered the punishment of officers who enlisted French natives in foreign regiments. Yet these measures were only partially effective.

Notwithstanding the presence of some French natives within the foreign regiments, these units retained their foreign character until their dissolution during the French Revolution. They received commands in foreign languages, adhered to foreign standards of drill and discipline, and served under the direction of officers who in most cases were almost exclusively foreign, even if the troops they commanded represented a mix of French and foreign soldiers.

The enduring presence of foreign corps within the army of France highlighted several significant ways in which warfare and the military realm helped to shape Europe and European empires during the Age of Enlightenment. For one, the foreign corps introduced considerable religious, racial, cultural, and linguistic diversity to both metropolitan France and the French empire. To be sure, the total number of foreigners in the Old Regime French army, who accounted for only about fifteen percent of the state's approximately 200,000 troops in the decades preceding the Revolution, represented a small proportion of France's total population of 26 million (Dupâquier 1970: 155). Yet the presence of even small concentrations of foreigners within the army was remarkable in an era during which France's absolute monarchy strove to cultivate an image of the kingdom as a religiously and racially (if not linguistically) homogeneous society.

Foreign troops contributed racial diversity to Enlightenment France, too. The Volontaires de Saxe regiment was composed primarily of recruits from eastern Europe, but it also included a company of black troops born in Africa, the Caribbean, South America, and India (Fieffé 1854: 1:280–1; Corvisier 1964: 1:273–4). Black recruits were scattered across several other foreign regiments as well (Tozzi 2016: 25). Black soldiers serving in the French metropole flew in the face of efforts by the state to restrict the entry of people of color into France proper during the Enlightenment.

The army's importance in diversifying French society extended to the French empire as well. Under the Old Regime, French colonies fell under the direction of the ministry of the navy rather than the army. The navy did not maintain as many foreign corps as the army, but it nonetheless relied under certain circumstances on foreign or black troops to assure the defense of France's imperial possessions.

In addition to diversifying the population of French settlements on the colonial frontier, the foreign regiments of both the army and the navy highlighted how imperial networks drove the migration of peoples and ideas across the globe during the Enlightenment era. That was particularly true in cases where the French army enlisted men born very far from where they served. In general, the available records provide little information to help determine precisely how troops from places such as south-east Africa and New England made their way into the ranks of French army units. It seems likely, however, that in some instances French military expeditions overseas facilitated the enlistment of such troops; for example, circumstantial evidence suggests that black troops who enlisted in regular French army regiments during the American Revolution were recruited by French officers from among local populations of people of color in the Caribbean islands where French troops were fighting. Yet troops from remote overseas locales also enlisted periodically in French corps starting several decades before the French army undertook major military expeditions in the Americas (and, on a smaller scale, to places in Africa such as Senegal) during the second half of the eighteenth century (Tozzi 2016: 26).

Foreign recruits introduced linguistic diversity to France and its empire, too. In addition to the German dialects of soldiers from Germany, Switzerland, and eastern France, troops from Ireland spoke Gaelic and English, soldiers from the Low Countries communicated in Dutch and Walloon, and variants of Italian predominated within foreign regiments associated with that nationality. Meanwhile, the languages introduced by recruits from eastern Europe and overseas, as well as the dialectic variations of French itself under the Old Regime, meant that the army was home to a truly expansive medley of different tongues during the eighteenth century (Tozzi 2016: 36).

France was not the only European state in the Age of Enlightenment that relied in large part on foreign troops to wage its wars. The Spanish and Austrian monarchies maintained Irish and Walloon regiments (Haythornthwaite and Younghusband 1994). The Dutch army recruited Germans and Swiss (Conway

2014: 24). The British army was exceptional in that it did not directly raise its own foreign regiments during most of the eighteenth century; however, the British state relied heavily on foreigners because it contracted with foreign states to supply troop contingents in wartime, as it famously did with Hessian units during the American Revolution (Conway 2014: 24).

THE ENLIGHTENMENT AND WAR: REASONS FOR WAR IN THE AGE OF REASON

So far, this chapter has highlighted several key themes associated with warfare in the Age of Enlightenment. First, the recruitment and organization of military forces, and the relationship between soldiers and the rest of society, underwent significant change during the period. Second, the nature of warfare varied widely and proved much less neat and orchestrated than the most famous pitched battles of the period imply. Third, the demographic and cultural composition of armies was complex. Rather than mirroring the society they served, military units, especially those that recruited foreigners, were among the most diverse organizations in the European world.

What did contemporaries think about these trends, and about warfare itself? What role did warfare play in the intellectual and political developments that emerged during the Enlightenment era? These seem obvious questions to ask, especially because the expansion of literacy and the public sphere during the Enlightenment made it easier than ever for elites and ordinary people alike to discuss war and armies.

The remainder of this chapter answers these questions by drawing on both literary sources associated with the "High Enlightenment," which reflected the thoughts of intellectual elites, as well as archival material that helps to illuminate what non-elites were thinking about warfare during the period.

Throughout the eighteenth century, philosophers such as Charles-Irénée Castel de Saint-Pierre (1713) and Immanuel Kant (1795) theorized that warfare could be abolished forever. Such ideas were far removed from reality, however. For the majority of the Enlightenment era, conflicts broke out frequently enough that peacetime for European societies and their overseas extensions was exceptional rather than the norm. The eighteenth century opened with the War of the Spanish Succession of 1701–14, which was followed by the wars of the Quadruple Alliance (1718–20), Polish Succession (1733–8), Austrian Succession (1740–8), the Seven Years' War (1756–63), and the American Revolutionary War (1775–83). These were just the conflicts that drew in multiple European states; in total, Europe witnessed sixteen major wars in the eighteenth century (Blanning 1986: 37).

The main reason why warfare proved so frequent in the eighteenth-century western world was that by the Age of Absolutism, military conflict had evolved into a low-risk and efficient means for absolute monarchs to settle scores with foreign adversaries. Financially, the cost of going to war was marginal because most European states after the military revolution possessed permanent standing armies, which they paid to maintain whether or not they were actively waging war. This did not mean that a state could transition from peacetime to wartime at zero expense; mobilization did require an increase in the size of the army. That cost money, since more troops required more pay and supplies. Yet the augmentation of army strength, which generally followed plans that royal ministers prepared ahead of time in case the country went to war, entailed only moderate increases. For instance, on the eve of the French Revolution, when France was at peace, its army's theoretical strength amounted to about 173,000 regular troops and 55,240 militia. Those figures would have increased to around 211,000 and 76,000 men, respectively, in the event that France went to war (Albert Duruy 1888: 8; Babeau 1890: 14). The additional recruitment—and, by extension, financial expenditure—that a declaration of war entailed under the Old Regime was certainly not negligible. But it was not exorbitant, either. If warfare contributed to the bankruptcy of the French state on the eve of the Revolution, the costs of maintaining large standing armies on an ongoing basis, rather than the expense associated with particular conflicts, was the primary cause.

Thus, mobilizing for war during the Enlightenment did not place a drastic new burden on the state's finances. This reality (which changed greatly during the era of the French Revolution, when armies became much larger) meant that there was no overwhelming financial incentive for avoiding war during much of the eighteenth century. On the contrary, *not* going to war on a relatively frequent basis would have seemed fiscally imprudent to most eighteenth-century royal ministers, given the huge expenditures that monarchs endured to maintain standing armies whether or not they were actually using them.

A second consideration that encouraged Old Regime monarchs to engage frequently in warfare was the limited risk, in terms of power as well as resources, that they assumed by doing so. Unlike the conflicts of earlier centuries, and many of those of more modern times, eighteenth-century wars were rarely existential in nature prior to the French revolutionary era. No monarch of a major European state lost his or her throne as the result of a war during this period. Instead, major wars within Europe usually revolved around the conquest or loss of "a few villages," as Voltaire quipped in his *Philosophical Dictionary* (Voltaire 1877–85: 18:143).

Conflicts on colonial frontiers tended to be more existential in nature, especially for indigenous peoples whom Europeans completely extinguished. In addition, the entire populations of European settlements overseas were sometimes destroyed during conflicts; this was the fate that befell the French Huguenots who settled Fort Caroline in Florida when it was attacked by Spanish forces in 1565, for instance. Yet wholesale massacres of European populations like these occurred only on small scales and grew less frequent by the eighteenth century. The potential devastation that could result from colonial fighting was of little concern for monarchs in far-off European capitals when they decided to go to war.

Nor did the destruction of eighteenth-century conflicts compare to that endured by European societies in earlier centuries, when marauding troops and economic devastation were common features of warfare, or to the devastation of twentieth-century mechanized combat. Eighteenth-century wars involved few battles. One major conflict, the War of the Bavarian Succession of 1778–9, included no significant engagements at all (Blanning 1986: 40). When battles did occur, they usually took place far from centers of population or economic activity, and they rarely lasted longer than a day.

This is not to say that Old Regime conflicts were cheery affairs for everyone involved. Locally, warfare frequently caused horrifying destruction to fields and villages. Battle could certainly prove deadly for the soldiers who engaged in it, even if Old Regime generals tended to be more sparing of their valuable grenadiers' lives than their successors during the revolutionary era (when frontal assault and overwhelming force became popular strategies for generals) proved to be. Yet dangers of this nature did not generally impact societies as a whole. Outside of the local context of battles, the quartering of troops in civilian homes (a practice that became uncommon as states invested in barracks during the military revolution) and the harassment of minority groups through initiatives like Louis XIV's anti-Protestant Dragonnades, armies and warfare caused comparatively little destruction during the Enlightenment.

ENLIGHTENMENT ATTITUDES TOWARD WAR

The lack of widespread destruction associated with warfare in the Age of Enlightenment helps to explain why contemporaries tended to express few reservations about war.

To be sure, war had its principled critics, especially among the highly celebrated Enlightenment philosophers of the era. Jean-Jacques Rousseau ([1755] 1917) lamented "the perpetual quarrels, the robberies, the usurpations, the revolts, the wars, the murders, which bring daily desolation" to Europe. Rousseau's critique expanded upon an earlier proposal by Saint-Pierre (1713) to establish "perpetual peace" in Europe, an idea taken up more famously near the end of the eighteenth century by Kant (1795), as noted earlier. For his part, Voltaire (who exhibited no qualms about meeting monarchs such as Frederick the Great of Prussia, the utter opposite of a peacenik, or Catherine the Great of Russia, also no stranger to war) never endorsed the pursuit of everlasting peace, which he viewed as infeasible. But Voltaire (1877–85: 19:320) nonetheless proved quite critical of war in some instances. In one sarcastic analysis, he called war an "infernal enterprise" in which "each leader of a band of killers blesses his battle standards and solemnly invokes God before going off to kill his neighbor" (Mason 1999: 311). Moral opposition to war was also evident in certain Old Regime texts. For example, César-Pierre Richelet used his 1680 *Dictionnaire françois* to define war in negative terms, giving usage examples that reminded readers that "war, disease and famine are the three scourges of God" (Branca 1999: 72). Finally, ecclesiastical critics such as François Fénélon (1850: 6:256) denounced war as "an evil that dishonors humanity."

Yet scattered opposition to war within certain erudite works authored by intellectual elites was not representative of widespread opinion. Some of the best known Enlightenment philosophers were inconsistent or reserved in their critiques of warfare. The baron of Montesquieu viewed war as detrimental to commerce, and vice versa (Howse 2006). But he expressed no principled qualms about war itself, which he viewed in Hobbesian terms as a natural, inevitable facet of human existence (Montesquieu [1748] 1900: 5). Voltaire criticized Montesquieu in the *Philosophical Dictionary* for being too supportive of preemptive war, but Voltaire's own views toward war varied over the course of his career (Mason 1999: 311–12). Voltaire never condemned war as much as he denounced the hypocritical nature with which monarchs of the time appeared to justify and conduct it.

Similarly, Denis Diderot and Jean le Rond d'Alembert, the editors of the *Encyclopédie*, a signal work of the French Enlightenment, included an essay on war that left little question as to whether war was something readers should oppose in principle (1751–65: 7:985). "Who can doubt that the art of war is not the greatest of all?" the article asked. "It is by war that liberty is perpetuated, dignity is maintained and provinces and power are protected." Written by military theorists, the essay read primarily as a manual explaining how to wage different kinds of war (Branca 1999: 73). To the extent that the *Encyclopédie* engaged the question of whether war served a useful purpose, it did so only to define the principles that characterized a "just" war (Diderot and d'Alembert 1751–65: 7:996–8). So long as a state waged war for justifiable reasons, the *Encyclopédie* implied, there was nothing wrong or lamentable about entering into a state of war.

Europe's population at large had little reason to be any less supportive of wars under the Old Regime than intellectual elites. Within the nobility, whose *raison d'être* during the eighteenth century still theoretically emanated from noblemen's role in fighting the monarch's wars, enthusiasm for war was ever-present (Bell 2007: 99). For their part, ordinary men and women, as noted earlier, were rarely impacted personally by warfare. It is true that war affected civilians in a roundabout way by leading to higher taxes, which, as noted earlier, sovereigns imposed to pay for the large standing armies they maintained. In

France, for example, the annual tax yield collected by the French state nearly doubled over the course of Louis XIV's personal reign, rising from 85 million *livres* to 152 million (Nolan 2008: 509). The increase was due in no small part to the cost of the king's wars and huge standing army. Yet the new royal taxes that Louis XIV's finance minister, Jean-Baptiste Colbert, introduced were not directly tied to warfare, and military affairs accounted for only one cause of the Bourbon state's chronic thirst for new sources of revenue. There is plenty of evidence that French peasants and artisans resented the high taxes they paid, which contributed to the popular disturbances that occasionally broke out in Old Regime France, such as the Flour War of 1775 (Bouton 1993). Yet there is no evidence that non-elites blamed warfare in particular for their tax burden, or that financial pressures ever caused them to resist the monarchy's efforts to wage war before the very end of the Old Regime.

On the contrary, ordinary people placed plenty of pressure on their sovereigns to go to war, especially after fissures in absolutist systems facilitated the emergence of politically meaningful public opinion starting in the mid-eighteenth century (Baker 1987: 210). While nationalism in European societies did not fully emerge until the very end of the Enlightenment era, national antagonisms by European peoples did factor into war-making. For example, mutual resentment between the peoples of Britain and France flourished under the Old Regime, especially among the generations that lived through the Seven Years' War and the American Revolution (Acomb 1950; Stone 1994: 142). This was especially true because these two conflicts were, to a considerably greater degree than earlier wars, international in scope and driven by national antagonism. Austrophobia thrived in France, too, and in fact only decreased after the "diplomatic revolution" of 1756, which transformed France and Austria from longstanding enemies into uneasy allies (Blanning 1986: 106–7).

THE FALLOUT OF PEACE: FRANCE AND THE DUTCH PATRIOTS' REVOLT (1781–7)

In some contexts, absolute monarchs' failure to take effective military action against foreign adversaries could undercut the legitimacy of their regimes. The best example of this phenomenon occurred in France during the late 1780s, when the monarchy's inability to intervene militarily in the Dutch Patriots' Revolt of 1781–7 illuminated the brokenness of absolutist policies in a way that helped to stoke the French Revolution.

On its own, the lack of French intervention during the Dutch Revolt might not have proven very significant for France. Ideologically, Louis XVI's court shared no interest with the Dutch Patriots, who began agitating in 1781 to reclaim the natural rights that they believed they had lost to the absolutist tendencies of Stadtholder William V (Schama 1977: 65–6). By 1783 the situation had evolved into an open war between the Patriots and the stadtholder's supporters, the Orangists. In September 1787, the localized war expanded to an international conflict when 26,000 troops from the Prussian army, renowned for their strict discipline and ability to maneuver with expert precision on the battlefield, invaded the Republic under the command of Charles William Ferdinand, Duke of Brunswick-Lüneburg.

The Prussian military intervention, which represented the response to an appeal for external help from the Orangists, drove the Patriots from their strongholds within a month and restored William V to power. The victory augmented Prussian influence over the Netherlands. It also extended British power in the region, since William Pitt's gold—specifically, 90,000 pounds' worth—had funded the expedition, a fact not lost on the Patriots (Te Brake 1985: 199). But this Anglo-Prussian collaboration represented no grave threat to French diplomatic interests. If anything, it helped to balance the longstanding tensions between Britain and France regarding the Netherlands by introducing Prussia, hardly an invariable British ally, as a third contender in the region (Schama 1977: 138).

Of much greater consequence for the French monarchy was the domestic fallout that resulted from its failure to do for the Patriots what the Prussians and British had done for the Orangists. French lack of support for the rebels, which was the result primarily of the Bourbon state's desperate financial situation during the 1780s, flew in the face of the encouragement that royal ministers in France had given to the Patriots by urging them on in their revolt (Schama 1977: 138). It was also at odds with public opinion inside France. French papers began reporting on events in the Dutch Republic in detail starting with the arrival in France in the fall of 1781 of copies of the first Patriot invective against the stadtholder's government, an anonymous pamphlet titled *To the Netherlands People* (Schama 1977: 138). The publication, which was the work of Baron Joan Derk van der Capellen tot den Pol, aimed to "raise the rabble against established authority," according to one contemporary French analysis, which was apparently doubtful of the legitimacy of the popular revolt then underway. Yet the same French writer tellingly attributed to van der Capellen's text "some rather accurate and detailed notions regarding the government" of the Dutch Republic (*Mémoires secrets* 1780–6; Schama 1977: 64). That interpretation revealed a level of sympathy with the Patriots' grievances against the regime.

Those sympathies grew as the crisis continued. The Count of Mirabeau lamented in November 1787, shortly after Prussian troops had overrun the Dutch Republic, that France professed support for the Dutch Patriots yet "rejected the most favorable occasions for abolishing the stadtholder's government and the House of Orange" because the court at Versailles had found itself "encumbered by internal divisions" (*Analyse des papiers anglois* November 11, 1787). Mirabeau's criticisms reflected, in part, sympathy for the tragedy of the Dutch Patriots' fate. Yet his greater concern was the embarrassment France had suffered internationally by failing to intervene in the Dutch affair.

The following year Mirabeau (1788) seized on the failed revolt to publish, in French, a 212-page monograph ostensibly addressed to the Dutch people. The text, which consisted primarily of a recounting of Dutch history, celebrated Dutch republicanism. For French readers, however, it served also as an attack on the Bourbon ministers who failed to assure Dutch freedom (Schama 1977: 138). By extension, it was a critique of the French state and a call for liberal reform inside France. To be sure, the amount of reform that Mirabeau and other liberal nobles deemed necessary to restore French prestige fell far short of the revolution that would soon appear on the horizon. Yet the state's continuing failure to intervene decisively in the crisis near its borders only discredited it further as the financial and political troubles inside France grew increasingly serious during the late 1780s.

France's non-intervention in the Netherlands was not a one-off episode. The affair represented the culmination of a long string of international embarrassments that stretched back to the early eighteenth century. France had lost nearly every conflict in which it embroiled itself since Louis XIV's death, with but two major exceptions: the War of the Quadruple Alliance (1718–20) and the intervention in the American Revolution. Following this string of recurring defeats and lackluster victories, Louis XVI's failure to intervene in the Dutch Revolt robbed the Bourbon state of the little diplomatic and military credibility it retained during the 1780s, both inside France and internationally. Similar inaction by the French state during the Austro-Turkish War of 1788–91 weakened the monarchy's prestige even further, especially because France had traditionally been a close ally of the Ottomans. The pattern of Bourbon military and diplomatic humiliation in the closing decades of the Old Regime "rendered credible critics' arguments that the country's institutions were in need of basic overhaul," as the historians Theda Skocpol and Meyer Kestnbaum (1990: 17) observed.

WAR AND POLITICAL CHANGE

If the Old Regime state's failure to make war when its subjects deemed it necessary undermined absolutist credibility, it was understandable that, given the opportunity, French subjects would demand the authority to decide issues of war and peace themselves. Calls for this right were a telling feature of the *cahiers de doléances*, the lists of grievances that approximately 40,000 communities throughout France submitted to the king in advance of the opening of the Estates-General meeting in May 1789 (Figure 1.5). The king's subjects seized upon the issue of war in the *cahiers* to help drive forward an agenda of political reform that would eventually undo the absolute monarchy entirely.

FIGURE 1.5: Opening of The Estates-General, Versailles, 1789 (1885). Credit: The Print Collector/Getty Images.

The *cahiers* recorded a diverse array of grievances, and war featured only occasionally in them. The majority of grievances in the *cahiers* centered on questions related to royal or aristocratic privilege or taxation. To the extent that military or diplomatic affairs arose within the documents, they usually involved unremarkable complaints or recommendations regarding regulation of the royal army and the *milice*, the unpopular conscript force in which the monarchy forced some peasants to serve under the Old Regime (Mavidal 1890: 1:723, 2:130, 5:655).

This did not mean, however, that the *cahiers* ignored the issue of war and peace. In some cases the authors of the *cahiers* seized upon financial concerns, the issue at the center of the crisis that had prompted the king to call for a meeting of the Estates-General for the first time since 1614, to promote the idea that the monarchy should share power with representatives of the nation in declaring war. Petitioners from the Third Estate in Ballainvilliers requested in their *cahier* that "no offensive war be undertaken unless, beforehand, the Estates-General appropriates, in consultation with the king, the resources necessary to wage it honorably" (Mavidal 1890: 4:337). This request reflected not only concern that financial default might result in further military embarrassment for France, but also fears that ill-advised wars could lead to exorbitant taxes.

Other *cahiers* made the case for representative government by leveraging war as an avenue of attack against absolute monarchy. For instance, the town of

Carcés requested that issues of "war and peace be voted in the Estates-General," provided the assembly was in session when the state needed to make such decisions (Mavidal 1890: 3:263). This *cahier* did not elaborate on the reasons why the Estates-General should have the power to approve or deny declarations of war or peace. The petitioners apparently took the legitimacy of such authority to be self-evident.

Yet more significant was the suggestion by the clergy of Peronne in its *cahier* that the king should agree to allow the Estates-General to meet on a recurring basis every five years. This was a bold request, since it aimed to restore the power that the Estates-General had enjoyed in France in earlier centuries, before Louis XVI's predecessors had effectively suppressed it by preventing the body from assembling frequently. The proposal would have transformed the institution into one that functioned something like Britain's Parliament. To justify the demand, the clergy pointed, among other considerations, to the importance of assigning to the Estates-General "the measure of authority that it requires regarding planning for war or other calamities" (Mavidal 1890: 5:352). The petitioners thus implied that the importance of the Estates-General's participation in debates about war was one reason why regular meetings should be restored.

Not all *cahiers* were so aggressive in demanding that the king surrender the powers of war and peace to representatives of the people. The nobility of the Paris region wrote in its *cahier* that the king, as the "embodiment of executive power," should have the right to take "the most prompt measures to assure the public defense," without requiring prior approval from the Estates-General for a declaration of war (Mavidal 1890: 5:240). Yet the language of the *cahier* on this point was significant. By assigning the king the right to make war only because he represented the "executive power," the nobility implied that the king's power was not absolute.

Admittedly, fewer than a dozen of the *cahiers* demanded greater freedom for the king's subjects in deciding questions of war and peace. It is unclear how widespread such ideas might have been in France. Still, the *cahiers* that did raise this issue, which emanated from communities spread across different parts of the kingdom, are evidence that the king's subjects in at least some cases viewed the right of the people to help decide war and peace as an essential component of sovereignty. This idea was totally at odds with absolutist politics.

WARFARE IN THE AGE OF REVOLUTIONS

The Enlightenment era began with the military revolution transforming the way European societies organized armies and conducted warfare. Those changes played a central role in reinforcing the absolute political authority of Europe's enlightened despots. As the Enlightenment era came to a close during the final decades of the eighteenth century, however, warfare assumed a political significance that helped to undo absolutism.

The revolutionary age ushered in a sharp break with many of the theories and practices of war that had predominated during the Enlightenment. In place of well-disciplined, meticulously trained professional troops, revolutionaries in America, France, and Haiti defeated their enemies using armies of relatively inexperienced "citizen-soldiers." The troops in revolutionary armies stood their ground on the battlefield because of political ideology and attachment to a revolutionary cause, not because they had undergone years of rigorous drill.

Revolutionaries also benefited from much larger armies. This was especially true in France, where by the end of the eighteenth century nearly a million men were under arms, far more than the 400,000 whom Louis XIV had commanded at the height of Old Regime France's military power. To fill the ranks of such large armies, the French revolutionaries introduced universal male conscription in 1798. Limited conscription of peasants for militia service had existed under the Old Regime. Some European powers with small populations, such as Sweden and Prussia, had relied on conscription prior to the age of revolutions. Yet wholesale conscription during the French Revolution significantly increased the extent to which warfare and the army impinged upon society.

Larger armies were necessary, in part, because warfare ceased to be limited. At stake were entire ideological systems, especially in the French and Haitian revolutions. Warfare had become existential.

Ironically, this turn toward unlimited warfare during the revolutionary age was made conceptually possible, in part, by prerevolutionary Enlightenment thinkers who argued that humanity could be perfected and warfare eliminated forever. Such ideas helped revolutionaries to justify all-out war by theorizing that one final, earth-shattering conflict might be necessary in order to eradicate absolutist societies and bring about the perpetual peace that seemed finally within reach (Bell 2007: 77).

All of these changes hallmarked the emergence of what historians David Bell (2007) and Jean-Yves Guiomar (2004) have called "total war." During the age of revolutions, states marshaled all of the resources at their disposal in the interest of waging war. Policies such as the *levée en masse* of 1793, which ordered men, women, and children alike to perform specific tasks in support of national defense, helped France to win its revolutionary war despite having all of Europe's other major powers—to say nothing of rebels inside the country—arrayed against it.

In many respects, the French revolutionaries pioneered the military innovations that characterized the revolutionary age. Yet their enemies adapted quickly enough. By the time the revolutionary age—and the Enlightenment era—came to a close with the defeat of Napoleon in 1815, armies across Europe were much larger than they had been before the French Revolution. They were composed in many cases of conscripts. Their activities had profound consequences for civilians, who risked not only becoming collateral victims of fighting but were sometimes actively targeted for retribution. War had indeed become total.

CONCLUSION

Warfare within European empires during the Age of Enlightenment took such different forms within different geographical and temporal contexts that it is impossible to speak of a singular culture of Enlightenment warfare. The culture of Enlightenment military institutions and ideologies was instead characterized by deep diversity and constant change.

At the outset of the Enlightenment era, conflicts within both Europe and on colonial frontiers tended to be bloody and brutal. In the seventeenth century, as a result of the military revolution, fighting within most parts of Europe became less destructive, even if it remained frequent. A different trend held true within European colonies, where ruled and regimented forces comprised solely of troops of European descent did not arrive until the latter half of the eighteenth century, if at all. The age of revolutions upended practices of warfare once again by inaugurating the era of total war, characterized by unlimited fighting and the marshaling of societies' entire resources to support the war effort. In many respects, total war remained the paradigm that shaped the conflicts of European societies, both within Europe and overseas, through the mid-twentieth century.

CHAPTER TWO

Trade

JUNKO THÉRÈSE TAKEDA

INTRODUCTION

The Age of Exploration saw the Portuguese and Spanish funnel unprecedented quantities of silver and gold into the early modern world economy. Poor investment choices, extravagant expenditures, and the British defeat of the Spanish Armada in 1588, however, hastened the waning of Iberian political power. The Dutch, British, and French took advantage of this crisis and competed for the next two centuries to acquire and monopolize trading territories in the Mediterranean, Asia, Africa, and the Americas. Meanwhile, rivalries among the "gunpowder" empires in Eurasia—Ottoman Turkey, Safavid Iran, Mughal India—and Muscovite Russia energized economic competition on a global scale and made dynastic geopolitics increasingly aggressive and complicated.

Trans-imperial trade was not a new thing in the early modern period. Robust exchanges stimulated by the Mongol empire in east and south Asian spices, textiles, and central Asian medicine, science, and engineering, in addition to the trans-Saharan gold, salt, and cowrie trade directed by the Mali empire had caught the eyes of European merchants, missionaries, and adventurers by the fourteenth century. Historians have identified the emergence of nine zones of commercial interaction by this point that linked the ends of the Silk Roads, North Africa, the Mediterranean, and the Pacific islands (Gerritsen and Riello 2016: 3–4).

What then, was different or novel about global trade in the period bracketed between the seventeenth and eighteenth centuries? As Michael H. Fisher elaborates in his essay on mobility in this volume, for the first time, improved navigational science allowed for long-distance trans-oceanic exchange.

Borrowing in large part from Asian technology, European explorers engineered and constructed bigger, faster, and streamlined ships while discovering groundbreaking information on the Gulf Stream, the easterly and westerly trade winds (Fernández-Armesto 2008: 412–13). New maritime routes made previously impossible direct physical, material, and cultural connections between Asia and the Americas, Europe and the Indian Ocean a reality. Whereas European maritime activity—dominated by the Venetians and other Italian city-states—had remained largely confined to smaller ships in the Mediterranean until this point, new technologies drove European expansion westwards and southwards to previously uncharted oceanic territories.

The use of such new sea-lanes launched a sea change in the dynamics of political and economic power between Asia and Europe, and introduced major transformations in the cultural life of European populations. Chinese, Indian, Persian, and Turkish manufacturing productivity had bested European output in quantity and quality for centuries. The establishment of Dutch, British, and French commercial presence in the Mediterranean, Atlantic and Indian Ocean worlds fostered cultures of mobility, and generated technological transfers from Asia to Europe that allowed bourgeoning European states to establish and improve industries, particularly related to textile production. European dynastic struggles to forcefully expand trading opportunities, combined with statist intervention to strengthen industrial output, played roles in destabilizing relations among Eurasian empires and upending the Asian monopoly on manufacturing. Corporate raiding of vast territories depleted resources, caused political instability, and resulted in environmental destruction, famine, and pandemics particularly in the Asian subcontinent. A violent Atlantic zone— marked by European colonization, a racialized slave economy, naval competition, exorbitant taxation rates, and prohibitory trade regulations—and a dark underworld of piracy, counterfeiting, and smuggling emerged and threatened to eclipse the formerly vibrant economies of the Mediterranean and Eurasian worlds.

Oceanic trade fundamentally altered the political, social, physical, and cultural landscapes of European states by the end of the eighteenth century. The efforts of state authorities, provincial and civic representatives to expand trade and commerce stimulated innovations in bureaucratic centralization of the kind that destabilized traditional social hierarchies of estates and orders. The Enlightenment, understood as the cultural byproduct of trans-imperial contacts and exchanges, spawned new philosophical explanations of the roles and value of merchants and laborers within commercial and political society, and energized debates about the proper role of the state to control or regulate the economy. Such discussions introduced new political vocabularies—of humanitarianism, universalism, democracy, equality, liberty, and the rights-bearing citizen—that threatened to unseat traditional political organizations, as made evident by the examples of the Glorious Revolution in England, the American War of Independence, and the French Revolution of 1789. These political developments also privileged western concepts of civilization, definitions of individualism, and standards of material and cultural progress used to rationalize European imperialism across the nineteenth and twentieth centuries. An examination of developments in early modern commercial exchange reveals the extent to which the physical and political mechanisms for modern western expansionism was built upon institutions, policies, and practices related to trans-oceanic trade established in the seventeenth and eighteenth centuries.

TRADE ENVIRONMENTS, DIPLOMACY, AND THE POLITICS OF GLOBAL EXCHANGE

While the overarching story of European commerce across the early modern period is one of the "rise of the West," the notion that European exploration and colonization was characterized solely by impositions of "western" supremacy is a mischaracterization. Certainly, violence plagued trans-imperial trade; conquest, colonization, and silver extraction in Central and South America, for example, resulted in the extinction and disappearance of indigenous populations and cities. But around the Mediterranean, Indian Ocean, south and east Asia, European states and trade monopolies oscillated between waging territorial wars, pursuing diplomacy, and engaging in commodity exchange. Europeans hoping to trade in Safavid Persia, Ottoman Turkey, Mughal India, Ming China, the Siamese Ayutthaya kingdom, or Tokugawa Japan often "played submissive role[s] within the complex hierarchies of royal and imperial courts" (Gosselink 2015: 24). The relative inferiority of European states in the early portion of this period becomes evident when we explore a few cases of trans-imperial trade between European and Asian empires, and the culturally ambiguous, pluralistic environments in which their merchants existed. While the largest and most powerful European trading colonies in Asia and Eurasia were administered by semi-autonomous trading companies, governors-general, and diplomats, and boasted large territories marked by palaces, gardens and hunting spaces, ports, shipyards, churches, hospitals, schools, and administrative offices, size did not translate necessarily into political or economic muscle (Gosselink 2015: 21–31).

Scholars have spilled much ink describing European trade companies and their role in fostering diplomatic and commercial connections between European states and the rest of the world in the early modern period. Following Vasco da Gama's arrival in Calicut in 1498, Portuguese merchants in the employ of the Estado da India, one of the first European corporate enterprises in the Indian Ocean, had begun organizing networks for collecting tolls, issuing passports, and arranging transportation of goods in south and east Asia. They also participated in private intra-Asian trade between Nagasaki, Goa, Malacca, and Macao in the early sixteenth century (Prakash 2009: 145). By the end of the century, British and Dutch East India trade overwhelmed Portuguese and Spanish commercial power. Following Dutch independence from Spain in 1579, the founding charter of the Vereenidge Oost-Indische Compagnie (VOC) in 1602 guaranteed the new company a twenty-one-year monopoly to trade in Asian spices. The largest and strongest European shipping and trading company in the early modern world, the VOC's fleet, numbering close to six thousand ships, transported a million Asian and European workers to its six hundred trading stations between the Cape of Good Hope and Japan during the span of the seventeenth century.

If we turn to Batavia, capital of the Dutch East Indies established near Bantam, in Java, the Dutch VOC certainly appears to be an economic and political powerhouse. Ruled by several Islamic kings, Java had emerged as a major commercial zone that linked the Indian Ocean trade with that of the South China Sea. The Dutch opened a factory in nearby Ayutthaya (Siam) in 1608, and received a Siamese embassy in Holland the same year. Led by Jan Pietersz, governor-general of the VOC, they established their headquarters in Batavia in 1619 (Figure 2.1). By the mid-seventeenth century, Batavia had become as large and prominent as a city-state. The VOC gradually spread its tentacles into the hinterland, developing farmland and established a vibrant

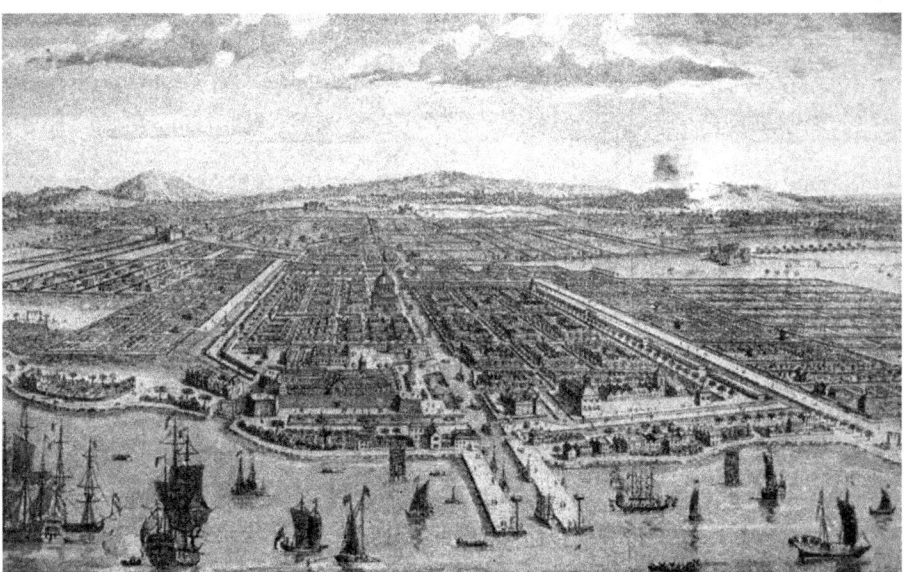

FIGURE 2.1: City of Batavia, headquarters of the Dutch East India Company in south-east Asia (Indonesia), in 1619. Credit: Universal History Archive/UIG via Getty Images.

sugar plantation economy with the help of Chinese inhabitants, day laborers, and slaves (Van Campen 2015: 40–9, 84–5).

The Chevalier de Chaumont, member of the French embassy to Siam in 1685, described Batavia thus:

> 'Tis like Venice, having canals which run through every street, and planted with great trees which yield an agreeable shade, as well to the canals as the streets. The houses are built as they are in Holland (and with the same cleanliness). There is a citadel (with four bastions). The town is enclosed with a wall, and a great ditch, but not deep. The surroundings are very fine, with country houses round about with very handsome gardens and fish ponds, wherein are admirable fish of all sorts (and many colours; I saw many both silver and gold). In this town are many exceedingly rich traders, who spare no cost for their delight; their freedom is the same as in Holland, particularly in regard to women . . . This town is a place of vast commerce, and its riches are so great that the inhabitants need not be sparing of their gold and silver. 'Tis extraordinarily well peopled and the Dutch keep a strong garrison; they have there near three thousand Moors from the coast of Malabar who are slaves, and several of the natives they keep under their obedience, who live about the town (Chaumont [1685] 1997: 29–30).

A commercial hub, Batavia was a "hybrid world." Like nearby Bantam and Siam, it attracted traders from "Europe, Persia, China, Japan, the Great Mogul's Empire, and diverse other parts (in the Indies)" (Chaumont [1685] 1997: 28). Europeans only comprised a portion of those who frequented the city or lived there permanently. In addition to the local Javanese, Armenian merchants, "free Asians" from Ambon, Makassar, and Malaysia, descendants of freed slaves from Golconda and Bengal, Chinese laborers, and slaves made Batavia their home, as did a large number of ethnically mixed populations. The traveler Nicolaus de Graeff noted, "the thing that amazes one most in Batavia is the splendid pomp and arrogance exhibited not just by the Dutch women but also by the mestizo and kastise women [born of a Dutch father and mestizo mother]" (Van Campen 2015: 41).

Batavia's opulence and cosmopolitanism, however, were not necessarily reflections of Dutch economic supremacy, but rather of compensatory responses to the VOC's struggles to be taken seriously in Asia. Portuguese and Spanish merchants who preceded them, or the English and French who arrived there later, claimed to represent powerful European monarchs and inflated their negotiating potential with royal patronage. The republican States General, which the VOC officially represented, had no singular executive head. This absence left Dutch merchants master-less and unprotected in a world where authority and privilege were derived from royal power. VOC merchants subverted their low political standing by breaking into intra-Asian trade and providing service as carriers, not only of European maps, clocks, globes, arms, glassware, and automatons, but also of Asian goods for Asian rulers and consumers. In other words, the Dutch capitalized off of the fact that they did not seem politically threatening or powerful; their usefulness to internal Asian commerce allowed them an opening to negotiate trade privileges and enter formally closed markets like that of China and Japan. They cemented their position within Asian trade through intermarriage. While some VOC employees entered into extramarital relationships with slaves and freed slaves, others married locally to take advantage of the commercial networks of their Asian spouses (Gommans 2015: 32–7).

By the end of the seventeenth century, rapid Dutch expansion in intra-Asian trade, marked by increasing diplomatic heavy-handedness, played a significant role in destabilizing their commercial power in south-east Asia. Following the forceful Dutch takeover of Bantam in 1682, the Siamese king Narai signed trade treaties with other European powers to check Dutch influence and aggression, and secure alternative sources for western arms and goods. In this context, the uptick in French diplomatic activity in Siam, demonstrated by Catholic missionary movements, Narai's Siamese embassies to France in the 1680s, the establishment of trade treaties with the French Compagnie des Indes Orientales, and the French embassy to Siam in 1685, was no coincidence (Smithies 1997: 3–6).

The low political profile of the Dutch, their reliance on preexistent Asian networks, and cultivation of cultural pluralism in the dawning years of company trade were hardly exceptional. The examples of Venetians and Frenchmen in Pera (or Galata), the large "international suburb" adjacent to Istanbul, illustrate similar dynamics of how Europeans traded and coexisted with other populations in the shadow of the Ottoman authorities that dispensed privileges to trade there. European states jockeyed for power and influence in the Turkish Sublime Porte, looking to out-trade one another by receiving Turkish *imtiyazat*, or capitulations that guaranteed physical protection, trade, and legal privileges for European nationals in the Ottoman empire. Capitulations sheltered them from local taxes and conscription, and placed European nationals under the legal jurisdiction of their state's consuls. While the gradual shift in political power differentials between the Ottomans and western Europeans led to increasing breaches in these trade agreements, initially, when first dispensed by the sultans, they demonstrated the dominance of the Ottoman empire.

The Turks who conquered Constantinople and made Istanbul their newly renamed capital developed centuries-long diplomatic and commercial ties with the Venetians. Despite the many wars waged between them, the Venetians populated Pera and remained the Turks' primary European trading partner until the later seventeenth century, when French trade assumed a monopoly in Levantine commerce. Several thousands of them—a large portion of them only nominally Venetian and coming from its *stato da mar* islands around the Adriatic—formed the Venetian trading nation in Galata. As in the case with the Dutch in Asia, the Venetians often assumed an acquiescent role in diplomacy. Venice's smaller size, its reliance on Ottoman grain, and its political fragility, magnified by the territorial and economic ambitions of its northern European neighbors and the Hapsburg empire, rendered critical the stability of its relationship with the Turks, and the renewals of their trade capitulations (Dursteler 2006: 4–7, 23–6).

French exchanges in textiles and colonial goods with the Ottoman empire soared following diminution of Venetian–Ottoman trade, across the latter part of the seventeenth century until the end of the French Old Regime in 1789. But this development, too, took time, and required France to begin its commercial relationship with the Ottomans from below. France secured a trade capitulation with the Turks in 1536, and its chief Mediterranean port of Marseille became an important node in the Levant trade with the founding of its chamber of commerce, Europe's first such institution, in 1599. But following early growth, the mid-seventeenth century witnessed a dramatic slump in Franco-Levantine commerce, when Venetian, Dutch, and English competitors crowded the Mediterranean and bourgeoning east Asian markets. Mercantilist protectionism introduced by the French crown, specifically by Louis XIV's controller-general Jean Baptiste Colbert, and a renewed Franco-Ottoman capitulation in 1673 gradually placed France at the helm of European trade with the Ottoman empire (Takeda 2015: 12–17). Commodity exchange between Marseille and the Levant grew threefold from 20 million *livres* in the 1720s to 60 million by 1789. While globally, the Indian Ocean and Atlantic economies overshadowed that of the Mediterranean, and Marseille found itself pulled toward those directions, its Levant trade remained competitive until the mid-eighteenth century (Eldem 1999: 14–17).

The French example also sheds light on the important role that regional non-company merchants played in challenging statist claims to commercial power. The French state and its merchants did not march in lock step. The political alliance of Suleiman and François I notwithstanding, the French state was a latecomer to Franco-Ottoman trade. Provincial merchants and bankers laid its groundwork long before the state's active involvement in the Mediterranean. Marseillais families (e.g., the Magallon, Couturier, Roland, and Rémuzat families) ran businesses in Istanbul for decades across the eighteenth century until the French Revolution of 1789. The influence wielded by these families demonstrates how the city of Marseille and its chamber of commerce monopolized French trading in the Ottoman capital. Marseille's fiercely independent merchant dynasties in the Levant remained distrustful of French royal plans for centralized governance in Mediterranean trade, and wary of representatives from other French cities who encroached on their trading privileges. They lobbied against the establishment of trading companies, royal convoys, and naval escorts for maritime commerce, and the expansion of trade privileges for other French ports. French merchants from municipalities other than Marseille or Provence were often prohibited from the assemblies of the French nation in Istanbul (Eldem 1999: 210–11; Takeda 2011: 24–49).

European private overseas activity was not limited to merchants. Artisans, craftsman, and artists also participated in trans-imperial exchange and contributed to the commercial connections between European and non-European states. Several Dutch artists, including Joost Lampen and Barend van Sichem, installed themselves in New Julfa, outside Isfahan, Persia, as early as the 1630s. Philippe Angel instructed Shah Abbas in painting while producing artwork for his court in the mid-seventeenth century. Other Dutch artists included Juriaen Ambdis, Adriaan Gouda, Hendrinck Boudewijn and Cornelis de Bruin (Floor 1979: 145–61). French Huguenot jeweler and merchant Jean-Baptiste Tavernier made six self-funded voyages from France to Persia and India between 1630 and 1668. Enlightenment philosopher Jean-Jacques Rousseau's father, the Genevan watchmaker Isaac Rousseau, lived in Istanbul for seven years as a "watchmaker in the seraglio," while his uncle Jacques Rousseau moved permanently to Isfahan, Persia in 1705. His son Jean François became French consul to Basra (Coller 2014: 61).

Traditional scholarship has stressed a symbiotic relationship between European oceanic trade and early modern statecraft. Historians considered as complementary, the two major transformations reshaping Europe at this time: the gradual expansion of commercial society and the rise of the modern state. The economics of early modern statecraft, or mercantilism, they argued, was premised on centralization, dirigisme, and micromanagement. Recent reconsiderations, however, have revealed that early modern trans-imperial trade cannot be studied by ignoring local angles and private activities. As Beverly Lemire has noted in her study on cotton, the center of early modern trade "was not the kingdom or principality prominent in national histories, but the great port or metropolis which drew necessaries and luxuries from near and far. What has been called 'an archipelago of towns' linked shipping routes and overland trails" (2009: 207). While state authority emerged as a formidable force in the seventeenth and eighteenth centuries, European commercial power relied as much on provincial merchant clans, adventurers, and renegades. The rise of oceanic trade depended on several categories of actors: the state, state-sponsored organizations, private traders, and entrepreneurs.

NON-STATE TRADE NETWORKS AND MINORITY POPULATIONS

Historians have recently applied network analysis and game theory to explore how interlopers, mercenaries, and diasporic communities organized themselves, monitored their activities, and built relationships based on trust and credit in Euro-Asian trade. They have shed light on informal ties among ethnically diverse populations of merchants who operated outside of their state of origin, or outside of state-sponsored organs all together. They have sought to answer how, in a rigidly hierarchical and segregated society, merchants, bankers, and agents from various ethnic and cultural backgrounds managed to work together across thousands of miles. Various examples abound. Huguenot refugees dispersed across the world traded under various flags. Dutchmen opted out of the Dutch VOC to participate in the Danish East India Company, French Compagnie des Indes, the Brandenburg Company or the Scottish Company (Glamann [1958] 1981: 9), or traded privately. And outside of state institutions, Italians in Lisbon, Sephardic Jews of Leghorn, and Hindus in Goa cooperated to exchange Mediterranean red coral with Indian diamonds as a coalition of private merchants united across ethnic and religious divides (Trivellato 2009: 224–50).

Various ethnic groups shared and circulated market information, benefited from established credit, and transported goods in what historians have identified as monocentric and polycentric trading networks. Persia's Armenian traders, India's Shikarpuri and Hyderabadi merchants are examples of groups who formed monocentric networks, operating out of one hub, while others, like the Sephardic Jews, organized themselves in several central clusters, including Leghorn, Venice, Istanbul, and London (Aslanian 2011).

A look at the New Julfan Armenians—one of the largest trade networks in the early modern period—demonstrates the importance of minority populations in trans-imperial trade. Armenians dominated raw silk production along the Caspian Sea and south-western Iran and monopolized silk-for-silver trading as soon as galleons loaded with colonial Spanish silver began arriving into European ports. At a time when western manufactured goods failed to attract interest among Asian buyers, Europeans acquired textiles, spices, gems, and raw materials from the East with silver bullion. Armenian merchants ran four trade circuits around the world, all connected to their hub outside of the Persian capital of Isfahan. These included: (1) the Indian Ocean trade, running from the Persian Gulf to India, on to Canton, Manila, and across the Pacific to Acapulco; (2) the Mediterranean zone, stretching from Ottoman-ruled Aleppo, Iskenderun, to the Italian ports, Marseille, and Cadiz in the Atlantic; (3) the northern passage to Dutch and British ports; and (4) the Persian-Russian Volga corridor from the Caspian Sea to Astrakhan, Moscow, Saint Petersburg, and Archangel (Aslanian 2011: 2–3). By the eighteenth century, Armenians, established as the primary exporters of Iranian raw and manufactured silks, transferred silk and calico manufacturing technologies to Europe.

While their fortunes waxed and waned at the mercy of various Safavid shahs, the Armenians initially benefited from the centralizing policies of Shah Abbas I (r. 1587–1629) (Figure 2.2). Abbas relied on new elites drawn from minority

FIGURE 2.2: Shah Abbas I "The Great," fighting against the Turks. Fresco, seventeenth century. Sutun Chihil Palace, Isfahan, Iran. Credit: PHAS/UIG via Getty Images.

populations to take back the throne from the Qizilbash military. He tapped Caucasians, Armenians, Georgians, and Circassians—designated as *ghulams*, or the shah's slaves—to perform functions in the Safavid military, political administration, and commercial society. Deporting approximately 300,000 Armenians in 1604 from the Persian frontier, he installed them in New Julfa, a suburb of his new capital of Isfahan, which he created to pull international trade away from the Ottomans and closer to India and the Persian Gulf. He granted them administrative and religious autonomy in exchange for drawing in revenue from the silk trade. He outlawed private sales of silk and limited silk exportation privileges to his Armenian *ghulams*. Silk helped the shah become, as Ina McCabe has noted, Iran's biggest landowner and chief merchant (1999: 1–2, 4–7, 26, 29, 123).

The Armenian trade networks, their geographic range, and their commercial, industrial, and technological contributions benefited more than the shahs and Persia. Their trade circuits joined previously disconnected markets of the Pacific world with that of the Mediterranean, Indian Ocean, and the Atlantic, and helped shape the first premodern global economy. As cosmopolitan cultural

FIGURE 2.3: Brothers Wetter's Indian textile factory by Joseph Gabriel Rossetti, 1764. Municipal Museum, Orange. Credit: Leemage/Corbis via Getty Images.

brokers and merchant-diplomats, they facilitated negotiations between imperial administrators, trading companies, and local interest groups. The materials and technologies they transported supported the development of European textile industries. Their prized raw silks fed bourgeoning manufacturers in France, England, and the Netherlands (Aslanian 2011: 3–5). In cities like Marseille, Armenians established a colony numbering in the hundreds by the 1670s, and shared with locals their recipes for producing *indiennes de Masulipatnam*, a calico with a particular shade of Turkish red dye. Despite prohibitionist regulations curtailing cotton printing, the city was home to thirty-three calico printing shops by 1733. One of its largest, owned by Rodolphe Wetter (Figure 2.3), employed over 700 workers who manufactured reproductions of calicoes from the Levant, India, and China (Karténian 2000: 85–92; Daumalin *et al.* 2003: 36–9; Raveux 2009: 2–12; Takeda 2014: 241–63). While European artisans comprised the bulk of the workforce in such factories, we cannot forget the critical roles played by minority communities like the Armenians, who disseminated Asian technologies and spawned western industrialization. The Armenian example highlights how trans-imperial economies did not purely involve trafficking of raw materials and manufactured goods; as Laura Mitchell elaborates in Chapter 3 of this volume, it involved global flows of knowledge.

MERCHANTS, ENTREPRENEURS, AND NEW VOCABULARIES OF POLITICAL ECONOMY

Early modern oceanic exchange materialized in tandem with new intellectual and philosophical frameworks for understanding, legitimating, and regulating such activities. The seventeenth and eighteenth centuries witnessed dramatic changes in the ways Europeans imagined and spoke of merchants and their value to society. These discursive transformations impacted European political economy and shaped oceanic trade policies. Across the seventeenth century, the emergence of favorable interpretations of mercantile exchange, merchants, and entrepreneurs helped legitimate trade and undercut religious stigmas against earthly pursuits. Meanwhile, governments introduced protectionist policies to stimulate exportation when domestic industries struggled to compete against Asian goods. But across the eighteenth century, economists worried about the negative effects of monopolistic global exchange began touting a "national commerce" that linked the metropole to the colonial periphery through free trade. They introduced concepts of the "nation" that associated the state's colonial and agricultural interests more closely with that of the homeland. As western European states like England industrialized and increased production, they mobilized the language of economic liberalism to gain access to more markets. These shifts held long-lasting consequences in the context of revolutionary warfare and the rise of state-led imperialism. The following examples of France and England demonstrate how in each country, administrators, scientists, moralists, and merchants devised various economic vocabularies and strategies to manage economic crises, collapsing bubbles, poverty, and unemployment (Stern and Wennerlind 2013: 9).

In France, religious arguments against usury and classical republican discourses against luxury traditionally led respectable families to eschew commerce. Legal barriers prohibited the aristocracy from involvement in mercantile activity, banking, and investing. The Dutch and English, who adopted positive attitudes toward commercial activity much earlier, thus easily outpaced French maritime trade. But by the 1660s and 1670s, French aristocrats searched for strategies to retain noble standing while investing in commercial ventures and developing their lands for agricultural trade. Jean Baptiste Colbert introduced loopholes for nobles wishing to contribute to oceanic trade. The *Declarations du Roy portant l'établissement d'une Compagnie pour le Commerce des Indes Orientales* (Royal Declaration establishing a Company for the East India Trade, 1664), for example, determined that the company would be comprised of "all willing Subjects, regardless of quality and condition, who would invest whatever sum they believed apropos (above the minimum subscription of 1000 *livres*), without loss of Nobility or Privileges" (Louis XIV 1664: 1–25). Colbert's *Code Marchand* (Commercial Ordinance) of 1673 stressed that international trade and banking were activities open to all meritorious subjects. An Edict of 1701 allowed any noble who did not hold judicial office "to undertake any type of wholesale commerce ... without losing their nobility" (Kessler 2004).

These reforms helped popularize new terms and vocabularies related to trade. Words like *entrepreneur* simply meant "redemptor," someone who undertook a large project, when it appeared in Jean Nicot's *Thresor de la langue francoyse* (1606) but became more specified by the end of the century. The first edition of the *Dictionnaire de l'Académie française* (1694) defined an entrepreneur as someone who managed the construction of public buildings and ships. Manufacturers, merchants, and administrators began referring to entrepreneurs as those who risked private assets on commercial, industrial, or martial ventures beneficial to the general good. They were seen as public-minded, useful subjects. Jacques Savary, co-author of the *Code Marchand*, highlighted that entrepreneurship, wholesale and international commerce were activities opened to men of all ranks. But he warned that they involved "risks" and "dangers," and therefore appropriate only for the "noble and honest" (Savary 1675: 408).

If we look at definitions for the term *entrepreneur* around 1750, we can observe a marked shift. Situated within indictments of mercantilist bullionism and imperial commercial warfare, unfavorable assessments of overseas wholesale trade and entrepreneurship helped reformers champion a political economy of agriculture and artisanal labor in the waning years of the Old Regime. The failures and bankruptcies of the Compagnie des Indes, Compagnie de la Méditerranée, Companie du Levant, Compagnie d'Occident, and the Compagnie du Nord, coupled with the crash of John Law's disastrous Mississippi Bubble in 1721, spawned critiques of entrepreneurship, speculation, and government-managed protectionism. Emergent modern philosophies of *laissez-faire* trade and economic liberalism grew out of these arguments. Classical liberal economists and Physiocrats equated regulatory micromanagement of commerce with stagnation. Denis Diderot and Jean le Rond d'Alemberts' famous mid-eighteenth-century *Encyclopédie, ou dictionnaire raisonné des sciences, des arts et des métiers* (1751–65) described entrepreneurial projects as unsustainable ventures that drained capital, required expensive properties, and abused government protections, privileges, and tax exemptions. It touted instead cottage industries, where artisans used local resources and seasonally harvested raw materials at low costs. It contrasted the hierarchical organization and unequal relationships that underpinned entrepreneurial projects against artisanal and agricultural ones that stimulated egalitarianism and liberty.

The Physiocratic program to replace France's Asia-focused trade with agricultural revitalization amounted to a substitution of one form of nationalist economic system for another. This shift appeared in the context of the rise of the Atlantic economy, and France's increasing dependence on its colonial Caribbean plantation labor for goods like sugar, indigo, and coffee. Reformers privileged republican mythologies of yeoman farmers, and increasingly shut out cosmopolitan foreign traders—whom they denounced as smugglers and thieves—from French commercial activities. Interestingly, this focus on agricultural output awakened French interest toward, and fascination with, Chinese agrarian advancements that they found to be superior to western ones. Physiocratic economists, who were ambivalent toward the globalizing tendencies unleashed centuries earlier by Asian industrial output and exportation, pushed reforms in agronomy and husbandry inspired by China to promote more restrictive ideas of French national economy. They dismissed a vision of a world where traders and merchants shipped Asian and European textiles, porcelains, and other luxuries across the globe at high costs. In its place, they offered a more static and isolationist world (Cheney 2010: 139, 175).

Despite the fact that historians have often contrasted Britain's economic successes against French failures in the Atlantic and Asian trade zones, these two states followed a similar path in economic policy. Both cases highlight how global trade, as Michael Kwass has characterized, "emerged in a profoundly illiberal environment" (2013: 16). French and British governments sought to expand the national economy, control the inflow of global imports, and enrich their respective states by legislating protectionist policies meant to strengthen domestic manufactures or fatten state-run monopolies that loaned the government exorbitant amounts of money. In England, the Navigation Acts, Calico Acts, Townshend Acts, Stamp Act, and Tea Act were all highly restrictive laws that padded royal coffers and protected domestic manufacturing.

Parliament issued a cluster of Navigation Acts between 1651 and 1663 in response to heavy losses to the Dutch in the Atlantic, Mediterranean, Levant, and east Asia trades following the lifting of the Spanish Embargoes. Renewed across the 1670s, these acts excluded the Dutch from English trade, restricted colonial trade to England, limited English trade to English vessels, and mandated a three-quarters English minimum for ship crews. Meanwhile, in the first two decades of the eighteenth century, British spinners, weavers, and dyers employed in domestic linen and woolens industries protested the cheap importation of Indian calico by the East India Company. They vandalized company offices, attacked women wearing imported calico, and petitioned Parliament, insisting that East India imports threatened domestic textile manufacturing. The resulting Calico Act of 1700 prohibited cotton importation, along with wrought silks from Persia, China, and East India; it slapped a fifteen percent duty on East India muslins; and it abolished English woolen export duties. By 1707, a fifty percent tariff on Indian goods was introduced. Parliament passed a stricter law against cotton consumption in 1721.

Meanwhile, regulatory laws particularly intended for Britain's American colonies faced increasingly politicized resistance across the latter half of the eighteenth century. The escalation of reactions against the Townshend Acts (1767–8), a combination of laws issued to better enforce the colonies' compliance with the Navigation Acts and to collect revenue to pay colonial administrators' salaries, led to the occupation of Boston and the Boston Massacre in 1770. The Tea Act (1773) was even more politically detrimental to

Britain. Parliament introduced the act to reinforce the Navigation and Townshend Acts and to prop up the struggling British East India Company by guaranteeing a colonial market for the company's tea surplus. But it fanned the flames of political opposition. Colonists in Massachusetts reacted with the famous Boston Tea Party (December 16, 1773) that helped spark the beginnings of the Revolutionary War (Figure 2.4).

By the latter half of the eighteenth century, when England had increased colonial holdings and its output of manufactured goods, liberal economic theories that attacked bullionism and criticized government interventionism began to take hold. Adam Smith famously commented that mercantile systems promoted the interests of the "rich and the powerful" over those of the laboring class after witnessing the deleterious effects that Glasgow's avaricious tobacco merchant lobbyists had on foreign policy and economic stability (Muldrew 2013: 375). Men of letters in the American colonies, like their Physiocratic intellectual comrades in France, critiqued the politics of mercantilism by turning to republican myths of farmer-citizens. Thomas Jefferson among others famously championed the ideal of republican civic virtue, and argued against monarchical and aristocratic regimes ruled by merchant, banking, and manufacturing elites.

THE BOSTON TEA PARTY—DESTRUCTION OF THE TEA IN BOSTON HARBOR.

FIGURE 2.4: December 16, 1773: A group of Bostonians dressed as Native Americans dump crates of imported British tea into Boston Harbor as a protest against the British Tea Act. Credit: MPI/Getty Images.

Revolutionaries used such theories to justify their wars of independence or rebellion against old regimes in the last quarter of the eighteenth century. Meanwhile, the repeal of the Calico Acts in 1774 and the formal end of the Navigation Acts in 1849 signaled the ascendancy of free trade philosophy, but this by no means meant that Britain had stepped away from protectionist ideas simply due to lofty Enlightenment ideals of equality, liberty, and public virtue. Rather, at a point where England cemented its status as the West's first industrialized nation, it touted free trade in order to gain entry into as many markets as possible, exploit the raw materials of its growing territorial empire, and increase the outflow of its exports.

RAW MATERIALS, COMMODITIES, AND THE CONSUMER REVOLUTION

When Europeans first arrived in south and east Asia, they hoped to trade in spices. Ledgers and invoices across the seventeenth and eighteenth centuries, however, reveal a marked shift in materials and commodities traded across this time. Papers for the Dutch VOC, for instance, indicate that until the mid-seventeenth century, the primary item purchased and sold was pepper, in addition to cinnamon, nutmeg, cloves, and cardamom. While they traded in other goods like sugar, saltpeter, opium, sappan wood, ebony, jewels, pearls, porcelains, and diamonds, exchange of textiles—cottons, silks, and woolens—skyrocketed across the seventeenth and eighteenth centuries.

Cotton manufacturing in the western world, famously tied to developments in slavery and industrialization in the West, only appeared in the Atlantic in the eighteenth and nineteenth centuries, but Indian merchants had introduced the plant and technologies related to its cultivation and manufacturing to China, Africa, central Asia, and the Mediterranean much earlier, between 800 and 1000 CE. Persian factories adopted Indian inventions like the spinning wheel, treadle loom, and cotton gin and drove cotton consumption across the central Asian empires. The Islamic conquest of Iberia brought cotton technologies into Portugal and Spain. By the fourteenth century, Venetian and Genoese traders in Cairo introduced the cloth to the Italian peninsula, while the rise of Portuguese maritime trade in the sixteenth century brought Indian cottons into Lisbon and Antwerp. At the same time, Europeans began taking modest steps to launch their own cotton textiles. Italians and Germans initially established themselves as the best European manufacturers of cotton and mixed cotton (woven with silk, wool, hemp cloth, or linens) handkerchiefs, ribbons, draperies, and veils in addition to garments and undergarments. But European quality paled in comparison to Asian imports, as Indian cottons continued to set the standards for excellence and affordability and drove trends for early modern consumerism (Lemire 2009: 210–13; Mazzaouli 2009: 63, 80–3; Parthasarathi and Riello 2009: 2–6).

Trade in Indian cottons by Dutch and British companies soared across the seventeenth and eighteenth centuries as they monopolized trade in the Asian subcontinent, which remained the primary exporter of cottons and printed calicoes through the period. The companies' massive haul was fueled by European consumers' obsessions for new patterns, prints, styles, and colors introduced by Indian manufacturers who were keenly aware of the demands and tastes of western audiences. But this surge in Indian textiles threatened the viability of domestic European manufacturers, prompting aggressive protectionist and prohibitionist policy-making, particularly in England and France (Lemire 2009: 220–5).

Meanwhile, raw and manufactured silk—the most coveted symbol of wealth and power in seventeenth-century Europe—became the VOC's most prized luxury article traded (Glamann [1958] 1981: 12–16). The majority of Europe's annually imported raw silks—eighty-six percent of the 200–250,000 kilograms—came from Persia, where successful sixteenth- and seventeenth-century Safavid conquests of Ottoman and Usbek silk-growing territories sustained unprecedented economic growth. In the seventeenth century, Persia annually produced over 2,200 tons of silk (Takeda 2015: 12–17). Beyond Persia, Bengal and China also provided European buyers with wild, raw, unspun and spun varieties of silk. As with cotton, these imports were critical to the development of European manufacturing, first in Italy, then in France and England.

Traffic in colonial goods also began climbing across the eighteenth century. Studies, for example, of French imports into Istanbul across the eighteenth century show a marked rise in colonial products from the West Indies. The shift toward global circulation of American products helped reduce Europe's and the Ottoman empire's dependence on certain Asian materials. While approximately seventy-five percent of French goods trafficked into Istanbul at the time consisted of manufactured textiles, colonial goods shipped across the Atlantic into Marseille then on to Istanbul comprised the majority of the remaining twenty-five percent. Colonial goods even began replacing local Ottoman products in the Turkish empire. Sugar, for example, formerly exported from Egypt and Cyprus, was replaced by higher quality refined sugar imports from Brazil and the West Indies. Coffee, which the Ottomans had been exporting to Europe through the seventeenth century, saw a similar reversal. At the turn of the eighteenth century, France annually imported around 12,700 quintals of coffee from Cairo. By 1713, the Ottomans banned coffee exports to prevent shortages within the empire, and within half a century, the Ottomans began importing American and "Frankish" coffee. By the end of the century, close to 1,700 tons of American coffee, priced at half the cost of Mokha coffee from Asia, reached the Levant. Other important colonial products from the Americas included indigo and cochineal, both used to produce high-quality pigments in textile manufacturing. As with coffee, colonial indigo replaced the Indian Ocean variety and trade, while cochineal, an American insect used to produce red dyes, became a substitute for lesser-quality locally sourced reds (Eldem 1999: 68–70, 74–80, 82–3). Such trends demonstrate the ascendancy of the Atlantic trade zone.

The period bracketed between 1650 and 1800 saw unprecedented growth in the ability for western and northern Europeans to acquire goods from various parts of the world, and to adopt Asian technologies to improve their own industries. This development affected more than the merchants and crews of the ocean-going ships that transported these materials. It propelled dramatic transformations in the gendered patterns of manual and industrial labor across western and northern Europe. The rise in numbers of middle-class consumers generated a need for more domestic service, a category of work that became feminized by the end of the eighteenth century. Because women outnumbered men in the seventeenth and eighteenth centuries and married later, they formed a substantial source of cheap labor for manufacturers. Female and child labor formed the bulk of textile manufacturing in England, Italy, France, and other European states. Female and child workers outnumbered their male counterparts in the woolen industry, as they did in linens, silk-farming, lacemaking, and knitting. Historians have compared European early industrial labor to that of current developing countries; newly introduced industries—like spinning and calico-printing—that required intensive labor relied heavily on female and child labor (Berg 1991: 1–4).

Commoners began consuming more global goods and decorating their homes and apartments with Asian or Asian-inspired porcelain, textiles, and furniture. They dressed and accessorized themselves in new and trending clothing and objects. They consumed sugar, coffee, vegetables, and spices from the colonies and from the East. Average lifespans increased with a more diversified and healthy diet, leading to population growth across Europe and Africa. Access to a wider array of literature, from travel narratives and almanacs to novels and pornography, helped increase rates of literacy and stimulate the circulation of new and revolutionary ideas.

The early modern consumer revolution provided new educational and recreational opportunities and outlets for both men and women. Historians have explored in detail how the burgeoning coffeehouse and theater cultures from the end of the seventeenth century shaped a new kind of Enlightenment public sphere for private people to participate in informed and rational discussions about politics, literature, and new conceptions of selfhood. Coffeehouses, long operative in the Ottoman empire, were introduced to Europe in the seventeenth century by Armenians, Greeks, and Jews, and quickly popularized as sites for intelligent conversation. London, for example, housed more than 700 coffeehouses by the eighteenth century.

Most importantly, new concepts of self-discipline and cosmopolitanism circulated in these spaces as early modern subjects familiarized themselves with rules of civility and politeness that sharply contrasted against the heavy-handed authoritarian rule of long-established regimes. In such places like the urban coffeehouses, debating societies, female-run literary salons, and outdoor shopping malls, early modern men and women sipped hot chocolate from the American colonies. They tasted Ottoman coffee from Chinese porcelains. They dressed in *chinoiserie* and *à-la-turque*. They sat in rooms adorned with Asian-inspired wallpaper and tapestries. And they experienced and practiced more democratic and egalitarian forms of self-governance that would ultimately help dismantle the rigid hierarchies of European society. In these and in other seedier spaces for socialization, like the public drinking houses and gambling salons of London, Paris, and Amsterdam, men and women of different social ranks crossed paths in ways unimaginable in the past, articulated their frustrations and dissatisfaction toward the powers that be, and helped shake the political stability of absolutist and monarchical regimes. The consumer revolution—a revolution in tastes, trends, and spending sparked by the circulation of global commodities—served as a springboard for political revolutions in England, the thirteen American colonies, and France (Figure 2.5).

Hardly limited to "the West," the uptick in western industrial activity and consumerism affected other parts of the world. China still boasted the world's highest population and concentration of industrial productivity in the eighteenth century. Despite the western world's interest in consuming Chinese teas, silks, and porcelains, the bulk of these products continued to be traded domestically, and by China's immediate neighbors. But for the first time in history, China began falling behind European scientific development. Whereas Chinese and Persian inventions—gunpowder, paper, paper currency, blast furnaces, rudders, catapults—had driven and shaped western technological innovations for centuries, Europeans made significant advances in astronomy, lens crafting, and mechanized time-telling (clock- and watch-making) that they exported to Asia. The movement of European commodities eastwards never paralleled in scope the mass importation of Asian textiles, crafts, and teas to the West. But Ottoman, Safavid, Ming, Qing, and Japanese elites expressed particular interest in European mirrors, glasses, mechanical toys and objects, clocks, watches, and firearms. The most famous example of Asian fascination with European science and technology, the Xiyang Lou "Western Mansion" in Beijing's Old Summer Palace, boasted Italian and French baroque architecture, interior designs and technologies, and a hybrid of French and Chinese garden pavilions, mazes, and bird sanctuaries. Commissioned by Qing Emperor Qianlong in the mid-eighteenth century, it was completed by a group of Jesuits: Italian court painter Giuseppe Castiglione, who designed and led construction; the Frenchman Michel Benoit who engineered hydraulics, garden fountains, and underground

FIGURE 2.5: Turkish merchants, detail from The Port of Marseille, 1754, by Claude-Joseph Vernet (1714–89). Credit: De Agostini Picture Library/Getty Images.

plumbing; and several Italian and German Jesuit artists who completed interior designs. While Europeans' fascination with an imagined "exotic" Asia led them to dress in Persian-style waistcoats, Ottoman-style turbans, Indian-style chintzes, and Japanese-style kimonos, Asians expressed interest in the allure of an "exotic" Europe.

While dressing as the "other" in Orientalized and Occidentalized sitting rooms and gardens might appear superficial and harmless, it was connected to a more troubling transformation in East–West relations. The eighteenth-century western productivity leap, characterized by the strengthening of European scientific, technological, and industrial power, held dire consequences for south and east Asia, Africa and the Indian Ocean world. It challenged China's economic supremacy. Europeans who originally traded Asian goods for silver increasingly turned to opium and arms for trans-imperial trade. They relied on a combination of indentured and slave labor, low-wage factory labor, and mechanized labor to produce cheaper domestic goods and offset their need for Ottoman, Persian, and Indian imports. This increased their drive to locate and dominate spaces for exploitative resource extraction. Thus the groundwork for nineteenth- and twentieth-century European imperialism and military expansionism was laid.

THE DARK SIDE OF COMMERCE: PIRACY, CONTRABAND, SLAVERY, AND EMPIRE

From the moment Portuguese and Spanish galleons took to the oceans, their bottoms loaded with American silver, privateers and pirates roamed in search of booty. Military aggression abounded on land and sea. Smugglers evaded tax farmers and ignored prohibitionist laws to distribute contraband tobacco and Asian textiles. Statesmen and administrators railed against the circulation of counterfeit coinage. Economic and political competition among burgeoning European nation-states fueled the Mediterranean and Atlantic slave trade (Kwass 2014: 1–14). Commercial concessions lay the groundwork for territorial expansion and conquest in the Asian subcontinent. Early modern trans-imperial exchange was hardly the peaceful *doux commerce* ("sweet commerce") that Enlightenment philosophers applauded.

The history of the seventeenth through eighteenth centuries in large part involves stories of crime, exploitation, violence, and rebellion. Mercantilist laws, which simultaneously tried to stimulate demand for colonial and homegrown goods while regulating the inflow of Asian imports, met with harsh resistance and spawned a cycle of repression, coercion, and rebellion. Interventionist responses—namely, prohibition and taxation—strengthened the fiscal military state, inadvertently energized underground illicit trading, and generated revolutionary political spasms. Investors from the second and third estates, merchants, professional transporters, retailers, and even members of government-backed monopolies smuggled goods, or helped gangs move, hide, and sell merchandise. A third of tobacco consumed in mid-eighteenth-century France was illegal. While riots erupted as silk-weavers in Spitalfields, outside of London, harassed women for wearing calico, attacked calico-printers, and destroyed their presses, contraband and counterfeit printed cottons abounded (Kwass 2014: 18–19; Stevenson 2014: 152–3).

Prohibitions, high tariffs, and rampant smuggling were directly related to the unprecedented expansion of paramilitary forces and the criminal justice system in eighteenth-century Europe (Kwass 2013: 18–20). Among the tens of thousands of people convicted and transported to labor camps, galleys, and colonies were also those who trafficked counterfeit monies. Accepting mercantilist assumptions that states increased power by maximizing their supplies of bullion, ministers of finance and controllers-general insisted that their merchants trade in manufactured goods rather than silver currency. But millions of coins leaked abroad as western merchants faced challenges exchanging their goods for superior Asian imports. Colbert once estimated that Marseille's merchants carried over two million coins annually to the Levant in addition to flooding the market with "false coins" (1679: 696, 455). Fake currency circulated as traders and local inhabitants desperate for cash and the means to acquire goods relied on clipped and altered monies, or committed the more serious crime of participating in counterfeiting rings and organizations. Given that a large proportion of those caught for the crime were lower class and artisanal workers, some historians have discovered that a considerable number of them were women; nearly half of all defendants in trials involving counterfeiting monies at London's Old Bailey between the years 1674 to 1749 were women. Because counterfeiting was theoretically understood as a crime of *lèse majesté humaine*, one that involved unlawfully copying the king's image and weakening his economy, offenders were tortured, hanged, beheaded, or sent to the galleys (Walshaw 2012: 45–57).

The mass incarceration connected to illegal trade and commerce served political purposes and profoundly changed European states and their institutions across the early modern period. The notion that subjects—and later, citizens—ought to be useful and productive members of society gained currency as economists, administrators, and philosophers equated the value of populations to their labor, and looked for new ways to manage the growing number of unemployed and displaced populations. Global competition in manufacturing and industrial output, population growth, and urbanization, combined with rising prices, heavy taxation, and famine threatened to push vulnerable groups teetering on the edge of poverty toward crime and vagrancy. In England, for example, the shifts in discussions about what to do with such populations had profound consequences for its colonial policies. In the seventeenth century, the notion that they ought to be transported overseas led to a rise in indentured servitude and bond-service in England's North American colonies. By the middle of the eighteenth century, a populationist focus on retaining and rehabilitating poor workers in England's industrial centers resulted in the heavier reliance on racialized slavery for agricultural labor across the Atlantic (Swingen 2013: 10, 46–55).

Perhaps nothing illustrates better the violence of commerce, the abusive potential of corporate power, and the blurred lines between trade and conquest than the long history of the British East India Company. Recent studies have highlighted how the trading corporation that was chartered by Queen Elizabeth I in 1600 became, in and of itself, a sovereign political community, a government within a government, a state, much earlier than its official assumption of territorial power in India in the mid-eighteenth century. Having cemented the privilege of jurisdiction over East India trade, English subjects in its employ, and their goods, it had its own courts, tax farmers, diplomats, and, by 1800, an army of over 200,000. Evidenced in the many loans that it advanced to the English government and the presence of a powerful lobby in Parliament, the company grew due to its alliance with the nation-state. Mercantilist policies and acts helped consolidate its power. But eventually, by the end of the eighteenth century, Britain transformed into a modern state and empire by coopting the functions, institutions, and territories of the company (Stern 2012: 3–7).

This militarized corporation, backed by the state, plundered India and set the stage for modern imperial rule. After defeating the French East India Company at the battle of Plassey (1757), the British company began its territorial usurpation of Bengal under the command of Robert Clive. Within a few decades, a few hundred company clerks effectively made themselves rulers of Bengal. Installing company directors and traders to collect tax revenues that formerly flowed to Mughal coffers, Clive enriched himself and his company, while the British members of Parliament, many of whom owned company stock, ensured its commercial privileges. The financial abuses of the company were particularly felt in the Great Bengal Famine of 1769–1773. Its taxation policies, coupled with its enforcement of export monoculture (indigo, tea, opium) depleted rice reserves and condemned the population to starvation while the company reaped the profits. Company excesses and abuses would continue to prompt environmental and biological disasters across the subcontinent into the mid-nineteenth century, when in 1858, the India Act legally transferred company territories to Queen Victoria.

The current age is perhaps an appropriate one in which to be reconsidering the violent politics and cultures of trade and commerce in the early modern world. Western nation-states continue to gamble on illiberal methods in their struggles with economic globalization. This has become more evident since the financial crisis of 2008 that amplified current arguments over government regulations and the efficacy of free trade deals, and that animated populist and nationalist movements weary of liberal democracy. Such movements embody a reaction against the cultures of mobility that have sustained the globalized worlds of yesterday and today. Meanwhile corporate raiding and private military activities continue to direct power and revenues to individuals willing to twist their relationships with governments to satisfy private interests. A study of early modern global trade and its effect on geopolitics, economic policies, demographics, industrialization, labor, and mentalities is particularly relevant in the present as we continue to search for ways to maintain and realize democratic, humanitarian, and egalitarian ideals from the Age of Enlightenment against the backdrop of an unstable global market.

CHAPTER THREE

Natural Worlds

LAURA J. MITCHELL

The Age of Enlightenment is unthinkable except in relation to the natural world. From Newton's keen observations to Rousseau's "noble savage," the game-changing thinkers of this period were preoccupied with the human condition in both metaphysical and material terms. Furthermore, the imperial competition that was coterminous with the Enlightenment significantly reshaped ecologies locally and on a global scale, continuing centuries-old processes of biological exchange and state-sponsored terraforming that accelerated dramatically after European conquests in the Americas. The period from 1650 to 1800 was also characterized by processes of modernization that took place with particular intensity in western Europe: nascent industries became increasingly concentrated in urban areas, changing the social makeup of cities; the related fossil fuel revolution enabled industrialization, creating a plethora of more widely available consumer goods; diplomats and philosophers developed a political system that regulated interactions among sovereign states; statesmen and increasingly powerful merchants strengthened legal and economic regimes based on private property; and cultural practices in large empires displayed increasingly syncretic characteristics.

The connected processes of empire-building and modernization had obvious environmental consequences, since "Stronger, more efficient early modern states and markets intensified and extended human impacts on the world's lands" (Richards 2003: 24). By the eighteenth century states were better organized and even more capable of managing people and natural resources than those of the seventeenth century, and they bumped up against the limits of sustainable growth given their available resources. Even in states as effective and well-managed as the Mughal empire and the Dutch Republic, environmental limits were real (Richards 2003: 56). Therefore, the benefits of a state being able to claim resources in other regions cannot be overstated. The spectacular changes of the nineteenth century associated with industrialization and the fossil fuel revolution were initiated in Britain, an empire that could rely on resources from around the world (Pomeranz 2000).

We have the benefit of hindsight—along with long-term data about climate, demographics, forest cover, and agricultural production paired with documentation about cultural changes such as diet, clothing, and artistic production—which gives historians perspective on the environmental consequences of early modern empires that were not always immediately visible to contemporaries. Work by Alfred Crosby (1986), Richard Grove (1995), and John Richards (2003) reveals the interplay between climate, resources, and forms of knowledge about the natural world that undergirded imperial expansion and its environmental consequences in the seventeenth and eighteenth centuries—many of which were detrimental in the long term. This dual attention to ecological origins and outcomes characterizes the field of environmental history as a whole (McNeill 2010), but it is especially important for understanding large-scale state-building and cultural interaction over unprecedented distances that differentiate early modern empires from their predecessors.

The exigencies of managing natural resources, exploiting new sources of material wealth, and circumventing constraints on population and economic growth—including the availability of arable land, agricultural production, and fuel—direct our attention to the environmental origins of empire. This perspective suggests rational policy-makers who sought to support state-building with the means available to them.

In contrast, the environmental consequences of political consolidation combined with territorial expansion—much of it in terrains and ecosystems distant and very different from imperial capitals—were simultaneously intentional and accidental, unevenly beneficial and deleterious. As the rulers of increasingly powerful states directed ambitious projects to generate more wealth, demonstrate the empire's prestige, expand their domains, and protect newly won resources, they rarely considered the effects on local peoples and ecosystems, let alone the potential worldwide implications.

As was the case with political, economic, and social changes in the early modern period, this was an era of intensification of the environmental consequences of human actions. Ordinary people felt these effects in the growing cities of the metropoles—both political capitals and emerging industrial centers—as well as in colonial hubs and hinterlands. The historically large land-based empires in China and Persia contended in this period with expanding Russian and Ottoman states, while the tentacles of overseas empire that characterized the most powerful western European states—Britain, France, the

Netherlands, Spain, and Portugal—meant that imperially driven environmental changes were not just widespread, but were truly global.

THE BIOLOGICAL OLD REGIME

Whether in fertile river valleys, tropical lowlands, or the earth's gently rolling prairies, general environmental conditions and the material conditions of production in 1650 were much as they had been in 1450 or 800. To be sure, regional variations and climate fluctuations played a significant role in human history, but the underlying relationship between peoples and their environment remained fairly constant in the pre-industrial world (Braudel 1996; Brooke 2014). In the biological old regime, population growth and economic activity were shaped by the limits of organic energy in any given ecosystem (Marks 2012).

Measurable climate variations, the most notable of which was the Little Ice Age, serve to underline the connection between environmental conditions and human endeavors, highlighting the constraints on a community's ability to change the resources available to it. Although human energy and ingenuity could harvest wild plants, clear forests and fields for agriculture, redirect the flow of water, exploit animal populations, and extract mineral resources, people and their technology could not blunt the effects of long-term warming and cooling cycles.

During the Little Ice Age, the earth experienced significant cooling due to atypically low solar activity. Lower temperatures prevailed from the fourteenth through the mid-nineteenth centuries, with the coldest period occurring between 1645 and 1715. Average temperatures in North America and western Europe in these seven decades were about two degrees Celsius lower than in the twentieth century. Glaciers and polar ice caps expanded; lakes, rivers, and even the Baltic Sea froze in the winters; summers were cooler and wetter, and the growing season was several weeks shorter than was typical before and after the chill.

This climate change led to crop failures, which in turn caused widespread famine. In some areas during this period, peasant revolts led to political instability (Parker 2008). Popular uprisings in Russia, Poland-Lithuania, and the Swiss Republic were all eventually quelled, but not without cost to the state. Elsewhere, population decline drove social and economic changes, shifting the ratio of rural to urban dwellers or increasing commercial activity. Societies with access to long-distance trade networks and those with diversified agriculture tended to cope better with the consequences of climate change than did more isolated communities or economies with a limited range of production. For example, Iceland lost half its population during this period; glacial activity and snowmelt damaged farms in the Alps and Scandinavia. The peoples of England

and the Netherlands, on the other hand, were able to import food and benefit from maritime activity, and so rode out the long cold cycle somewhat more comfortably, though they were not unscathed. England endured fourteen food riots between 1647 and 1649, violent outbreaks that were enveloped by the Civil War (1642–51)—political foment that did not really subside until the end of the Glorious Revolution in 1689. Similarly, political upheaval transformed the government of the Dutch Republic, after which the two seafaring powers fought a series of wars that were, in part, over access to resources and control of shipping routes that brought valuable goods from afar.

The Dutch Republic was on sound economic footing—despite the protracted conflict of the Eighty Years' War that ended in 1648 because "the Dutch greatly expanded the amount of protein and profits they took from the sea and from the inland waterways" during that period (Richards 2003: 50). But overfishing reduced both freshwater and ocean fish—especially the crucial herring stocks of the North Sea—while reclamation projects needed to create more arable land served to increase the salinity of the remaining inland streams and lakes. So after about 1650, the Dutch economy needed additional strategies to increase the resources it could wring from the land and the sea. Ongoing land reclamation was one solution. From the early sixteenth century until 1815, the Dutch Republic reclaimed about 250,000 hectares of land, increasing arable land by one-third (de Vries and van der Woude 1997: 31). Combined with the more efficient extraction of local peat for fuel and the ability to cheaply import coal from Germany, England, and Scotland, the Netherlands was able to support unprecedented growth throughout the early modern period. By the end of the eighteenth century, "the alluvial lands of the Dutch Republic were among the most intensively managed and exploited in the world" (Richards 2003: 53) (Figure 3.1).

It is important not to isolate political events in the seventeenth century from dramatic environmental changes. Large-scale land reclamation projects, including draining the Fens in south-east England and the creation of polders in the Netherland are evidence of human–environmental relationships in flux. In both cases, as with the Enclosure movement in England, which also gained momentum in this period, local political organization was key to environmental management. Even with such dramatic reshaping of local landscapes and the reorganization of access to resources such as wood, game, pasturage, and arable land, human activity was constrained by the limited energy available to sustain daily life in any given ecosystem.

Before the Industrial Revolution, all peoples lived within this biological old regime in which human and animal muscle power were the prime movers, aided by water and wind, and in which the energy in food and fuel came from the sun, captured by plants (Crosby 2006). Existing technologies limited the storage and transportation of transformed solar energy and of wind, water, or

FIGURE 3.1: Jan Leeghwater, Dutch mill builder and hydraulic engineer, 1608. Print by W. Steelink, 1870. Credit: The Print Collector/Getty Images.

bio-power, although textiles meant that plant fibers—like seeds—could be stored from year to year.

The English political economist Thomas Malthus described the consequences of these constraints in a 1798 essay in which he identified population growth as the variable in an otherwise static equation of natural resources and energy required to produce sustenance for a community (Malthus [1798] 1958). The Malthusian trap imposed very real limits on growth that colonial resources and nascent industrialization were only beginning to transcend in England at the end of the eighteenth century, a result that would not become clearly evident until after Malthus' death in 1834. It is telling that despite teaching at the East India Company's administrative college, Malthus' mental resource landscape did not include the potential benefit of imported staples or commodities, despite the fact that products from colonial "ghost acres" were already meeting metropolitan needs that local agricultural capacity could not (Pomeranz 2000). Like his contemporaries, Malthus could not yet imagine a future in which technological breakthroughs—especially the fossil fuel revolution—would lead to production that exceeded needs and facilitate the global circulation of goods and people. Technological innovation—a decidedly cultural process—enabled empires to be more productive with the resources they had, ensuring political stability and making lasting marks on the environment as ghost acres and industrialization combined decisively to pierce the growth ceilings of the biological old regime, first in Britain then in other parts of western Europe and North America.

Despite the fundamental constants of life in the biological old regime, there were significant regional differences that influenced population growth, economic productivity, political frameworks, social organization, and culture. Across Europe, the need to let fields lie fallow and the reality that staple crops grew only during the summer led to relatively low agricultural production and high food costs compared with societies in south and east Asia. The limits on food production were one factor in Europe's ongoing political fragmentation. Many competing states of different sizes fought for control of land, resources, and people throughout this period, despite the emergence of a negotiated multistate political system after the Peace of Westphalia in 1648—a system complicated by violent religious debates and religious plurality that coexisted uncomfortably with interstate relationships premised on similarity of governance and state structures.

The states of western Europe organized relations among themselves differently than states in other regions, so increasingly powerful economies and governments were near neighbors, but no single one of them could exert dominance over the others over the long term. At the same time, new institutions—notably the structures of capitalist economies, centralizing governments, and quasi-state structures such as chartered companies—acted together to intensify human effects on the natural world in Europe and other regions. The convergence of European state politics and global intensification of resource use meant that imperial expansion led to unprecedented environmental changes. John Richards makes the case that "the western European presence around the world, and western Europe's resource demands at home, caused important environmental effects in many world areas during the sixteenth century through the mid-nineteenth century" (2003: 17).

We must be careful, though, not to ascribe all human-driven environmental change to European dynamism. Victor Lieberman convincingly documents a widespread Eurasian process of political consolidation with evidence from Japan, Burma, Siam, Vietnam, France, and Russia (Lieberman 2003). Meanwhile, region-specific environmental histories document the dramatic consequences of imperial policies and trans-imperial trade on nature around the world (Slezkine 1994; Elvin 2006; Marks 2006; Biggs 2012; Jones 2014; Khazeni 2014; Fedman 2015). This scholarship lays the groundwork for a comparative study of imperial environments that would put the rich literature on European maritime expansion into conversation with studies of environmental change engineered closer to home in places such as Japan, Vietnam, Russia, and Persia. Suffice to say that the environmental consequences of empire were not limited to European powers, nor is this a story about what European empires did to the rest of the world, although those empires played a decisive role in the early modern period.

Local ecologies strongly influenced economic productivity, underpinning important differences among empires. As Robert Marks argues, "In the biological old regime, productive agriculture was Asia's competitive advantage, even in industry" (2012: 60). Rice-growing regions had much higher yields than grain-growing ones. Rice can glean nutrients directly from water, so its growth does not deplete the soil. Consequently, rice farmers do not need to leave fields fallow, or move on to new terrain after exhausting their existing land. What's more, the warm climate of south China can support three growing seasons a year, a feat that impressed eighteenth-century European travelers. This agricultural productivity was not confined to China, which goes a long way toward explaining the major population growth in India, Japan, and China during the seventeenth and eighteenth centuries (Marks 2006: 285).

From the time of the Delhi Sultanate—the first large-scale consolidation of political power in south Asia—Indic rulers encouraged intensified land use, promoted settlement and forest clearing, and sought to increase tax revenue by both extending and intensifying cultivation (Figure 3.2). After Babur defeated the

FIGURE 3.2: Harvesting of the almond crop at Kand-i Badam (Bhawani), sixteenth century. © The British Library Board.

last Lodi sultan, the new Mughal rulers assumed control of a vibrant economy based on the expropriation of peasant-produced surplus and continued the process of state-building based on territorial assimilation. Mughal wealth depended on agriculture and land-based expansion, not maritime exploits. By 1690 the empire consisted of almost all the Indian subcontinent, except the southern tip. "The state's primary environmental impact lay in its unremitting pressure to increase cultivation and its revenues from that cultivation. To do this ... the state ... struggled with a long-term process of socialization directed at the rural aristocracy ... [T]he Mughal Empire ... carried out these tasks successfully for a large population and an immense territory" (Richards 2003: 32).

These transformations included Mughal expansion into Bengal—a terrain actively being changed by the shifting course of the River Ganges, which moved the areas reliably replenished with alluvial soils from regular flooding. An activist state propelled Bengal's advancing settlement frontier, demonstrating more interventionist power than the previous Afghan rulers had shown. Consequently, the early modern Bengali economy benefited from frontier-driven growth, a process that lasted well into the nineteenth century. A significant aspect of Mughal state consolidation was the transformation of the wetlands of eastern Bengal into a new wet rice landscape (Crosby 1972).

Other large land-based empires reacted to different environmental challenges. In the Ottoman empire, whose territories were already extensive in the seventeenth century, the challenge was to maintain agricultural production in the face of climate change. Sam White argues that the Little Ice Age nearly brought down the Ottomans at the beginning of the seventeenth century and imposed limits on economic growth and political centralization until the nineteenth century. As the empire grew, its inhabitants pushed the limits of the locally available resource base. The effects of war and natural disasters were compounded by climate change, which along with "... nomadic invasion, rural insecurity, and flight from the land drove a vicious circle of demographic and agricultural contraction" that shaped the "loosely governed and thinly populated" empire (White 2011: 1–2).

The Ottomans faced particular environmental challenges ruling Egypt, where control of water has shaped human settlement and practices of governance for millennia. Alain Mikhail argues, though, that "Water ... is only one part of this environmental story of Egypt. Timber, plague, animals, wind, grain, and microbes" all played a major role in shaping seventeenth- and eighteenth-century political changes (2011: 1). In Ottoman-controlled Egypt, imperial administrators exchanged Nile-irrigated grain for imported timber, which was necessary for rural irrigation infrastructure, a significant transaction because "the status of a dam or canal in Egypt had wide imperial consequences" (Mikhail 2011: 3). Shifts in the administration of natural resources accompanied a change in political rule at the end of the eighteenth century, marked first by the

French occupation, then by the nominally independent rule of the Muhammad Ali Pasha dynasty, starting in 1805.

As Egypt went from being the most economically important region in the Ottoman empire to becoming an autonomously governed polity, forced labor for large-scale infrastructure projects decreased peasants' quality of life and led to the death of over 300,000 Egyptians. In the long eighteenth century, Egyptian peasants went from "having quite a bit of room to maneuver in an Ottoman imperial system to essentially having none in an Egyptian one. As they came to suffer more and more under this new political system, so, too, did the Egyptian rural environment" (Mikhail 2011: 4).

Expanding empires sought new sources of wealth even as they worked to maintain agricultural production in order to keep the populace fed and reasonably loyal to the crown. As they exercised their duties, rulers of contiguous territories did not have to contend with the huge range of climate and ecological diversity, or the extremely long delays in communication that were inherent to maritime empires. They could not, however, benefit from the variety or novelty of resources that came with European colonization in Asia and the Americas.

COLUMBIAN EXCHANGES AND AFTERMATHS

The nutritional benefits of the Columbian Exchange for Afroeurasian populations have been well documented. Maize and potatoes, in particular, enabled communities in Africa and Europe to blunt—but not eliminate—the food production advantage achieved through wetland rice cultivation in China and India. Growing populations—clearly connected to higher agricultural production—had many knock-on effects, including technological innovations and urbanization. The benefits of new foods were evident to contemporary observers in the eighteenth century. Adam Smith, for example, extolled the virtues of potatoes: "[T]he food produced by a field of potatoes is . . . much superior to what is produced by a field of wheat . . . No food can afford a more decisive proof of its nourishing quality, or of its being peculiarly suitable to the health of the human constitution" (1776: 67–8). Smith's paean overlooks the class and geographic implications of "earth-apple" consumption, however. Potatoes fed peasants and the nascent working class; potato cultivation happened away from imperial capitals, and was not part of the bucolic landscape aesthetic in Dutch, French, or British paintings, unlike pastures or fields of wheat. The humble American potato was crucial to the growth of Europe's maritime empires, but its significance was downplayed in imperial idiom and iconography.

The cultivation of new foods clearly mattered for imperial expansion, but the causal relationship among increased food production, improved nutritional yield, and population growth is still unclear. Although the availability of new foodstuffs after the Columbian voyages is undisputed (Goucher 2013), scholars periodically revisit the question of whether improved crop production caused population growth, or whether expanding communities pushed the innovations that led to more food. A recent contribution to this debate argues unequivocally that the arrival of the potato accounts for about one-quarter of Afroeurasia's demographic expansion and urbanization between 1700 and 1900 (Nunn and Qian 2011: 593). The data is persuasive, but crop production and nutritional value alone do not explain the complexity of post-Columbian environmental change in Europe and Africa.

New agricultural production processes accompanied crop diffusion. Joel Mokyr argues that potatoes were part of "an entirely new system of tillage" in which the tubers, along with grains and livestock, "were *joint* products, the output of each determined by the quantities of labour, land and capital" as well as by the intertwined output of the other two products (1981: 12, original emphasis). Maize cultivation, too, caused farmers to reshape their landscapes, reorganize communities, and devise new foodways. The quick and easy genetic adaptability of maize meant that Afroeurasian farmers were able to modify it to local conditions soon after it crossed the Atlantic, leading to the global diversification of the crop. Because all parts of the plant—the kernels, leaves, stem, stalk, silk, and roots—are edible, maize yields more food per unit of land and labor than other grains, which explains why maize cultivation spread quickly in Africa (McCann 2005: 6).

Farmers grew corn in the seventeenth and eighteenth centuries for consumption as a vegetable (eaten on the cobb), as a grain (stored in kernels and ground for flour), and as animal fodder. Cooks took up the new product and created various dishes quite different from the baked tortillas and fried pupusas of the Americas, most notably maize-flour porridge eaten as a staple in many cultures: Italian polenta and *kenkey*, *pap*, or *ugali* in west, southern, and east Africa. This food sustained populations in places that expanding European empires sought to control—as did potatoes in Ireland. In Europe and Africa, the expanding imperial reach of early modern empires resulted not just in the circulation of commodities new to both the eastern and western hemispheres and a change in local diets, but also to the transformation of agricultural practices.

The environmental consequences of the Columbian Exchange were not limited to the changes that accompanied new staple crops in Afroeurasia. British merchants' advantageous exploitation of the Atlantic trade in American commodities meant that the British economy accelerated relative to her European rivals (Acemoglu *et al.* 2005). At the same time, more frequent and cheaper access to drug foods—sugar, tea, coffee, and tobacco—improved general welfare in England before the nineteenth century (Hersh and Voth 2009), entrenching the unequal repercussions of the global redistribution of plants.

The Columbian Exchange also facilitated the strengthening of European imperial power in the Americas. Spanish forces defeated the powerful Inca and

FIGURE 3.3: The Vergenoegd Farm of Mr. Lochner (South Africa). Watercolor by Jan Brandes, 1778. Public domain: courtesy of the Rijksmuseum, the Netherlands.

Aztec empires prior to 1650, but the consequences of the Great Dying lingered for centuries afterwards. Old World pathogens—especially small pox, measles, malaria, and yellow fever—decimated American populations that had not acquired immunity to them. The widespread depopulation not only facilitated military conquest, it lent credence to the fictional ideology of "empty land" available for imperial acquisition (Figure 3.3). In North America, British colonists were largely unaware of—or uninterested in—indigenous land use practices or claims to resources (Anderson 1994). Settlement expanded in fits and starts from the earliest colonial outposts in Virginia, Massachusetts, and previously Dutch-controlled New York, motivated by imperial ideology that sought to remake landscapes according to European aesthetics and productive norms (Pratt 1992).

Similarly, in India, Australia, and South Africa, colonial administrators were either ignorant of or willfully overlooked local resource uses, a practice we now see had deleterious long-term consequences (Iqbal 2006; Mitchell 2009; Gammage 2013). Even in places where indigenous resistance temporarily halted or pushed colonial frontiers back, the consequences of settlers' "portmanteau biota" continued to spread introduced plants and animals into new environmental niches, leading Alfred Crosby to famously ask (and answer) "why the sun never sets on the empire of the dandelion?" (1986: 7, 270). The conquerors' plants, animals, and pathogens did as much work as governors and farmers—if not more—to achieve the environmental and political transformation of distant territories into outposts of empire with recognizably European characteristics.

The Columbian Exchange is one clear example of the connections between imperial expansion and the environment, but it was not alone. Biological interactions and environmental change as a result of imperial activity were hard at work around the world, propelled by both maritime and terrestrial empires in this period. These changes in the production and trade of agricultural and other commodities had decidedly cultural consequences. The social importance of tea drinking in Britain, coffee house life and its attendant circulation of new print materials in western Europe, exchanges of cotton cloth that influenced clothing in Europe, Africa, and Asia, and the proliferation of fur clothing spurred by increased access to Pacific and Siberian hunting grounds, all demonstrate the cultural consequences of environmental exploitation by empires.

IMPERIAL HEARTLANDS TRANSFORMED

Imperial ideology is fundamentally about rationalizing conquest and extraction. Justifying the expropriation of land, resources, and people was central to imperial policies, since some sense of legitimate acquisition—other than the persuasive power of brute force—was a useful tool in an empire's arsenal. All imperial rulers faced the challenges of uniting diverse populations and managing varied ecosystems (Burbank and Cooper 2010). The tremendous size and geographic reach of early modern empires made these biologically rooted challenges especially acute, however, and led to unprecedented changes in landscapes, knowledge production, and daily life in imperial heartlands. These changes were especially evident in western Europe.

Pointing out Europe's disproportionately large role in this process is not to "succumb to mindless Eurocentrism," in John Richards' pithy phrase, but rather to "acknowledge an obvious fact" (2003: 17). The growing power of western European empires spread a set of local, culturally specific ideas about how the world works—in both natural and human realms—around the globe. Understanding how imperial planners thought about the environment, managed natural resources, and regulated relationships between people and the physical landscape in Europe is a necessary precursor to understanding the global changes that accelerated after 1600.

The general narrative of European environmental history is one of long-term degradation and rural depopulation due to centuries of overuse (McNeill 1992). Deforestation is central to this story, with scholars giving particular attention to changes in the nineteenth century tied to industrialization (Rajan 2006). There were, however, important antecedents in the seventeenth and eighteenth centuries that point to struggles not just over the use of woods but also of pasture, water, domestic animal products, wild game, and marine resources. These local histories of contested resource management have clear connections to the larger ambitions of early modern empires around the world.

Looking at the state's efforts to manage forests in France and fisheries in Spain we see the nexus among ideology, resources, and people that shaped the environmental consequences of imperial policy.

Legislation promulgated in the reign of Louis XIV influenced French resource management until the twenty-first century. A landmark 1669 ordinance subordinated local forest use to the needs of the state, especially the military. Finance minister Jean-Baptiste Colbert orchestrated a plan to more efficiently manage domestic resources for the benefit of the crown, noting that "France will perish for want of wood," since timber shortages disadvantaged French maritime interests compared with her rivals in Britain and the Netherlands (cited in Matteson 2012). Colbert's plans prioritized growing tall, slow-growing hardwoods necessary for shipbuilding, especially oak, but also elm and fir. The ordinance regulated cutting and planting cycles, mandating up to 100 years of growing time for some oaks. The growth and preservation of tall trees kept locals out of the forest and curtailed customary practices such as harvesting forest litter, shrubs, and small trees for firewood and domestic timber. This approach benefited imperial interests overseas but pitted peasants and landowners against royal—and then republican—administrators for centuries. Sporadic violence was punctuated by periods of sustained resistance to government controls on land and resource use, underscoring the point that the costs and benefits of empire were rarely distributed evenly.

Revolutionaries in Paris took up the cause of popular resource use. Republican claims of liberty included relaxing forest restrictions between 1789 and 1799 by delegating decisions about woodland use to local authorities. This reprieve for peasants was short-lived, though, and forest use restrictions returned with renewed vigor in the nineteenth century (Matteson 2015). Contested access to resources remained a governance problem for the French state. Local people assassinated a forestry official every year from 1840 to 1900 (*Les Eaux et Forêts du 12e au 20e siècle* 1987: 494).

Histories of forest management have taken center stage in French environmental histories, but other domestic resources were contested, too, including wool, water, and grain (McPhee 1999; Locher and Quenet 2009). In Spain, the crown not only granted land and labor rights in return for support from noble families; royal purview also distributed monopoly rights to some resources while leaving other regions or products unregulated. The dukes of Medina Sidonia—the oldest ducal title in Spain—enjoyed monopoly rights to fish the annual bluefin tuna migration off the coast of Cádiz. This seasonal fishing required large-scale butchering and salting processes, which were based in the town of Conil. Bluefin are large; adults typically weigh over 800 pounds. They are also strong, fast, and athletic animals, considered by current-day anglers among the most formidable of game fish. Harvesting large numbers of bluefin with pre-industrial technology required intensive seasonal labor, investment in specialized nets for the *almadraba* fishing technique, highly choreographed maneuvers by boats at sea, and skilled fishermen—in short, a lot of capital and organization, something wealthy lords could muster and most competitors for the fish could not. Nevertheless, the dukes zealously asserted their monopoly on the *almadraba*—a method in which multiple boats hauling large nets essentially "herd" the schooling fish to the shore, where wading men with gaffs kill the animals and teams haul them onto the beach (Phillips 2017).

For the weeks of the tuna migration, staffing the *almadrabas* presented challenges. Spanish literature depicts the seasonal communities as dangerous places, not just because men were wrestling in the waves with huge animals. Pirates threatened from sea and the laborers' camps were rough and sometimes lawless places (Phillips 2004: 132). Managing the endeavor was clearly worthwhile for the dukes, who relied on the profits. The annual tuna catch generated nearly two million *reales* a year for the house of Medina Sidonia in the last quarter of the sixteenth century (2004: 130). The fish—and monopoly access—were clearly a resource worth protecting (Figure 3.4).

For the dukes, "protecting" the tuna meant maintaining order among the laborers and keeping interlopers from hauling off fish. In the seventeenth century, though, they were faced with a new problem: long-term, marked decline in the annual catch. Whether because of changing migration patterns, overfishing, or a shortage of labor during wartime, the dukes saw a real reduction in their tuna-based income. At the same time, local fishermen increasingly challenged the dukes' exclusive access to the fish, while costs for labor and salt rose. The dukes continued to assert their monopoly rights and to extract what fish—and money—they could from the Atlantic. The depth of the problem came to the fore in 1728. Carla Phillips' poignant telling of the preparation for that spring's catch shows that the duke and his agents were experimenting with new approaches to nets and labor recruitment, but to no avail. A major storm

FIGURE 3.4: Tuna preparation depicted in "Conil de la Frontera," from Civitates Orbis Terrarum. Georg Braun and Franz Hogenberg, sixteenth century. Credit: DEA/R. MERLO/De Agostini Picture Library/Getty Images.

coincided with the tuna swimming past Conil; the year's catch was a financial disaster (Phillips 2004). Even monopoly rights were no guarantee of income from a precarious resource.

It is perhaps exceedingly obvious to point out the material foundation—whether forests, fish, or agriculture—required to support a state of any size. But insights of materialist history remain especially relevant as we consider the challenges confronted by a government that seeks to scale up from local to imperial administration. Having resources in the state's heartland and managing them, whether for the good of the state and the economy, or in times of loss—as in the diminished ducal tuna haul—was no guarantee of long-term survival or geopolitical success on a global stage. Natural resources and environmental management were central to early modern empire-building. Luckily for Spanish ambitions, the state's economy, princely power, or nascent imperial reach did not rest only on tuna.

Like other states that expanded from local to imperial dominance, the united crowns of Aragon and Castille based their strategies for governing vast territories and managing distant resources on existing practices in the heartland. Zealous intervention characterized the husbanding of resources as diverse as French forests, Mediterranean fish, central European silver, Songhai gold, and even Turquoise in Persia and Afghanistan. Meanwhile Ottoman, Mughal, and Qing rulers used tax policies and local proxies to encourage greater agricultural production. Expanding states took these resource management tools and other strategies of rule with them into newly conquered realms.

TRANSFORMATIONS ABROAD

Iberian customs granting land and tenant labor for service to the crown undeniably shaped the earliest European expansion in the Americas politically, economically, and culturally. The Spanish crown parceled out Caribbean territory to conquistadors, who then sought to establish the same modes of agricultural production and social hierarchy that characterized their homeland. The resulting creation of haciendas and encomiendas may not have resulted in uniform or deep control of American land or people, but the practices, however unevenly established, initiated fundamental changes in land rights and uses in the western hemisphere. In fact, land use and changes in property regimes were foundational to imperial expansion in all the maritime empires, including the Dutch East India Company settlement in South Africa (Mitchell 2009).

But transformations in land ownership were not the only economic interventions into colonized landscapes. The steady increase in the number of slaves imported to the Americas was also tied directly to environmental changes (Voyages n.d.). Increased sugar production in Brazil and the Caribbean led to a seventy percent price drop between 1645 and 1680. This was good news for consumers in Europe, but posed a challenge to colonial planters who had to further increase their volume to continue making money. The resulting intensification of sugar production in the eighteenth century led to the clearing of forests to make way for plantations, which concomitantly required more labor to plant, harvest, and process the cane.

The introduction of the plantation system of production in the Americas accompanied other changes: the introduction of private grazing land, horses, cattle, pigs, and monocrop agriculture—especially sugar. These changes supported colonial endeavors and ultimately limited indigenous productive capacity wherever foreign powers developed plantations. This form of commercial agriculture was not only an imperial endeavor, but was an especially effective form of domination and production, implemented by colonial officials and private investors alike. The combination of slave labor and commodity production that came to characterize the Atlantic plantation complex was a unique configuration (Curtin 1998), combining the reorganization of labor and the near extermination of local populations, the concentration of capital, and the large-scale transformation of the environment.

Despite their prevalence, Atlantic plantations and their owners only had a tenuous grasp on the land and peoples claimed as imperial subjects. The brutality of slavery ensured production but also engendered widespread resistance. Runaways, local revolts, maroon communities, and the constant specter of violence permeated French, Dutch, British, Spanish, and Portuguese colonies, imposing limits on what owners or governments could accomplish. These similarities across plantation colonies in the eighteenth century are striking (Burnard and Garrigus 2016). Given the challenges of managing an unwilling slave labor force, planters invested systematically in technology, constantly looking for ways to keep their estates profitable and more effectively control the forces of nature (Rood 2017).

In light of the labor problems, the threat from tropical and semi-tropical diseases that limited European imperial advances (McNeill 2010), and an ecosystem that resisted clear-cutting and overgrew planted land at the same time that it produced sugar, tobacco, cotton, and indigo, the deeply intertwined image of Atlantic plantations and the Garden of Eden in imperial imaginations is surprising (Grove 1995; Linebaugh and Rediker 2000). But planters clung to the myth (Figure 3.5). Scotsman Thomas Cumming named his plantation in Guyana "Garden of Eden," the devilish challenges of running and holding on to it notwithstanding (Hamilton 2005: 71).

The intention to completely transform landscapes, Edenic or otherwise, into plantations and the willingness to invest the requisite time, capital, and labor—even if it was the effort of enslaved others—reveals the extent to which European ideas about nature supported imperial ideology. Hierarchies of race, in which "Hottentots" and other "savages" ranked well below Spanish peasants

FIGURE 3.5: Plantation in Surinam. Oil Painting by Dirk Valkenberg, 170. Public domain: courtesy of the Rijksmuseum, the Netherlands.

or English yeoman farmers, overlapped with Christian theology that gave humans dominion over the birds and trees (Mitchell 2012). The plantation project on the scale of the Atlantic complex, however daunting, was justifiable in the context of European imperial expansion.

European attempts to develop or control existing plantations in regions other than the Americas had limited success. After the Dutch East India Company conquered the Banda islands—then the world's only source of nutmeg and mace—in 1621, VOC officials took control of the nutmeg plantations. Colonial rulers sought to reorganize them according to Dutch agricultural practices and introduced a forced labor system that had more in common with Atlantic slavery than Asian or Indian Ocean systems of bondage, a transformation described as a "Caribbean cuckoo in an Asian nest" (Winn 2010). To work the plantations, the VOC imported slaves, indentured laborers, and convicts to replace Bandanese workers—many of whom had been massacred in the Dutch invasion.

Wherever it occurred, plantation agriculture was detrimental to indigenous communities, although peoples in some regions initially benefited from new opportunities to trade in natural resources. Such trade was particularly important in climate zones not well suited to profitable semi-tropical crops such as sugar, indigo, or tobacco, or to European farm staples such as wheat or oats. "Commercial hunting," argues John Richards, was the most lucrative way to exploit the northernmost regions of the Americas" (2003: 463). Furs from American beavers, foxes, and martens, along with deerskins, provided substitutes for dwindling fur supplies in Europe. Although new textile techniques provided some alternatives, these more densely woven woolens were not as warm as fur in the increasingly cold winters of the Little Ice Age. So the North American fur trade—part of what Richards calls the world hunt of the seventeenth and eighteenth centuries—was important for European markets. It also transformed indigenous and colonial social relationships and ecosystems in North America and Siberia.

European empires competed in the Americas, each carving out a sphere of influence while working to limit the trade of their rivals. The French established settlements and trading posts in the Saint Lawrence River system, the Dutch connected with Native Americans on the Hudson and its tributaries, and the English penetrated the Connecticut and Delaware river valleys. European traders introduced flint and firearms to Amerindian hunters, changing the local technological landscape. More reliable fire-starting and more efficient hunting tools helped hunters meet the growing demand for furs.

The advent of commercial hunting changed local practices, disrupting the Algonkian practice of coalescing into family groups for the winter and summer hunting seasons, for example. As game became scarcer in the Saint Lawrence River regions, hunters had to disperse more widely, so individual families began to mark out their own territories, asserting property rights (Richards 2003: 473). Such changes in local resource use are often overlooked in colonial environmental histories that focus directly on resource extraction or settler-driven transformations, such as clearing woodlands for agriculture, or the introduction of new species into an ecosystem.

The knock-on effects of hunting were not limited to North America, or to the expansion of maritime empires. Russian conquest in Siberia similarly exploited animal resources rather than trying to establish farming in an environment not suited for the endeavor (climate considerations did not always appropriately influence colonial agricultural plans). Granted, hunting and commercial fur preparation had long been central to the Russian economy (Martin 1986). The expanding Tsarist state directly asserted control over the land, resources, and people of Siberia from the seventeenth century, fueled by the fur trade (Richards 2003: 523–5). Yuri Slezkine (1994) convincingly shows the relationship between environmental exploitation and economic conquest on one hand, and significant cultural change—among both indigenous Siberian peoples and Russian imperial planners—on the other. The quest for furs, implemented as the exercise of imperial dominance imposed by military force and materially demonstrated through the payment of tribute in furs by conquered peoples, led directly to the Christianization and cultural Russification of Siberians such as Samoyed, Yukaghir, and Evenek peoples. Meanwhile, the incorporation of linguistically and ethnically diverse populations into the Tsardom meant that Russian administrators developed new categories of classification, new approaches to census-taking, and an ideology that firmly connected subordinated peoples with economic metrics such as resource extraction. The absorption of "native hunters" into the Russian polity differed from the European treatment of indigenous trading partners in North America, who were not incorporated into colonial settlements or considered part of the colonial population—except in some cases in New France.

Imperial policy—directly influenced by merchants and planters—linked change in European heartlands to changes in colonial territories. The seventeenth- and eighteenth-century consequences of the Columbian Exchange are perhaps the most remarkable changes, but not the only ones evident in the historical record. Scholars remain especially focused on the transatlantic connections because those dynamics contributed so directly to processes of modernization. Kenneth Pomeranz's work (2000), for example, sheds new light on the connections between the large-scale trade in natural resources and Britain's use of her colonies—the "ghost acres"—to escape the Malthusian trap of early modern growth. Britain's lucky conjuncture combined access to resources, innovations in governance and technology, private property rights, and maritime trading success to support unprecedented levels of economic production and population growth. But at the end of the eighteenth century, even those fortuitous advantages could not indefinitely surpass the limits imposed by the biological old regime. Despite the considerable global changes rooted in early modern imperial expansion—including nutritional benefits across Afroeurasia, timber for British shipping, American sliver infusing the Chinese and western European economies, and the increasing use of coal—energy regimes in every empire continued to depend on plant matter fueled by the sun.

NATURE, THE ENLIGHTENMENT, AND COLONIZATION

Despite the preponderance of scholarship on the connection between imperial economics and environments, colonial extraction was not only about resources. Knowledge, too, flowed through imperial circuits as a result of lopsided interactions in both imperial outposts and capitals. Understanding local environments was partly a necessity of rule, facilitating the management of distant and initially unfamiliar places and enabling profitable expansion. As Richards succinctly puts it: "Knowledge of the natural world conferred power over previously unused natural resources across the globe" (2003: 20). Ideas born from imperial interactions influenced European thinkers in non-materials ways, too. Rousseau's noble savage would be unthinkable without reports of living "savages" and their often quite reasonable treatment of European explorers or merchants. Similarly, the increasingly empiricist agronomes and physiocrats of the mid-eighteenth century turned to information from tropical islands to think about the consequences of economic activity on the natural world (Grove 1995).

Equally important, the field of natural history depended on detailed observations of the natural world at home—in the case of thinkers such as Isaac Newton, Blaise Pascal, or René-Antoine Ferchault de Réaumur—and the collection of information from imperial territories that fueled the work of scholars such as Carolus Clusius, Carl Linnaeus, Joseph Banks, and the Comte de Buffon (Fara 2004). The connection between emerging science and imperial expansion after 1600 is well documented (Cañizares-Esguerra 2006; Schiebinger 2007; Bleichmar 2012). The Columbian Exchange was especially dramatic because there had not been sustained contact between the eastern and western hemispheres of the globe for millennia. Europe's encounter with flora, fauna, and people who previously were unfamiliar led not just to an exchange of crops, microbes, and material culture but also to the transfer of ideas and the development of new technologies. The tiny cochineal beetle purchased in a Mexican market enabled European textile manufactures to create the "perfect red," changing dyeing materials and techniques (Greenfield 2009). Maria Sybilla Merian's botanical drawings based on observations in Surinam contributed to emerging natural history debates and challenged gender norms for professional artists (Davis 1997; Reitsma 2008). The need for more accurate navigation prompted the British Parliament to offer a prize for the development of an accurate measure of longitude while at sea, a prize claimed by clockmaker John Harrison in 1762 (Sobel 1998; Richardson 2010).

Other early modern exchanges, however, were also consequential for the circulation of plants, foodstuffs, and knowledge, though not nearly as disastrous for entire populations as the Columbian disease effects in the Americas or the slave trade—on which Atlantic exchanges depended—in Africa. Clusius, for example, depended on merchants and officials traveling with the Dutch East India Company to send seeds, bulbs, and plant specimens to him in Leiden, where he established a renowned botanical garden. His sixteenth-century precedent laid the groundwork on which seventeenth- and eighteenth-century scholars continued to build (Cook 2008). Linnaeus developed an unparalleled collection of specimens to support his efforts to devise a complete taxonomy of the world's living things, provided by students he sent out across the world expressly to find exemplary types and discover new species (Hansen and Hansen 2007). The English acquisition of Linnaeus' collection after his death speaks to the increasing importance of scientific knowledge in imperial rivalries and in the calculations of imperial planners. Banks took up the global collecting mantle, overseeing the development of the Royal Botanical Gardens at Kew and orchestrating scientific-imperial missions from London, including Captain James Cook's voyages (Drayton 2000). Meanwhile, Georges-Louis Leclerc, the Comte de Buffon, oversaw the Jardins du Roi in Paris, which included a significant menagerie of exotic animals. He benefited from the expeditions of Louis Antoine de Bougainville in the Pacific and François le Vaillant in southern Africa, among others, to develop broad knowledge which he published in the 36-volume *Histoire Naturelle*.

These large-scale collecting projects were only part of the ongoing reconfiguration of European landscapes, foodscapes, and environmental priorities—all influenced by colonial specimens and information. Menageries, botanical gardens, curiosity cabinets, and markets in Europe were transformed by the arrival and sustained importation of raw materials from the Americas, Africa, and Asia. Colonies changed agricultural landscapes in Europe, too, even after the arrival of post-Columbian foods. Richard Grove shows that colonies were effective laboratories for agronomic science, places where the efficacy of new techniques could be assessed without encountering the same resistance that domestic farmers would put up with (Grove 1995). He further argues that European ideas about environmental change, degradation, and the foundational concepts of modern environmentalism emerged from imperial interactions with colonial landscapes. "Economic motives and global networks involved in the diffusion of exotic plant and crop species . . . were vital both to the dynamics of agricultural improvement and to the evolution of a global environmental awareness" (Grove: 1995, xi).

This emerging environmental thinking included the realization that ecosystems could change—for better and for worse—and that species could decline. "By the eighteenth century, primarily because of systematic observation and recording of data, some intellectuals began to perceive the impact of human activity on the natural world" (Richards 2003: 20). There was a gradual awareness of species change and species decline, which came to a head in the early nineteenth century with definitive arguments about extinction that continue to shape our current understanding of evolution and demise. Although this is generally considered to be an idea rooted in modern western science, there are earlier and broader imperial contexts for ideas about extinction, suggesting that this was not an observation or idea with a single genesis. Chinese official Deng Qi'nan speculated about the extinction of animals in Guangdong in an 1811 report for the Qing emperor (Marks 2017: 122). Deng recorded his remarks about the disappearance of elephants, buffalo, centipedes, and deer from the prefecture where he was posted a year before Georges Cuvier's *Discours sur les révolutions de la surface du globe*, a touchstone publication for western thinking about extinction.

Of course, both Deng and Cuvier relied on earlier observations to chart a trajectory of decline, but they were not alone in drawing conclusions that species distributions changed, or speculating that extinction was possible. Russian observers of Pacific marine animals mentioned extinction as early as 1760 (Jones 2014). Both Pierre Poivre, the French Intendant of Isle de France and Réunion from 1767 to 1772, and Robert Jacob Gordon, the Dutch commander of the VOC garrison at the Cape of Good Hope from 1780 to 1795, lamented the decline in the number and diversity of animals in their respective colonial terrains.

CONCLUSION

Empirical observations by Deng, Cuvier, Poivre, Gordon, and others led to rational explanations that sought to fit the diversity of the natural world into emerging universal paradigms. Such thinking is commonly associated with the Enlightenment. Finding examples of this intellectual process connected to imperial expansion—but not only to Europe or European empires—disrupts Europe-centered approaches to early modern empires and to environmental histories. Even in Europe, Enlightenment thinking, investigations of natural history, and approaches to natural resource management were increasingly mediated through empire in the period between 1650 and 1800. What's more, these processes were not confined to Europe. Intentional policies to support the state's effective environmental management were also evident in the Ottoman, Mughal, and Qing empires.

Imperial governance, territorial expansion, and daily life in both frontier areas and metropolitan capitals were multiply entangled with the natural world. The quest for resources—especially the sustenance needed for growing populations in order to escape the constraints of the biological old regime—was of course an important motivation for states to acquire new territory (this strategy worked even better if the empire could claim land it believed to be uninhabited, or populated by people the empire was not responsible for feeding). The unexpected windfall of timber, silver, or ghost acres cannot, however, account for imperial ambition in the first place, or entirely explain the marked change in human–environmental relations in the early modern world.

The development of new knowledge regimes based on empirical observation and detailed record-keeping led a more robust understanding of the environment. It also interacted in complex ways with large modernizing empires that sought increasing control of the natural world. Record-keeping about the environment became enmeshed in the record-keeping of nascent bureaucratized states. Gaining, categorizing, and communicating new information was central to imperial strategies of rule.

Through this codification of information, resource management strategies developed in specific local circumstances became enshrined in state-level laws, which in turn were exported throughout empires. In this way, site-specific practices of labor control, tenant farming, plantation agriculture on large single-owner estates, and commercial hunting practices spread beyond their sites of origin.

The records created by this process show that human ingenuity when confronted with new ecosystems, human adaptability to new food sources, and human inability to respond to new disease regimes had discernable effects on the environment. Enlightenment knowledge production also influenced the outcome of sustained face-to-face interactions among African, American, Asian, and European peoples who met through the forces of empire. Even before the turn to fossil fuels, imperial officials, subjects, and enslaved peoples traveled great distances and adapted to new environments. Exchanges both planned and unintentional spread crops, weeds, animals, and pathogens. Although meeting the needs of a growing population and increasing political power were explicit goals of early modern empires, seventeenth- and eighteenth-century leaders did not plan to pierce Malthusian ceilings or initiate the kind of inter-hemispheric, multilayered transmissions we retroactively call the Columbian Exchange. Rulers did, however, explicitly seek transactions or conquest that provided commodities, produce, rare resources, information, and technology—in short, products from the environment along with knowledge of how to get and use them. Trying to achieve these goals inadvertently led to the transformation of ecosystems across the globe.

CHAPTER FOUR

Labor

ABIGAIL SWINGEN

By the middle of the seventeenth century, the global empires of the western world addressed their labor needs in a variety of different ways. Most relied on some form of unfree labor, ranging from workers whose status meant temporary un-freedom, to those whose enslavement was perpetual and hereditary. This spectrum of unfree status was culturally embedded into the ways that many early modern societies functioned and for most early moderns, the existence of unfree labor was normative. In some cases, unfree labor helped states to function in military and bureaucratic capacities, and in others, unfree laborers worked in mines and agriculture and created wealth for the empires they served. Across empires, the period 1650–1800 witnessed the entrenchment of unfree labor on an unprecedented scale. Although this era is commonly associated with the emergence of Enlightenment ideals of individual liberties in many parts of the Atlantic world, it coincided with the vast expansion of the transatlantic slave trade and the hardening of colonial laws governing enslaved Africans in the Iberian, British, and French empires. Despite the massive intellectual and cultural shifts happening among European and colonial elites, unfree status remained common and in many cases became more widespread during this period.

In addition, imperial labor regimes were transformed significantly during this era. For example, by the seventeenth and eighteenth centuries the Ottoman empire relied heavily on unfree labor, mostly to fill the bureaucratic and military needs of the state. These unfree laborers ranged in status from those who were likely to be emancipated to those who would pass along enslaved status to their offspring. By the 1600s, most slaves in the Ottoman empire were obtained in raids along frontier regions, particularly those of Russia, eastern Europe, and the Black Sea. Although some enslaved people worked on agricultural estates and in certain industries like silk weaving, generally the Ottoman slave system was not designed to generate wealth, but to protect the empire militarily (Inalcik 1979: 28–38).

In the case of the Russian empire, both chattel slavery and serfdom had existed for centuries. Russians not only enslaved foreign war captives, but were notorious for being willing to enslave their own populations. Unfree laborers served in a variety of capacities in the Russian empire, both as laborers and soldiers; by the early 1600s, a good portion of the army was made up of slaves. Interestingly, the number of serfs who worked as agricultural laborers declined throughout the seventeenth century as people voluntarily sold themselves into slavery as a way to avoid being taxed by the state. Noting this loss of revenue, by the late 1600s, the imperial government technically turned all enslaved agrarian workers into serfs. According to historian Richard Hellie, the status of serfs declined precipitously thereafter and "evolved into near-slavery" (Hellie 2011: 275). This style of serfdom on agricultural estates expanded throughout the Russian empire during the 1700s and remained legally entrenched until 1861.

In the Americas, European empires also based their labor regimes on cultural familiarity with unfree labor. But ultimately the unfree labor regimes looked much different from the Ottoman and Russian cases. Both the Spanish and the Portuguese in the sixteenth century first turned to enslaving indigenous American populations, but by the late 1500s had mostly shifted to relying on enslaved Africans forcibly brought across the Atlantic Ocean, a trade that had been exploited by Portuguese merchants since the late 1400s (Russell-Wood 2009). In Spanish America, enslaved Africans worked not only on sugar plantations and in silver mines in Mexico and Peru, but also as skilled and domestic laborers in cities and towns, sometimes building military fortifications or working for imperial authorities (Blackburn 1997: 135–43; Elliott 2006: 100–1). By the 1600s, the wealth of the Spanish empire became the envy of other European powers and a model for imperial expansion based on the forced labor of enslaved Africans. Interestingly, the Spanish were not direct participants in the transatlantic slave trade and were instead dependent upon other Europeans to provide their colonies with enslaved workers. Since 1518, the Spanish crown issued an exclusive contract every few years to provide its colonies with enslaved African laborers, called the *asiento de negros*. For the first 150 years of its existence, the *asiento* was usually in the hands of Portuguese merchants (Postma 1990: 29–31). According to official records, from 1492 to 1595 about 51,300 enslaved Africans were imported into Spanish colonies (Figure 4.1). Real numbers were undoubtedly larger because of a flourishing illegal trade.

The idea that the Spanish had a limitless need for enslaved laborers, combined with the vast wealth of their silver mines in Mexico and Peru, made the *asiento* particularly coveted by European slave trading nations during the seventeenth century. This essay will consider how the *asiento*, and Spanish demand for unfree labor in its American empire more generally, influenced how other European

FIGURE 4.1: Map of the Caribbean, antique Spanish atlas, eighteenth century. Credit: goldhafen/Getty Images.

imperial powers, particularly the Dutch, British, and French, conducted themselves in terms of trade, war, and diplomacy. The essay will show how the unique dependence that the Spanish empire had on other Europeans to provide it with unfree labor via the *asiento* influenced how these other empires developed their own slave trades and altered the dynamics of labor supply and demand in the colonies. Focusing on the *asiento de negros* to understand unfree labor in colonial America from 1650 to 1800 emphasizes how issues of labor contributed to an interconnected world of trade in human beings, both licit and illicit, which cut across European national and imperial boundaries. At the same time, focusing on the *asiento* emphasizes the various ways that European powers, despite how entangled they might have been on the American frontiers, were still very much beholden to national imperial boundaries, laws, and regulations. As Junko Takeda emphasizes in this volume, state institutions played a key role in maintaining, often violently, networks of trans-oceanic trade. Arguably this was felt most acutely in the trades for unfree labor.

THE *ASIENTO DE NEGROS* AND IMPERIAL LABOR

The use of enslaved Africans as laborers was widespread in many American colonies by 1650. Part of the ready acceptance of slavery in earlier decades had to do with an ingrained culture of violence in European societies. Concepts of enslavement, or at least unfreedom, were also widespread. Historian David Eltis has argued that early modern Europeans saw Africans as "others," so different from Europeans that their eligibility for enslavement largely went unquestioned (Eltis 2000). But as Vanita Seth's essay in this volume attests, such notions of racial difference were by no means hardened by this time period. The vast exploitation of the transatlantic slave trade by the Dutch, British, and French from 1650 to 1800 certainly contributed to the entrenchment of these concepts. Thus during the time period considered here, there was very little questioning of the enslavement of Africans, although the legal framework surrounding this had yet to fully form until the later part of the period.

Although by 1650 the Iberian monopoly over colonization and trade in the Americas had been broken, the *asiento de negros*, with its promise of guaranteed sales of enslaved Africans, came to be understood by other European imperial powers as a way to benefit from Spanish American wealth. Indeed, jealousy of Iberian-American prosperity directly influenced the imperial designs of other European countries. The Netherlands, for example, formed in revolt against Spanish Habsburg rule. The seven primarily Protestant provinces of the Low Countries that formed the Netherlands orchestrated a long and bloody rebellion against the Spanish beginning in the 1560s, which lasted off and on until 1648. Historian Benjamin Schmidt has noted that this experience of throwing off "Spanish tyranny" deeply informed how the Dutch conceived of their own imperial exploits (2009: 168–72). Beginning in the 1580s and 1590s, the Dutch sent hundreds of ships to the Caribbean to trade illegally with Spanish merchants, and Dutch privateers also frequently plundered Spanish ships and ports (Rupert 2012: 28–32).

The Dutch also hoped to undercut Portuguese dominance of overseas trade, especially their control of the transatlantic slave trade. At the turn of the seventeenth century, the Dutch organized two trading companies that were designed to remove the Portuguese from their trading outposts in south-east Asia and the South Atlantic. In 1602, the Dutch formed the East India Company (VOC), which experienced success in the spice trade in south-east Asia. In 1621, they formed the West India Company (WIC) (Schmidt 2009: 173). The WIC was granted a monopoly on all trade in the Americas and the western coast of Africa. The hope was to dislodge the Portuguese from the sugar and slave trades and weaken the Iberian crowns. The WIC was conceived of as both a military and a commercial enterprise (Postma 1990: 16–18; den Heijer 2003: 80–6; Rupert 2012: 34). After a series of failed attempts to conquer north-eastern Brazil from the Portuguese, in 1630 the WIC successfully seized Pernambuco, took over sugar plantations and mills abandoned by Portuguese planters, and established a functioning colony that sent a significant amount of unrefined sugar to the Netherlands for the next two decades (Blackburn

1997: 194; den Heijer 2003: 89). Brazil's sugar plantations lacked adequate supplies of labor, however, and at first the Dutch relied on raiding Portuguese slave trading ships and diverting slave cargoes to Brazil (van Welie 2008: 57). But this was not sustainable, and therefore in 1637 the WIC-appointed governor of Brazil, Johan Maurits, launched a successful conquest of Portuguese-controlled Elmina Castle on the Gold Coast of Africa. Then in 1641 the WIC seized the center of the Portuguese slave trade, Luanda in Angola. For the next four years, the Dutch WIC delivered between 2,000 and 5,000 enslaved Africans annually to Brazil (Postma 1990: 21, 1992: 286, table 2; den Heijer 2003: 90–1).

In a remarkably short period of time, with the support of the Dutch government, the WIC had supplanted the Portuguese in the South Atlantic. In addition, the WIC had established trading outposts and colonies in North America in New Netherland (Manhattan), and on Caribbean islands such as Saint Martin, Saint Eustatius, and Curaçao (Figure 4.2). But Dutch dominance of the South Atlantic did not last. In 1645, Portuguese colonists in Brazil organized a successful revolt against WIC rule and by 1654 had pushed the

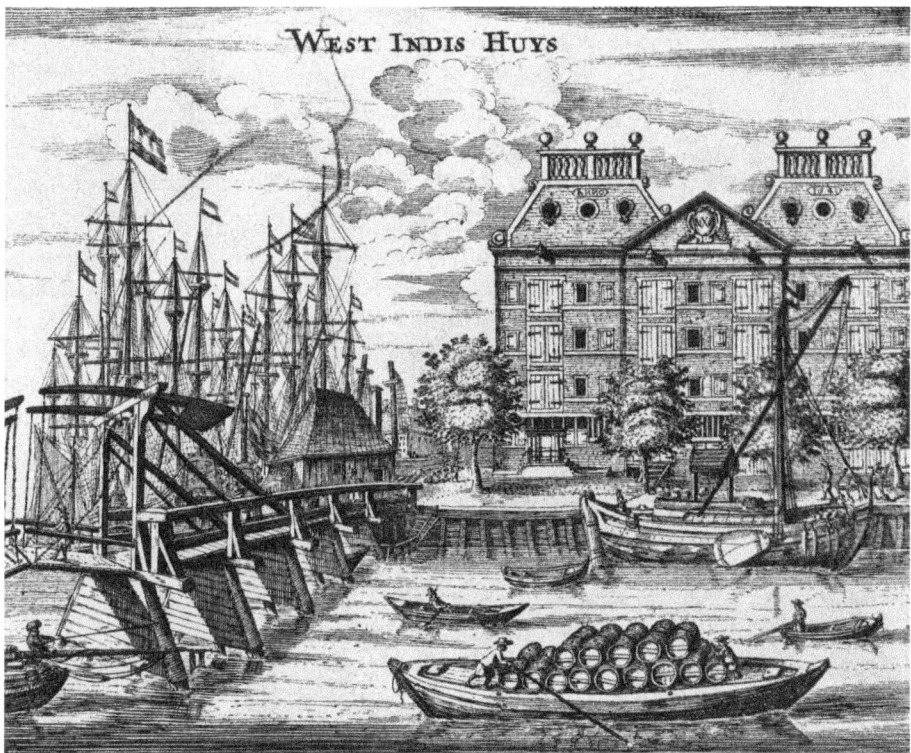

FIGURE 4.2: Men rowing canoes through Amsterdam. Warehouse of the West India Company in Amsterdam, the Netherlands. Built in 1641. Credit: Bettmann/Getty Images.

Dutch out (den Heijer 2003: 87; Schmidt 2009: 176; Rupert 2012: 34–6). In addition, in 1648 the Portuguese successfully regained Luanda in Angola (Thomas 1997: 185). It seemed that the WIC's colonial experiment in the South Atlantic had ended in failure.

Despite these losses, however, the Dutch remained firmly ensconced in the transatlantic slave trade in the middle of the seventeenth century, and soon would profit from the *asiento*. Significantly, the WIC held onto its Caribbean acquisitions of Saint Eustatius and Curaçao (Schmidt 2009: 176; Rupert 2012: 50–2). Even more importantly, the Dutch quickly reestablished themselves in West Africa, notably in Loango, in the Congo region north of Angola (Thomas 1997: 186). Although they lacked any real demand for labor in their own small colonies, the Dutch were well-positioned by the mid-1600s to dominate the slave trade to other European empires, particularly that of the Spanish. The WIC never held the *asiento de negros* but for the remaining decades of the 1600s merchants who held the contract would regularly subcontract to traders connected to the WIC. Often merchants of Portuguese, sometimes Sephardic Jewish, descent who were based in Amsterdam held the *asiento* during the 1670s and 1680s. The WIC used Curaçao as its base of operations because of its location near the northern coast of South America. Slaves were delivered to the island, held and "refreshed" in company barracks for a few weeks or months, and then sent to Spanish American port cities for re-sale (van Welie 2008: 82; Rupert 2012: 76–85). During the second half of the seventeenth century, despite bankruptcy and reorganization in 1674, the WIC delivered about 74,000 enslaved Africans for the *asiento* trade, with nearly 50,000 coming through Curaçao. In addition, the Dutch regularly sold slaves in other European colonies, especially English and French islands in the Caribbean. Overall, it has been estimated that Dutch merchants through both legal and illegal means delivered approximately 186,000 slaves from West Africa to the Americas from 1650 to 1700 (Postma 1990: 33–4, 1992: 287, table 3; van Welie 2008: 55, table 2, 61; Rupert 2012: 60, 78–82).

It was during the second half of the seventeenth century, as the Dutch came to dominate the transatlantic slave trade, that the *asiento de negros* began to play a significant role in international diplomatic relations (Rupert 2012: 60). In large part this centrality of the *asiento* to the imperial designs of European powers, particularly the English and the French, had to do with the continued demand for slave labor in the Spanish colonies as well as the ability of the Spanish to pay for slaves with bullion. Spanish colonial demand for slaves, coupled with the perceived wealth of the Spanish empire, made the *asiento* so coveted by other European powers that they were willing to go to war over the right to sell slaves to the Spanish by the early eighteenth century. As the remainder of this essay will show, this indicated a major commitment on the part of a number of European states to expanding the transatlantic slave trade.

FREE AND UNFREE LABOR

The English and French both started to conquer and settle their own colonies in the Americas during the early seventeenth century. Neither English nor French colonies had particularly auspicious beginnings, but within a few decades their colonies in North America and the Caribbean were not only viable but in some cases extremely profitable. French imperial expansion began in earnest with the establishment of colonies on the Caribbean islands of Saint Christopher, Guadeloupe, and Martinique during the 1620s and 1630s (Figure 4.3). The French also established colonies in North America around this time, mostly in the Saint Lawrence River region of Québec. Such enterprises were first organized by chartered companies, which attempted to people these colonies with migrants from France. They recruited free migrants and unfree servants who indentured themselves for a period of time in exchange for the cost of transportation (Blackburn 1997: 281–2). These servants, or *engagés*, usually agreed to a three-year contract. During the first few decades of settlement, *engagés* could expect to receive some money and a small plot of land upon the successful completion of their term of service, but also agreed to

FIGURE 4.3: Map of Martinique created by Matthieu Seutter. Details: Merchants and Native American Indian. Musée du Nouveau Monde. Credit: De Agostini Picture Library/Getty Images.

severe limitations on their mobility (Huetz de Lemps 1991: 174–5). In the West Indies, *engagés* performed a variety of agricultural work, including the cultivation of tobacco, and in Canada they worked as agricultural laborers as well as in the fur trade.

Individual merchants, planters, trading companies, and the Catholic Church were all involved in sponsoring the delivery of *engagés* during the 1600s, and most went to the West Indies. The *engagés* tended to be young and male, and came from all over France and from a variety of socioeconomic backgrounds (Mauro 1986; Boucher 2008: 145–9). The number of emigrants leaving France for the Americas was never substantial, however, and labor shortages remained a significant problem. In Canada, the French attempted to fill this need in part by utilizing enslaved indigenous people. Historian Brett Rushforth has analyzed a significant Indian slave trade within the Great Lakes region during the mid-to-late seventeenth century. Indigenous groups allied with the French would often offer enslaved members of enemy groups to French fur traders and missionaries, who would then sell them in Montreal and Québec (Rushforth 2012: 138, 154).

Around the same time, a number of planters in the French Antilles began to cultivate sugarcane, something they possibly learned from Dutch planters expelled from Brazil during the 1650s (Stein 1979: 7). This transformed demand for labor in the French West Indies. Growing sugarcane in the early modern period was a labor-intensive enterprise that required a large labor force as well as big plantations to be profitable. Tending the crop was both tedious and backbreaking; it required constant vigilance to keep out weeds and vermin over the course of its eighteen-month growing season. Once harvested, the cane had to be ground and boiled within a very short period of time for the sugar to be extracted, work that was extremely dangerous (Dunn 1972: ch. 6; Stein 1979: 7–8). Although the French government attempted to make servitude more appealing to migrants by decreasing the amount of time of a typical indenture from three years to eighteenth months, beginning in the mid-1600s, fewer French people were willing to indenture themselves for a life of hardship in the colonies. In part this occurred because there was less land available in the islands for servants to claim at the completion of their contracts. In addition, the harsh environment and poor working conditions for *engagés* in the West Indies had become notorious back in France (Huetz de Lemps 1991: 175–82; Boucher 2008: 268–71). Thus just as demand for labor began to skyrocket, there were fewer servants available. Instead, French planters relied on enslaved Africans.

Enslaved Africans had been a presence in the French West Indies since the 1630s, and the first French slave trading company, the *Compagnie du Cap Vert et du Sénégal*, was established in 1633. By 1660 there were about 8,000 enslaved Africans in the French islands, and about 16,000 European inhabitants (Huetz de Lemps 1991: 181; Boucher 2008: 155). But the transition to growing sugarcane and the expansion of French settlement to a significant portion of the large island of Saint Domingue by the last third of the seventeenth century dramatically transformed labor demand. French finance minister Jean-Baptiste Colbert created the *Compagnie des Indes Occidentales* in 1664 as a way for the French state to monopolize and profit from the sugar and slave trades. Although this company was quickly disbanded, the effect of trying to limit French colonial trade to the home country was successful, and almost all raw sugar produced in French islands was now sent to France for refining under a "mercantilist" policy of *exclusif* for the remainder of the century (Figure 4.4). Despite the existence of these policies, French planters depended heavily upon Dutch and English merchants for enslaved Africans during the seventeenth century (Blackburn 1997: 282–5; Boucher 2008: 155, 273). Still, French traders managed to deliver about 40,000 enslaved Africans through both legal trade and smuggling from 1651 to 1700 (Eltis 2001a: 43, table 1).

FIGURE 4.4: View of a sugar plantation in the West Indies. Public domain.

By 1685, there were approximately 25,000 enslaved Africans in the French Antilles. That year King Louis XIV issued a declaration concerning the governance of slaves in terms of religion, economics, and family life. This decree, later known as the *Code Noir*, laid the legal foundations for the physical and psychological control of slaves in the French colonies. For example, all slaves had to be baptized by the Catholic Church, could not participate in local markets without their masters' permission, and could not gather together with slaves from other plantations (Rushforth 2012: 125–31). Although it was never stringently enforced, the *Code Noir* became a symbol of how the French imagined an ideal empire in which enslaved laborers were strictly and violently governed. It is telling that although by 1685 the French Antilles had not yet fully developed into slave societies, imperial authorities felt the need to issue these regulations and envisioned an empire in which the use of enslaved Africans on sugar plantations would serve as its economic backbone.

The next few decades were transformative in terms of labor demand in the French American colonies, particularly Saint Domingue. The French state also expanded its involvement in the transatlantic slave trade, which was directly related to international affairs. When King Carlos II of Spain died without an heir in 1700, Philip of Anjou, the grandson of Louis XIV, inherited the Spanish throne. The vast riches of the Spanish American empire were now controlled by France, which significantly upset the diplomatic balance in Europe and contributed to the outbreak of the War of Spanish Succession in 1702. These events also brought the *asiento de negros* into French hands and in 1702 the *asiento* was granted to the *Compagnie de Guinée*. The French company was supposed to deliver 3,000 slaves to Spanish American ports per year, but it was never able to meet this obligation. The company's directors regularly asked permission to purchase slaves from Dutch or British traders to help fulfill the contract, but the Spanish crown was unwilling to grant such a concession (Stein and Stein 2000: 133).

Although French control of the *asiento* was not successful, during the early eighteenth century the French slave trade transformed dramatically. Some scholars have argued that what turned France into a slave-trading nation was its control of the *asiento* in the first decade of the 1700s (Stein 1979: 11; Boucher 2008: 2). Whereas before 1713 the slave trade was ostensibly restricted to those who purchased licenses from trading companies such as the *Compagnie du Guinée* and the *Compagnie du Sénégal*, after the loss of the *asiento* to the British in 1713 (see later) the slave trade was essentially opened. This coincided with a significant increase in demand for labor in the French West Indies. From 1700 to 1715, the population of enslaved Africans in the French West Indies increased from approximately 30,000 to 50,000 (Stein 1979: 14; Blackburn 1997: 294–5).

FROM SERVITUDE TO SLAVERY

English imperial designs were also in large part inspired by a desire to profit, legally or illegally, from the riches of the Spanish empire (Appleby 1998: 60–1). England's first "successful" settlement in North America along the James River in Virginia was established in 1607 by the Virginia Company, which had been granted a monopoly on all North American settlement and trade by King James I. Infamously, this experiment nearly ended in failure. Populated by men better suited for military pursuits than those involving the hard labor of settlement and agriculture, the Jamestown colony lost nearly ninety percent of its first colonists to disease and starvation (Morgan 1971b; Games 2008: 127–31).

What saved Virginia, it is well known, was the discovery in the late 1610s that tobacco grew extraordinarily well in the warm, humid region. The English had developed a taste for smoking and chewing tobacco in the late sixteenth century, importing it from Spanish and Portuguese colonies, often via Dutch merchants. The ability to bypass imperial competitors for these kinds of commodities was another major motivating factor in English overseas expansion. This was difficult in Virginia, however, because there were never enough laborers to work the tobacco plantations. In the first instance, channeling the labor of Native Americans in the region was not an option because of deep-seated hostility between the two groups. In addition, there was an inability among some English settlers to see Native Americans as people who could or should be enslaved or forced to work; that was what the Spanish had done, and the English, at least in theory, liked to think of themselves as not behaving as the Spanish had in the New World (Guasco 2007: 394–5). It should be noted, however, that the English utilized enslaved indigenous populations where they could, especially in later decades in colonies such as the Carolinas and the West Indies. Eventually, the Virginia Company organized a system in which it contracted with private merchants who transported servants to Virginia and delivered tobacco back to England. The merchants bore the up-front transportation costs and would sell the servants' contracts to planters or merchants in Virginia for a set period of years (usually between four and seven). Between 1619 and 1624, nearly 4,000 people, including children suspected of being orphans rounded up from the streets of London, were delivered to Virginia. Most died within a matter of months because of the unfamiliar climate, disease, and the harsh work regime in that planters frequently worked servants to death (Johnson 1970; Morgan 1971a).

Although the Virginia Company was dissolved by the English government in 1624, this system of indentured servitude became the basis of how the English sent servants to their colonies for the remainder of the seventeenth century, including to the West Indies. The English established settlements on Saint Christopher in the Leeward Islands (Saint Kitts) in 1624 and Barbados in 1627.

By the time the English arrived, there were few native Caribs left on the islands, so there was no significant native population to attempt to utilize for labor. The proprietors of these colonies, desperate for labor to establish tobacco, cotton, and indigo planting, turned to some of the same merchants who had been involved in the indentured servant trade to the Chesapeake region. These merchants quickly set up a robust servant trade to the English West Indies, and many also established their own plantations (Brenner 2003: 115–66, 173–81; Menard 2006: 52–9). By the 1630s, colonial merchants delivered between 800 and 1,000 servants from London annually to Barbados (Beckles 1989: 15–16, 34, table 1.6; Dunn 1972: 52–3). As in the *engagé* system, servants were often promised land at the completion of their terms.

Within a decade, however, even this annual influx of servants was not enough to keep up with labor demand in Barbados. Although English planters had been relatively successful growing tobacco, indigo, and cotton, problems of quality persisted, which limited profits. By the 1640s, they turned with increasing frequency to cultivating sugarcane, which in a few years dramatically transformed the economy and culture of the English West Indies, like it did the French Antilles. Not surprisingly, as the crop became profitable, demand for labor in Barbados intensified. In addition to servants from Europe, throughout the 1640s Barbados planters purchased ever-growing numbers of enslaved Africans primarily from Dutch traders, although some English merchants were also involved in the trade. Servants continued to be delivered to the island as well, and by 1650 there were approximately 12,800 enslaved Africans in Barbados and 30,000 European inhabitants (Menard 2006: 25, table 4).

These transformations contributed to a major shift in imperial policy on the part of the English government. After the English Civil War (1642–7), the execution of King Charles I in 1649, and the establishment of a republic, imperial concerns began to take center stage for the state. This marked a significant alteration in terms of policy; up until the 1650s, almost all English colonial endeavors had been orchestrated and funded by individual proprietors or semi-private chartered corporations. Under the leadership of the army general Oliver Cromwell, the government aimed to expand England's overseas possessions by conquering territory from the Spanish. Cromwell and his Protestant compatriots were deeply anti-Catholic and extraordinarily jealous of Spanish success in the New World. Importantly, many of Cromwell's closest advisers were colonial merchants who resented Spanish attempts at maintaining a monopoly on trade and settlement in the Americas. Many of these merchants were involved in the servant trade to Virginia and Barbados, and hoped to expand colonial markets in sugar, tobacco, and slaves. They convinced Cromwell that the English could successfully conquer territory from the Spanish in America, and in December 1654 an expeditionary force of 3,000 men sailed from England to the West Indies (Kupperman 1988; Swingen 2015: ch. 2).

The original plan of the "Western Design," as the expedition was known, involved conquering Santo Domingo in Hispaniola. The English forces missed their target by nearly thirty miles, however, and after a few weeks of utter chaos as ill-equipped troops fell sick and died from exhaustion and malnutrition, they re-grouped and sailed for Jamaica in May 1655. Jamaica was far less important to the Spanish, with only a few hundred inhabitants and no real local economy. The English managed to take the island in a matter of days. At the time, few in England were happy with the conquest, but in the long run it marked a significant turning point in imperial designs by the English state. At the center of it all was the desire not only to conquer territory and siphon wealth from the Spanish, but to expand markets in the servant and slave trades (Swingen 2015: 53–5). In the coming decades, Jamaica would play a key role in the expansion of the English slave trade, and the *asiento* in particular.

After the restoration of the monarchy in 1660, directly profiting from the slave trade became a central concern of the English government. Up until this point, English merchants had mostly been peripherally involved in the transatlantic slave trade; as mentioned earlier, most planters in Barbados and the Leeward Islands likely purchased enslaved Africans from Dutch merchants. Wary of Dutch success in the Atlantic, in 1660 King Charles II issued a charter for the first of three African trading companies granting a monopoly on all trade between West Africa and the American colonies. The African companies were closely run by the king's brother, the Duke of York (the future James II; Figure 4.5), and

FIGURE 4.5: James II (1633–1701). © National Maritime Museum, Greenwich, London.

were intimately connected to the English crown (Davies 1957; Swingen 2015). When the African Company was reorganized in early 1663, selling enslaved Africans to the Spanish became an explicit goal. Shortly after petitioning the king to grant licenses to Spanish merchants to allow them to trade in English colonies (normally they were forbidden to do so by the Navigation Acts, which limited colonial trade to English merchants and ships exclusively), Charles II issued instructions to the governors of Barbados and Jamaica informing them that they had to honor licenses granted to Spanish merchants who wished to trade in their colonies. The hope was that Spanish traders would bring in "moneys, bullion, and goods and freely to buy Negroes there" (King Charles II to Francis Lord Willoughby, National Archives, CO 1/17 no. 7, February 26, 1662–3; Zahedieh 2001: 8–9). The Portuguese holder of the *asiento* during the 1660s, Domingo Grillo, even subcontracted with the African Company to deliver 3,500 slaves to help him fulfill his obligation. This subcontract, however, was not legal and had to be abandoned (Thomas 1997: 213). But clearly there was hope that the English could profit from the *asiento* just as they expanded their involvement in the transatlantic slave trade.

Over the course of the 1670s and 1680s, Jamaica became the focal point of such efforts (Figure 4.6). In addition to the legal trade in slaves sanctioned by the African Company, a number of Jamaica's planters, merchants, and colonial officials profited handsomely from contraband trade in a variety of goods and especially slaves to the Spanish. Indeed, by the late 1600s, English, French, and Dutch merchants throughout the Caribbean regularly used the *asiento* trade as a way to smuggle other goods into Spanish markets (Stein and Stein 2000: 114, 122). This was an extremely lucrative enterprise for Jamaicans. According to historian Nuala Zahedieh, enslaved Africans who would sell for £17 to English planters could be sold to the Spanish for close to £40 because of high demand. She estimates that at least one-third of all slaves brought to Jamaica during the 1680s were sold to Spanish merchants (Zahedieh 2010: 878; see also Eltis 2000: 207). The various holders of the *asiento* during the 1680s, in fact, usually stationed agents in Jamaica to take advantage of the slave trade there. Often this trade involved the most important colonial officials on the island. Sir Thomas Lynch and Sir Hender Molesworth each served as governor of Jamaica during the 1680s and each collected hefty profits from legal and illegal slave trading with Spanish *asientistas* (Zahedieh 1986: 589–91). They both encouraged the Royal African Company to send even more slaves to Jamaica to benefit from this trade. They also (despite orders from London to the contrary) did very little to discourage illegal slave traders, called "interlopers," reasoning that they also helped the *asiento* trade. Molesworth described the *asiento* as "so considerable a trade . . . the benefit whereof the whole Kingdom of England doth participate" (Molesworth to William Blathwayt, National Archives, CO 138/5, p. 107, September 25, 1685).

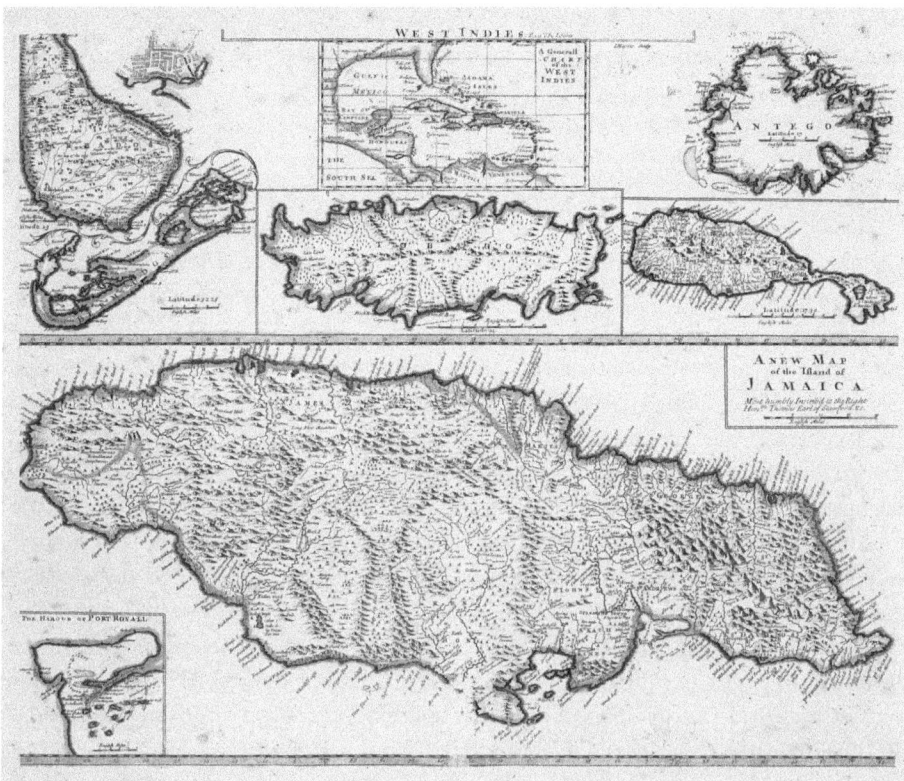

FIGURE 4.6: Central America, Jamaica, West Indies, 1721. Credit: Historic Map Works LLC/Osher Map Library.

To benefit from the *asiento*, the African companies had tremendous influence over colonial governance. Company directors had a vested interest in making sure that colonial officials supported its monopoly, as well as its desire to profit from Spanish trade. They often directly influenced colonial appointments as well as the removal of officials who were seen as not supportive enough of the company (Swingen 2015: 113). The Royal African Company was commercially successful throughout the 1670s and 1680s. Its market share increased steadily at the expense of Dutch traders as well as interlopers (Carlos and Brown Kruse 1996). According to historian David Eltis, the company delivered nearly 80,000 slaves to the English West Indies from 1672 to 1688, which represented roughly sixty percent of the total slave deliveries to those colonies (Eltis 2001b: 196–200, table 10–1). The African Company delivered about 7,000 enslaved Africans to Spanish colonies in the years before 1700. As Eltis argues, undoubtedly this is a gross underestimate because numerous English interlopers participated in this illicit trade and many slaves purchased by English planters were then re-sold to Spanish merchants (2000: 207–9). By the late seventeenth century, the English had designed their slave trade to cater to the Spanish as much as their own planters. This would influence how the English interacted with other European imperial powers and by the eighteenth century contributed to the outbreak of war.

TRADING THE *ASIENTO* IN THE AGE OF COMPANIES

The survival of the Royal African Company's monopoly could only last as long as its governor, King James II, was in power. After the king's removal in the Glorious Revolution of 1688–9, the African Company's monopoly that had been granted at the behest of the king's prerogative was now in legal limbo because of Parliament's new supremacy over many affairs of state, including overseas trade and colonization. As a result, the transatlantic slave trade was effectively open. The African Company organized a lobbying effort to convince Parliament to reaffirm its monopoly privileges. The company's critics, including a number of merchants and planters who had long opposed the company's monopoly, also campaigned throughout the 1690s and early 1700s to keep the slave trade open (Pettigrew 2013; Swingen 2015: ch. 6). In addition to petitioning Parliament, each side published a number of pamphlets in an attempt to persuade public opinion. Pro-company publications emphasized the need for a monopoly joint-stock corporation to organize the trade, whereas those opposed highlighted the virtues of keeping the slave trade free from such restrictions. Importantly, both pro- and anti-company pamphlets praised the transatlantic slave trade as essential to the economic well-being of the empire. As one anti-company author wrote, "It will be of absolute Necessity to have [the colonies] plentifully supplied with Negroes, by whose Labour and Strength all the Commodities of those Countries are produced, which Production is all clear Gains to this Nation, and better than the Mines of Gold and Silver are to the Spaniard" (Anon. 1697).

Interestingly, many of the company's detractors also argued that because of the monopoly, the *asiento* trade from Jamaica had been weakened and was at risk of disappearing altogether, to the great detriment of that colony's economy. John Cary, a Bristol sugar merchant who wrote extensively on trade, was particularly critical in this regard: "By the slow steps of the *African* Company," he wrote in 1695, "and the Hardships they have put on the Interlopers or private Traders, the number of *Negroes* imported thither hath been so small, and so much below our promises and the *Spaniards* Expectations, that this profitable *Assiento* or Factory hath for some time stood on Tiptoe, ready to wast it self to another Island, as it certainly had done long since if the Interlopers had not given a better Supply than the Company" (Cary 1695: 77). In other words, only a trade unrestricted by monopoly could keep up with demand from English planters and Spanish merchants and bring benefits to colonies like Jamaica. In the end, rather than reinstate the monopoly, in 1698 Parliament passed an Act that opened the slave trade to all participants so long as they paid a ten percent duty to the company on all goods shipped to Africa (Swingen 2015: 173–8). The Act proved impossible to enforce, however, and expired in 1712. For the remainder of the eighteenth century, the British slave trade was open to any merchant who wished to participate.

The demise of the African Company's monopoly in the 1690s brought concerns over the *asiento* trade and its perceived importance to the English empire into sharp relief. These developments played a major role in contributing to the reemergence of war between England and France in 1702. As noted earlier, after the death of the Spanish King Carlos II in 1700, Louis XIV of France claimed Spain and its vast empire for his grandson, Philip of Anjou. This included the *asiento*, which in 1702 was in the hands of the French *Compagnie du Guinée*. French control of the *asiento*, some historians have argued, "triggered open warfare" in the War of Spanish Succession (Stein and Stein 2000: 120). This conflict between the two major European slave-trading powers set the tone for the remainder of the eighteenth century, as Britain and France regularly fought with each other over imperial concerns, particularly profiting from the slave trade.

After seven years of war, a pamphlet appeared in London entitled *Proposals for Raising a New Company for Carrying on the Trades of Africa and the Spanish West-Indies*. It argued that in order for the British to benefit from the slave trade, they should create a new company that "unit[ed] the Trades to *Guinea*, and the *Spanish West-Indies*." It continued, "If we consider the *Spanish* Trade only, and of what vast Advantage to the Nation the keeping to our selves the *Assiento* may be, which is no other way to be preserv'd than by the Preservation of this Trade; this Consideration is of it self sufficient to obviate all Pretences. By that, we shall have a perpetual Supply of Gold, Silver, and other useful Commodities . . ." (Anon. 1709: 4–5). According to the author, by combining the interests of British and Spanish colonial labor demand in the form of a trading company, British dominance of the transatlantic slave trade would be secured.

This pamphlet, published in 1709, was produced at a time when debates about how best to manage the slave trade had been the talk of the political nation for twenty years. A number of well-placed politicians sought to seize a unique opportunity. In 1711, Sir Robert Harley, Earl of Oxford, serving as Chancellor of the Exchequer and Lord High Treasurer, proposed the creation of a new trading company, the South Sea Company (Figure 4.7). The company was designed to solve a major credit crisis caused by the nation's ballooning war debts, which were at least £9.4 million. According to Oxford's plan, creditors, including soldiers and sailors owed wages and suppliers to the armed forces whose bills the government had yet to pay, would have these debts exchanged for stock in the new company. As an incentive to investors and creditors, the new joint-stock corporation was established with a monopoly on trade to and from Spanish America (Wennerlind 2011: 197–201). Oxford knew full well

FIGURE 4.7: "A New and Exact Map of the Coast, Countries and Islands within the Limits of the South Sea Company," Herman Moll. Public domain.

that not only would peace soon be negotiated ending the war, but that the terms would be beneficial to Britain by including the *asiento*. As one supporter at the time remarked, "I must admit it to be an uncommon method to raise the public credit by exposing to the whole world the immense debt of nine millions ... yet what ill consequence can it be, when the vast ocean of the South Seas, and the infinite treasures of America are (inter alia) assigned for that satisfaction?" ("Remarkes upon the Act *None Annae R.* for Erecting a Corporation for carrying on a Trade to the South Seas," n.d., British Library, Harley MS 6393, pp. 3–6). The idea of the "South Seas," particularly Spanish America, continued to have a powerful hold on the British imagination as a source of potential wealth. Government creditors would earn money and the nation's debt would be funded from the slave trade. With the founding of the South Sea Company, the *asiento* was presented as being in the British national interest.

The South Sea Company's charter was approved by Parliament in September 1711, and a few days later preliminary peace negotiations between Britain and France were signed. In 1713, after the ratification of the Treaty of Utrecht, Queen Anne granted the *asiento* to the company. British control of the *asiento de negros* was the culmination of decades of official and unofficial policy regarding the slave trade and international (and intercolonial) relations. Supporters emphasized that the result for Britain would be the preservation of "lasting Credit," and an influx of "real Treasure, such as Gold and Silver" into the imperial economy (Anon. 1711: 4, 8). The creation of the South Sea Company with the specific purpose of managing the *asiento* was also designed to hinder French participation in the trade. As we have seen, the French had held the *asiento* since 1702. Daniel Defoe, one of the most prolific propagandists for Oxford's government, wrote that French control of the slave trade to the Spanish American colonies was designed "to keep *Old-Spain* in a perpetual Dependence [on France]," and that the French hoped for nothing more than "to revive her lately baffled Project of an *Universal Monarchy*" (Defoe 1711: 8–9). Thus British control of the *asiento* was seen as patriotic and would hinder the nefarious designs of the French king.

In 1713, the South Sea Company agreed to deliver 4,800 *pieza de indias* annually to Spanish American markets, which were to be sold at an agreed-upon rate and import duty. (A *pieza de india* was the unit for measuring a slave's economic value. A healthy adult slave was usually valued at one *pieza*, and younger, older, or less healthy slaves were valued at one-half to two-thirds of a *pieza*. Thus 4,800 *pieza de indias* could mean more enslaved people in absolute numbers than 4,800 would suggest.) In the first instance, the company turned to the Royal African Company to help fulfill the terms of the contract (Figure 4.8). Although the African Company's political influence and profitability had diminished considerably by the 1710s, it still held a number of forts on the west African coast and had contacts with African merchants, resources that the South Sea Company lacked (Swingen 2015: 190–2). Spanish authorities allowed the South Sea Company to station between four and six agents in strategic Spanish American cities, including Havana, Santiago de Cuba, Panama, Cartagena, Veracruz, Portobello, and Buenos Aires. The company also sent men to Barbados and Jamaica to serve as agents and acquire slaves in those colonies (Palmer 1981: 59–60; Finucane 2016: 15, 25). In addition, the British won the right to send one "permission ship" laden with British goods for sale at the annual market fair at Portobello without duties or customs fees. No previous contract

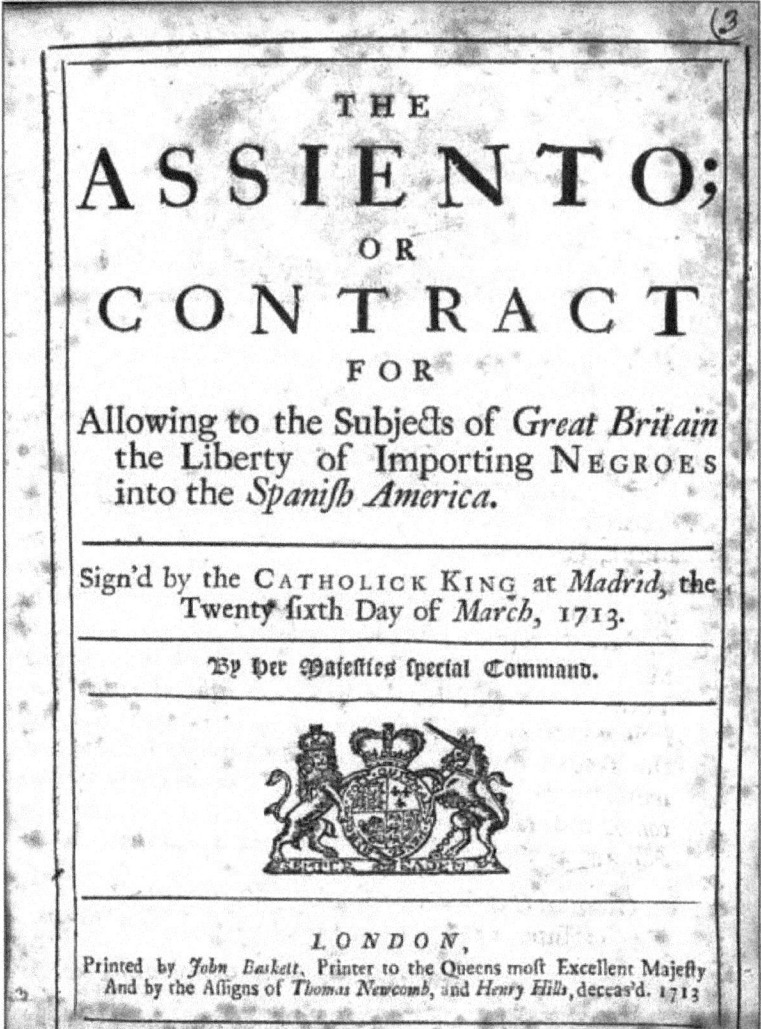

FIGURE 4.8: Cover of the English translation of the *Asiento* contract signed by Britain and Spain in 1713 as part of the Treaty of Utrecht that ended the War of Spanish Succession. Public domain.

had allowed such access to Spanish markets beyond the slave trade (Stein and Stein 2000: 138–9).

There were numerous problems executing the *asiento* to the satisfaction of either the Spanish or the British, however. There were constant issues of mistrust and miscommunication between British agents and their Spanish counterparts. Often, Spanish officials would impose unofficial taxes or would insist upon inspecting company ships and cargoes without notice. In addition, both British and Spanish agents regularly participated in smuggling, which significantly cut into the company's profits (Palmer 1981: 79, 130). The official *asiento* trade also met with outright hostility from British colonists, especially in Jamaica, because the South Sea Company's trade undercut their ability to sell slaves to the Spanish illegally. As one British critic of the *asiento* wrote, "the private Trade from *Jamaica* to the Coast of *New Spain*, has been very considerable, and brought more Mony into her Majesty's Dominions in a Year, than the [*asiento*] contract can" (Wood 1714: 6). In retaliation, the colony's assembly imposed an export tax on each slave "refreshed" at Jamaica and reexported by the company. British imperial authorities intervened and ordered the duty rescinded (Palmer 1981: 62–8; Swingen 2015: 193–4; Finucane 2016: 30–1). Despite these obstructions, the South Sea Company's proportion of the total British slave trade usually registered somewhere between fifteen and twenty-five percent. Historian Adrian Finucane has calculated that the company delivered over 34,000 enslaved Africans into Jamaica and Spanish American ports from 1713 to 1739 (Wennerlind 2011: 222–3; Finucane 2016: 181–2, n. 50).

In addition to these obstacles, the *asiento* trade was regularly disrupted by outbreaks of war between Britain and Spain, first between 1718 and 1720 and then again most significantly in 1739. The South Sea Company and the *asiento* trade played a major role in the debates leading up to the outbreak of this later conflict, known as the War of Jenkins' Ear (Finucane 2016: 124–6). Many in Britain who supported war against Spain argued that the *asiento* did not live up to its promise of bringing profits into Britain and was more trouble than it was worth. The South Sea Company was often portrayed as not only adding little of value to the British imperial economy, but of hindering profits in the colonies because of the restrictions the *asiento* placed on contraband trade. "Whilst the *Spanish* Coast was supply'd with Negroes from *Jamaica* by private Persons," argued one pro-war propagandist, "it was upon the Whole a very profitable Trade to the Concern'ds [*sic*]. It may likewise be made appear beyond Contradiction, that the Number of Negroes then supply'd the *Spaniards*, amounted annually to three times as many as have been sent them by the Company in any one Year since they have been in Possession of the Contract" (Anon. 1739: 11). After nearly three decades of controlling the *asiento*, many in Britain were underwhelmed with the results. For those who wanted war, the *asiento* was neither worth the effort nor the expense of maintaining cooperative relations with Spain. The *asiento*, rather than being coveted, was by the mid-1700s understood by many as a hindrance to British imperial interests. The War of Jenkins' Ear morphed into the War of Austrian Succession and continued until 1748, at which point neither Britain nor Spain were willing to renegotiate the *asiento* contract. In the coming decades the Spanish would again turn to other European powers, especially the French, to supply their colonies with slaves.

THE *ASIENTO* FROM ENLIGHTENMENT TO REVOLUTION

Competition with the French over sugar and slaves, the origins of which were intimately connected to the politics of the *asiento*, framed much of Britain's imperial interests for the remainder of the eighteenth century. The British not only wanted to limit French imperial success, but they also hoped to hamper Dutch participation in the *asiento* trade (Goslinga 1977: 4–5). British control of the *asiento* seemed to have this desired effect. The French had relied heavily on Dutch traders based on Curaçao to deliver slaves required by their *asiento*, but once the South Sea Company controlled the contract, Curaçao's role as a hub in the slave trade to the Spanish diminished significantly (Jordaan 2003: 246; van Welie 2008: 64; Rupert 2012: 99). From 1700 to 1716, approximately 16,000 slaves were delivered to Curaçao by the WIC; from 1717 to 1729, that number dropped to 2,500. For the remainder of the eighteenth century, roughly 15,700 enslaved Africans were brought to Curaçao on Dutch ships (Postma 1992: 287, table 3, 293, table 8). By the 1730s, the WIC's monopoly was dissolved and Dutch "free traders" started to outperform the WIC in Guyana and Surinam (Postma 1990: 202–3; den Heijer 2003: 102). The Dutch remained heavily involved in the transatlantic slave trade for the remainder of the eighteenth century, particularly to the expanding sugar colonies in South America such as Surinam, Guyana, Berbice, and Demerara, as well as to Saint Eustatius. Both Curaçao and Saint Eustatius continued to be used as places of transit in the slave trade, mostly for illegal trade to French and British colonies. Historian Johannes Postma has argued that it was during the era of "free trade" after 1730 that "the volume of the Dutch slave trade reached its peak," sometimes reaching between 5,000 and 9,000 slaves per year. He estimates that Dutch slave traders delivered nearly 200,000 enslaved Africans across the Atlantic from 1730 to 1803 (Postma 1990: 209, 2003: 129, table 5.3).

The French also expanded significantly their participation in the transatlantic slave trade during the mid-1700s. To provide a sense of how much the French slave trade grew at this time, during the 1720s, approximately twenty-three ships left French ports each year bound for West Africa and the slave trade, and by the late 1730s that number increased to over fifty ships per year. The vast majority of enslaved Africans on French ships were bound for Saint Domingue, which grew exponentially as a sugar-producing colony and soon became "the most valuable colony in the world." Between the years 1737 and 1743, French merchants brought nearly 110,000 enslaved Africans into the French West Indies (Stein 1979: 21–3). Throughout the 1700s, France became Europe's leading re-exporter of finished sugar, surpassing the Netherlands and Britain (Dubois 2009: 144).

For the remainder of the eighteenth century, France's primary competitor in the transatlantic slave trade was Britain. These two countries were frequently at war during the 1700s, which would often disrupt trade while at the same time give smugglers new opportunities. At times of war, French planters often turned to British slave traders, despite open hostilities between the two countries (Stein 1979: 26). In fact, the British and French often fought over control of their lucrative sugar plantation colonies. During the Seven Years' War (1756–63), for example, British forces occupied Martinique and Guadeloupe as well as Québec. Because of pressure from British sugar planters who feared competition from better quality French sugar, however, the British returned the islands to the French in peace negotiations (Thomas 1997: 274). During the war, the British once again became involved in delivering enslaved Africans to Spanish colonies. In 1762, British forces occupied Havana and, for the better part of a year, British slave traders monopolized the slave trade to Cuba, significantly transforming that colony into one dependent upon sugar and slaves. British occupation came to an end with the Treaty of Paris in 1763, but two years later British merchants were given a subcontract by the Spanish company then in charge of the *asiento* (Thomas 1997: 272; Finucane 2016: 153–4). In the wake of the war, sugar production in both French and British colonies skyrocketed, particularly in Saint Domingue and the small Dutch colonies ceded to Britain, such as Surinam and Demerara (Davis 1966: 161–2). British and French slave traders continued to deliver tens of thousands of slaves to the colonies for the remainder of the 1700s. The French slave trade reached a peak during the 1780s, when an average of 37,000 enslaved Africans were delivered to the French colonies per year. In the year 1790 alone, nearly 60,000 slaves were brought to Saint Domingue (Stein 1979: 38; Geggus 2001: 125–6). The British delivered equally staggering numbers of slaves to the Americas, totaling some 1.6 million Africans from 1750 to 1800 (Eltis 2001a: 43, table 1).

It is one of the most horrific ironies of human history that the transatlantic slave trade reached its peak during the eighteenth century, a time known for the emergence of "Enlightenment ideals" such as the inalienable right to individual liberty. And yet some seven million enslaved Africans were forcibly delivered to the Americas during the 1700s, mostly by European traders. The major political revolutions of the late 1700s were each intimately connected to slavery, the slave trade, and notions of enslavement and freedom. The American Revolution (1776–83), for example, although rhetorically based on notions of liberty from imperial authority, actually entrenched slavery in the new United States more concretely in law than had been the case under British rule. Many historians have argued that the American Revolution signaled the beginning of the demise of slavery in Britain's Caribbean colonies, albeit for different reasons. Eric Williams, for example, makes an economic argument that slavery was no longer profitable by the late 1700s, whereas Christopher Brown has argued that the political debates surrounding the American Revolution gave abolitionists in Britain a moral and political language to argue for ending the slave trade (Williams 1994; Brown

2006). Britain continued to try to monopolize the slave trade to its colonies throughout the period until British participation in the slave trade became illegal in 1807. Slavery itself was not outlawed in British colonies until 1834.

The French Revolution (beginning in 1789) was also intimately connected to notions of human rights and individual liberties. It had some of the most radical immediate results. By 1791, a massive slave revolt was underway in Saint Domingue, and by the following year a significant portion of the colony was controlled by former slaves under the leadership of Toussaint L'Overture. A combination of French and British forces attempted and failed to retake the island in 1793, and by 1794 the emancipation of slaves throughout the French empire became law. This did not end the question of slavery in French territories, however, as war raged in Saint Domingue and the consequences of the Revolution rocked the other French colonies as well. Slavery was in fact reinstated by Napoleon Bonaparte in 1802, although he was unable to implement this plan in Saint Domingue. In 1803, French forces sent to the island were defeated by Jean-Jacques Dessalines, who declared the creation of the independent nation of Haiti on January 1, 1804. The Haitian Revolution thus transformed "a slave colony into an independent black state in just over a decade" (Dubois 2009: 144–5). However, slavery remained legal in the French colonies of Guadeloupe, Martinique, and Guiana until 1848. This was truly a period of both enlightenment and enslavement.

Although by the late eighteenth century the *asiento de negros* no longer played a significant role in international politics or imperial competition, it clearly contributed to the ability of the French and the British to dominate the slave trade throughout the 1700s, beginning with the War of Spanish Succession. Competition over access to Spanish American markets framed the imperial designs of many European powers, most explicitly those involving the slave trade. The existence of the *asiento de negros* sold by the Spanish crown to individual merchants or corporate entities was an example of how institutions and states, alongside entangled networks of individuals and communities, shaped the European empires of the early modern world. The expansion of the transatlantic slave trade and the role it played in European imperial designs highlights the massive iniquities and inconsistencies of the Enlightenment Age.

CHAPTER FIVE

Mobility

MICHAEL H. FISHER

MOBILITY AND ENLIGHTENMENT EUROPEAN EMPIRES

The period 1650 to 1800 saw important continuities in the technologies and also the cultural valuations of mobility and mobility control, as well as significant and interacting new developments, especially those inherent in the Enlightenment and in the process of European global imperialism. As all the chapters in this volume reinforce, mobility (with different degrees of coercion and choice) included people's physical movement but also changes in their economic class, and culture, as well as the movement by people (intentionally or inadvertently) of fauna, flora, and inanimate substances within Europe and globally. Within many parts of competing European empires, in Europe and overseas, men and women continued longstanding patterns of mobility, and cultural valuations of it. But increasingly, some people advanced ideas that valued both a range of types of mobility and also technological and scientific improvements. These created dramatically new means to move themselves, their cultures, and their possessions. Over this period, the world's human population had doubled to more than a billion by 1800, and mobility had become a world phenomenon as never before in history.

Historically, empires expand as rulers of one social or ethnic group extend their sovereignty over others. Informal empires do not claim sovereignty but nonetheless economically or culturally control people living outside of their official borders. So, all empires contain multiple groups within their dynamic domains—territories and populations sometimes diffusely bounded and not necessarily contiguous. Further, asymmetrical power relations among each empire's multiple groups and classes shape voluntary or involuntary territorial, socioeconomic, legal, and cultural movement. Some empires enforce more rigid and coercive controls on mobility than others, often using religious, racial, gender, class, or other culturally constructed grounds to encourage, force, or block immigration or emigration for particular types of people. Through treaties (usually following disruptive wars or political marriages between imperial families), rulers occasionally trade territories, making the people living in them suddenly subjects of a different empire. Within each empire, patterns and cultures of mobility affect men and women of various classes differently, including aristocrats, commercial or professional middle classes, peasants, serfs, indentured laborers, and slaves.

As the global context shifted over this Enlightenment period, some individuals, communities, and socioeconomic classes thrived and pressed for their own upward social and economic mobility. Particularly in western Europe, rising social groups and classes developed the concept of the national kingdom or nation-state, in which they themselves were the primal inhabitants and collective rulers of their bounded territory, and other groups should be limited in their upward mobility or expelled or become objects of state or capitalist control.

Some of the most striking new cultures and forms of mobility, and also stringent mobility control, emerged from and enabled the intercontinental expansion of European formal and informal empires over almost the entire non-European world through various types of imperialism. While the earliest European overseas imperial expansion had already been undertaken by the Spanish and Portuguese kingdoms, over the Enlightenment period, northern Europeans carried out the most dynamic intercontinental expansions. Indeed, several emerging nation-states transformed themselves into continental or intercontinental empires, through formal or informal rule, forcing, limiting, or attracting various kinds of mobility on their diverse new subjects overseas. In particular, the Dutch Republic, England, and France combined formal and informal empire over much territory and many people in North America, the Caribbean, Asia, and Africa.

Much of this later European expansion came through early multinational capitalist corporations. In overseas colonies, the meanings of the Enlightenment differed from those emerging in Europe: many Europe emigrants claimed human rights for themselves, but did not accord them to the subordinated population. In less densely populated regions of the non-European world, a range of Europeans settled and established formal imperial rule, driving away, exterminating, or subordinating the remaining local inhabitants. In lands with larger or more resilient populations, especially in mainland Asia and coastal Africa, European empires ruled indirectly or directly by conquest and by offering to particular parts of the local society limited upward mobility into the imperial establishment as collaborators, employees, servants, or spouses.

Overall, European empires also created global arenas for mobility unprecedented in human history. Growing numbers of Europeans traveled to the colonies, either sojourning or settling there. Additionally, substantial numbers of Americans, Asians, and Africans were forcibly moved or culturally induced to travel to Europe or to other colonies of European empires. Further, some upwardly and outwardly mobile Europeans and non-Europeans articulated innovative ideas about the world around them and about the meaning and value of mobility itself. In particular, the writing and mass printing of autobiographical travel narratives, novels, and other kinds of non-fiction and fiction literature both encouraged mobility by their contemporaries and are also revealing evidence for later historians. Thus, many, but not all, key aspects of, and cultural attitudes toward, mobility within many European empires within Europe and globally in 1650 were markedly different from those of 1800.

INTRACONTINENTAL MOBILITY AMONG EMPIRES WITHIN EUROPE

Over this period, human mobility among empires within Europe was in some ways constrained by cultural, technological, and political limits while in others it expanded rapidly. In many rural parts of Europe, some important attitudes toward mobility and also forms of overland transportation did not change much. Many villagers saw no reason to travel far from their homes. Marriages customarily transferred brides from one patrilineal household to another within communities. Outsiders arriving in villages often meant danger from coercive tax collection or the disruptions of war or disease. In much of eastern Europe, empires tried to bind peasants hereditarily to the land, with serfdom only slowly abolished over the late eighteenth century (in the Russian empire not until 1861). Further, most rural roads remained earthen tracks only seasonally passable by foot, on animal back, or in heavy, slow-moving wooden carts.

Even for elites who could afford horses and carriages, many rural journeys remained arduous, time-consuming, expensive, and dangerous, not to be undertaken without strong motivation. For the most part, even private carriages and public coaches (even the small but growing number of cross-country post or mail coaches) did not use spring suspensions to ease the constant jolting.

Nonetheless, despite the hardships of overland travel, there were substantial movements of various classes. Changes came at different rates in different European empires, due to shifts in climate, diseases, socioeconomic forces, technology, and politics, among a range of other factors. High epidemic death rates created labor shortages and available fallow fields. Some villagers migrated seasonally since agricultural systems had peak labor demands. As the exact time of harvest for some crops varied from locality to locality, some agricultural laborers moved in short waves, from their region to the next before returning, while laborers from the second region moved beyond after their harvest. Peasant rebellions mobilized villagers, often around a charismatic leader or cause, which states punitively used force to crush. Pastoralists moved with their herds, often in transhumant patterns of higher land in summer and lower in winter. The eighteenth century also saw a significant rise in the number of popular pilgrimages to Catholic holy sites, especially Rome, Santiago de Compostela in Spain, and Jerusalem in the Ottoman empire.

Expanding urbanization, particularly in western Europe, drew in ever more substantial numbers of people from the countryside. The abolition of serfdom across western and central Europe had freed peasants legally to leave their land and seek better living conditions elsewhere, on newly available farmland or in cities. Many of the most entrepreneurial or desperate villages also increasingly regarded longer term physical mobility as a means of upward economic or even social mobility. Unskilled and skilled laborers from the countryside found an insatiable demand in expanding towns and cities. High urban mortality rates perpetuated the labor shortages there. Rising aristocratic and middle-class wealth meant a constant market for male and female servants, often immigrants from villages. Growing regional and long-distance commerce meant more traveling merchants and an expanding middle class with rising consumption patterns of products and labor.

Trade and craft guilds valued physical mobility during the early part of a man's career. So, men seeking to join guilds still had to move to their master's household as apprentices, take to the road for years as journeymen perfecting their crafts from other masters, and then be accepted as established masters themselves where there was sufficient demand. The expansion of artisan production (especially of new kinds of consumer goods like fine textiles) and the rise of commercial and consuming classes accelerated the pace and broadened the scale of rural–urban migration. In addition, mines and artisanal workshops and then—in the later part of this period—early mechanized factories attracted male and female workers from the surrounding countryside to nascent industrial centers, especially in north-western Europe. Expanding universities across much of Europe also attracted young elite men as students, many of them then moving out as teachers themselves. Some parts of the law and medicine professionalized, requiring aspirants to travel and live in training sites. Even some autocratic rulers recruited leading Enlightenment thinkers to move to their courts and exchanged ideas by correspondence with others.

Political forces both limited and also powerfully forced or encouraged mobility. From the Thirty Years' War (1618–48) among an array of Protestant and Catholic rulers and communities until the end of this period with the French Revolutionary wars (starting in 1792), vast armies of state-commanded soldiers and their often larger numbers of less controlled camp followers marched across Europe, displacing huge numbers of refugees (see Tozzi in this volume). The martial flow, ebb, consolidation, and fragmentation of European empires displaced populations but also created incentives and opportunities for immigration and settlement.

The Treaty of Westphalia (1648) signed by King Louis XIV of France (r. 1643–1714) and the "Holy Roman Emperor of the German Nation," Ferdinand III (r. 1637–57), among other rulers, became the basis for international diplomacy. Further, this Treaty sought to regulate the movement of troops through the signatories' territories and the negotiated rather than martial settlements of territorial and financial disputes. This Treaty also guaranteed the "full Liberty of Commerce, a secure Passage by Sea and Land" for merchants, some freedom of religion, and the right of emigration of subjects to a neighboring state rather than having to convert to the particular religion of the local ruler. It also shrank the borders of the Spanish empire by accepting the independence of the Dutch Republic as an emerging nation-state, a political model that would eventually spread across much of Europe and eventually overseas.

Despite this 1648 Treaty, displacing national and international wars and expulsions based on religious or ethnic identity continued. In 1649, English Parliamentarians tried and publicly executed King Charles I (r. 1625–49), during a decade of civil wars based on class and religion that ended with the flight of King Charles II in 1651. In France, displacing civil wars based largely on religion lasted for seven years after this Treaty. Then, in 1685, the Catholic French King Louis XIV revoked the nearly a century old Edict of Nantes (which had promised tolerance to Protestants), thereby impelling 400,000 French Calvinists (Huguenots) to emigrate to Protestant lands across Europe or to North America.

In some regions, from the beginning of this period onward, various new kinds of mobility became technically more efficient and also culturally more attractive. Western Europe in particular saw the first substantial non-urban road construction and improvement projects in fourteen centuries, since the Roman empire. These were usually main arteries between political or economic centers built through state funding or state-sanctioned private capital initiatives. During the 1660s and 1770s, French King Louis XIV and his leading minister Jean-Baptiste Colbert (1619–83) expensively constructed a few improved royal roads and bridges but their maintenance thereafter lapsed; new French royal initiatives did not sporadically resume until the 1740s. In England, from 1695 onward, Parliament authorized a series of private entrepreneurs to construct, maintain, and profit from turnpikes (toll roads), speeding travel for those who could afford it and were willing to pay. But growing numbers of entrepreneurial highwaymen kept even this travel dangerous, especially at night. Particularly in continental Europe, multiple political units meant multiple tolls that slowed the transport of goods, making them more expensive.

Mobility on inland and coastal bodies of water around and within Europe also showed both continuities and some dramatic changes, especially due to cultural, economic, and technological developments. Throughout, vessels continued to be constructed of wood and propelled by wind or by human or animal labor. They also remained heavily dependent on tides and water currents and flows. But various newly developed technologies significantly improved some coastal, inland, and overseas transport. Economically and culturally, fishermen, watermen, and sailors have historically depended on mobility, with specialized expertise and jargon that distinguishes them from their contemporaries living on land. Over time, shipwrights and naval engineers learned from seamen and from their own experience and professional training how to construct various types of vessels that each met particular needs.

Rivers have always enabled water-borne transportation. Some regions naturally have more economically useful rivers than others. Some European states, hydraulic engineers, and commercial entrepreneurs developed and applied evolving technologies to improve upon natural flows, thus enhancing the productive value of existing rivers and cultural attitudes toward them. In some regions, interconnected networks of locks and dams diverted and controlled the movement of water in long-distance, planned systems. Although still mostly drawn by manpower or by horses, and so traveling at a walking pace, specially designed long, narrow, shallow-draft canal boats were not subject to tides or winds and could transport cargo or passengers far more inexpensively than overland means. The topography and economies of the low countries and England were particularly adaptable to canal building and more systematic, scheduled coastal and inland waterway transportation. In France, rivers naturally tended to have strongly seasonally variable flows that were less adaptable to hydraulic controls. Hence, the French state constructed fewer canals, with some notable exceptions, most notably the building (1667–82) of the 240km canal (now named Canal du Midi) linking the Atlantic with the Mediterranean.

Based both on empirical and (increasingly) trained naval architecture, a variety of north-west Europeans developed specialized merchant vessel models. For instance, during the seventeenth century, the newly created Dutch Republic proved to be one center for innovative developments in coastal as well as inland waterborne mobility. Dutch culture valued efficient use of available resources: limited supply of farmland and timber but easy access to the Baltic and North Sea for commerce and fishing. Hence, Dutch shipwrights evolved standardized designs for *fluyt* or *fluitschip*: lightly constructed but purpose-built, flat-bottomed, and relatively inexpensive sailing ships that required fewer seamen to transport larger volumes of grain or other bulk cargo, either along the relatively shallow Dutch coast or on ocean-going voyages (Figure 5.1). This distinctive vessel helped the Dutch control trade from the expanding agriculture around the Baltic to the growing towns and cities of north-west Europe. This

FIGURE 5.1: Dutch Fluyt (1642). Public domain. Courtesy of the Rijksmuseum, the Netherlands.

design also formed the basis of the seagoing merchant navy of the Dutch East India Company (see Fatah-Black in this volume).

Dutch shipwrights also enhanced the efficiency of their deep-water fishing with *buizen* or *Harringbuis*: small (60–100 tons, about 20 meters long) but hardy vessels, especially efficient for their purpose. Dutch fishing fleets of up to 1,000 vessels dominated the herring fisheries of the Baltic, North Sea, and North Atlantic. Seamen and their families lived aboard, often for an entire summer and fall fishing season, using drift gillnets, then gutting, salting, and barreling the catch aboard. Other specialized vessels transshipped these barrels at sea and carried them to coastal markets. In the offseason, *buizen* also transported from the French and Iberian coasts cargoes of grain or salt, vital for preserving their fish.

Various competing European empires kept eastern Europe in territorial dispute, causing distinctive large-scale forced and voluntary population movements. The Ottoman empire had long been dynamically advancing its armies and administration across south-eastern Europe, along the Mediterranean, as well as east against Iran and into the Indian Ocean. Much of the Ottoman army and administration depended on its forced recruitment system of Christian subjects from the Balkans as military or domestic slaves. But this system enabled cooperative and skilled slaves the opportunity for upwardly mobile careers. The Ottomans schooled them in Turkish language and culture and assigned each to a branch of the imperial administration. Some became state-regulated Greek Orthodox Christian clergymen but the most promising converted to Islam and served in the imperial administration as scribes, officials, or soldiers. The latter eventually became Janissaries, "New Troops," the world's first major professionalized regiments: all wearing the same distinctive uniforms, living in official barracks, paid regular salaries, trained to march in step to martial music, and disciplined as masters of the most innovative and effective cannon and other firearms available (see Tozzi in this volume). At times, these Janissaries controlled the imperial household, and thus the empire. The most skilled or fortunate individuals among these slaves could personally rise high in the imperial service. A slave woman could gain power as Queen Mother if her son inherited his father's throne (see Wiesner-Hanks in this volume). Many of the highest officials were converts from Balkan families. For instance, an originally Albanian family, the Köprülü, provided a series of powerful viziers during the second half of the seventeenth century.

The Ottoman empire's territorial expansion largely peaked with its failed 1683 siege of Vienna against the Holy League of Habsburg, German, and Polish forces. This was followed by the Ottoman empire's contested retreat from Hungary in 1699, moving its imperial boundary, army and administration, and loyal populations back into the Balkans. The victorious Hapsburg, Hungarian, and Polish empires each then expanded by moving their armies and subjects into those territories formerly under the Ottomans. For instance, the Habsburg monarchs encouraged substantial immigration into the Hungarian steppe by giving free land to soldier-settlers who agreed to serve against the Ottomans.

For its part, the Russian empire forcefully expanded its territorial boundaries and increased its power by encouraging (or compelling) mobility on some of its subjects, while at the same time working to prevent mobility among others. While a multi-ethnic state with combined European and Asian identities, the Russian empire had as its core Slavic culture and the Russian Orthodox Christian Church. However, the imperial Romanov dynasty (1613–1917) itself included non-Slav, non-Orthodox immigrants.

Emperor Peter the Great (r. 1682–1725) innovatively, and autocratically, imposed a number of mobility policies. For some, he looked to Enlightenment thinkers and western European models. Famously, he personally traveled to learn central and western Europe's latest technologies. Then, he deliberately let the old Russian order of boyars die out and created a new Russian nobility, based on Prussian, Danish, and Swedish models. He graded elites who served him into fourteen aristocratic ranks. But Peter's new aristocracy eventually became hereditarily fixed without a service requirement (a pattern officially confirmed in 1762). Starting in 1703, Peter brought in tens of thousands of conscripted laborers to construct St. Petersburg rapidly. He compelled his new aristocrats to build mansions based on a uniform architectural template and to live there (at least part-time). This northern capital became the base for his Northern War (1700–21) which gained control over the Baltic and ended a century of Swedish imperial domination there. Yet, Peter also continued serfdom that legally bound peasants in the Russian heartland to their masters' service. Most estate owners kept their serfs from moving, but some transplanted whole villages, for example to populate new centers of artisanal production.

Throughout Europe, various aristocrats moved from their natal homes to become emperors or empresses in distant lands and over ethnic groups quite distinct from their own. A striking number of European emperors began their lives in one land and ended ruling another. In some cases, immigrating royalty made efforts to adapt to the culture of their new subjects. For instance, while expanding a global empire, the English accepted as kings the Scottish Stuarts in 1603, Dutch William III of Orange in 1688, and the German House of Hanover in 1714. Likewise, Czar Peter III (lived 1728–62, r. 1762) had immigrated from the Lutheran Protestant German duchy of Holstein-Gottorp to Russia at age fourteen to be imperial heir-apparent, where he learned some Russian and converted to Russian Orthodoxy. Simultaneously, the Swedish parliament also offered Peter succession to that throne in 1742, but he was already claimed by the Russian empire (instead, the Swedes eventually enthroned his Holstein-Gottorp second cousin, King Adolf Frederick, elected heir 1743, r. 1751–71).

Many empresses also immigrated through political marriages. The personal career and policies of Empress Catherine (r. 1762–96) illustrate both mobility and mobility control (see Wiesner-Hanks in this volume). She was born Sophia, a Lutheran Protestant princess of the German principality of Anhald-Zerbst. Her family sent her to Russia at age fifteen for her arranged marriage with future Czar Peter III, her second cousin. In addition to studying Russian, she converted to Russian Orthodoxy and was rechristened Catherine. While she strongly disliked her future husband, she determined to succeed in her rise to imperial status. As she recalled: "My heart did not foresee great happiness; ambition alone sustained me. At the bottom of my soul I [believed] sooner or later I would succeed in becoming the sovereign Empress of Russia in my own right" (Catherine 2005: 31–2). Indeed, only six months after her husband Peter's enthronement in 1762, her supporters deposed and executed him, making Catherine the ruling empress. While she corresponded with Voltaire, she also ruthlessly asserted autocratic power (Figure 5.2).

Empress Catherine expanded her empire by 500,000 square kilometers in eastern Europe and central Asia by both military aggression and also by imposing different laws about mobility on each of her many diverse subject communities. During Catherine's reign, Russia annexed large parts of Poland in 1772 and sponsored or induced the immigration of German-speaking

FIGURE 5.2: Catherine II Empress of Russia portrait, engraved for the Eclectic by Geo. E. Perine, N.Y. Public domain. Retrieved from the Library of Congress, https://www.loc.gov/item/96516267/.

agricultural settlers to expand its power around the Volga. Catherine's armies also conquered much of south-east Europe, winning access to the Black Sea in 1774 from the Ottomans, and annexing the Crimea in 1783 (successfully defended in 1787–91). She and other Russian rulers encouraged Slav farmers to settle in the Balkans and eastward across Asia.

Catherine decreed mobility controls on other classes and communities among her subjects. While not as favored as Russian Orthodox Christians, Roman Catholics received some protections and rights of movement. But Russia's five million Jews could not obtain citizenship, paid heavy extra taxes, and had to live within "the Pale." Created by Catherine, the Pale's boundaries changed over time but its territories are today mostly in Poland, Ukraine,

Moldova, Belarus, Lithuania, and western Russia. The growing number of Muslims under Russian imperial rule would continue to be subject to various forced migrations. This empire eventually extended its Slav settlement, military power, and political authority over various khanates east of the Caspian Sea, and on to the Pacific coast and Alaska.

Other European land empires also encouraged immigration and then permanent settlement of selected agriculturalist communities. Relatively thinly populated, eastern Europe had been an expanding agricultural frontier for centuries, draining swamps and clearing forests to make productive agricultural land. For instance, both Frederick William I (r. 1713–40) and his son Frederick II "the Great" (r. 1740–86) induced large numbers of German Protestant farmers to settle plague-depopulated and newly opened farmlands of eastern Prussia. Their menfolk then were recruited and regimented as highly disciplined infantry to march out and expand Prussia's boundaries militarily.

The largest state-forced migrations across Europe since the Thirty Years' War came during the French Revolution and consequent continent-wide wars at the end of this period. In 1789, failed harvests had weakened an already bankrupt French government and mobilized peasant discontent, intensified by a new class of revolutionary leaders (many inspired by Enlightenment ideas). The Revolution drove many French aristocrats into exile or to the guillotine, including Louis XVI and his family. For the ensuing pan-European wars, the Committee of Public Safety proclaimed *Levée en Masse* (general conscription):

> From this moment until that in which the enemy shall have been driven from the soil of the Republic, all Frenchmen are in permanent requisition for the service of the armies. The young men shall go to battle; the married men shall forge arms and transport provisions; the women shall make tents and clothing and shall serve in the hospitals; the children shall turn old linen into lint; the aged shall betake themselves to the public places in order to arouse the courage of the warriors and preach the hatred of kings and the unity of the Republic (Committee for Public Safety [1793] 1908: 184–5).

This raised a national army of 800,000 male citizens, with the rest of the population supporting them, thus replacing the older royal model army (mostly professional mercenaries, often imported) (Figure 5.3). France then sporadically conquered continental Europe under an immigrant from Corsica, Napoleone di Buonaparte (lived 1769–1821), who rose through the army officer corps and crowned himself Emperor Napoleon in 1804.

Within Europe, empires both had means to prevent mobility and also increasingly caused people at all levels of society to leave their homes and change their status. Simultaneously, attitudes among various groups toward mobility, and their capacity to move, shifted in many, but not all, ways. Further,

FIGURE 5.3: Characters of the French Revolution. Musée de la Ville de Paris, Musée Carnavalet, Paris, France. Credit: Le Sueur Brothers.

this period saw increasing globalization, as people (as well as goods and ideas) traveled within the new arenas created by European imperialism around the world.

INTERCONTINENTAL MOBILITY IN OVERSEAS EUROPEAN EMPIRES

European informal and formal overseas empires in Africa, the Americas, and Asia created many new diverse kinds of mobility via new trans-oceanic corridors across the Atlantic, Indian, and Pacific Oceans. Almost all humans either participated in or resisted these new Eurocentric world systems. European world empires moved a growing number of products as well as people from Europe, to Europe, and among their colonies (see Takeda and Mitchell in this volume).

In a process that Alfred Crosby named the "Columbian Exchange" (1972), species that had evolved on the long isolated American continents were transported on European ships to Eurasia, Australia, and Africa, and the converse, with substantial beneficial or detrimental effects. For instance, American-origin maize/corn and potatoes became widely planted staples in European empires or their colonies in Asia and Africa, wherever environmental conditions permitted. These crops supported increased populations, although not necessarily healthier ones. Further, when plant diseases, like the potato blight, were later unintentionally also imported to Europe, these increased populations faced famines, leading to widespread emigration, especially to the Americas. Far larger volumes of sugar from Caribbean plantations also altered European diets. Tobacco originating and grown in the Americas undoubtedly had long-term negative health effects globally. Conversely, European people, diseases, cultures, and technologies of transportation and warfare penetrated lands and societies across the earth.

Wherever in the Americas, Asia, Africa, or Australia that European empires established their influence or official colonies, local communities were affected, leading to large-scale voluntary or involuntary mobility. Gradually the economies and societies of much of the world shifted; many of the largest cities outside of Europe today were originally created by European colonialism and populated by immigration from the surrounding countryside. In informal imperialism, for instance in most of inland Africa and China, European merchants and their local collaborators reshaped the economy and key parts of society. In formal European empires, European traders, settlers, officers, and officials attracted indigenous people to translate, guide, fight for, and otherwise serve them.

The military and commercial capacity of European ocean-going ships developed significantly through empirical and also planned scientific accumulations of knowledge and technology, making possible these expanding European formal and informal global empires. In the Mediterranean, the Ottoman empire (among other states) had perfected oar-driven galleys for warfare. But this naval engineering expertise also limited its capacity to expand into the more turbulent Indian Ocean. Further, when its fleets of ships pushed outward there, they met with more powerful and faster Portuguese warships.

By the beginning of this period, the Spanish and Portuguese monarchs had been for over a century extending their realms across the Atlantic to the Americas and along coastal Africa and Asia, in uneasy alliance with the Catholic Church. Their sturdy carracks and galleons could withstand ocean storms and carry sufficient provisions for longer voyages. Iberian navigators also learned to predict the prevailing wind and water currents that could safely carry them to and from North and South America and also south along and then around the African coast into the Indian Ocean. By 1650, Spanish royal colonies ranged from the Philippines to much of South America, the Caribbean, and Florida. The Portuguese king held Brazil and trading enclaves along the east and west coasts of Africa and India and scattered as far east as Japan. Both empires tried to control mobility into, within, and out of their colonies.

Many Iberians responded to the push of impoverishment at home (made worse by inflation due to the inflow of American silver and gold) and to the pull of promised wealth in a colony. By the mid-eighteenth century, some 700,000 Spaniards had emigrated to New Spain and the Philippines and about 500,000 Portuguese emigrated to its Brazilian, African, and Asian colonies.

Not all Europeans were permitted to settle, or even visit, these colonies. Even Iberians had to prove that they were Catholic, not of Muslim or Jewish descent, and thus worthy of immigration. Since settlers were disproportionately men, but families seemed to the authorities to be more reliable, male colonists legally had to bring with them their wives. Their private letters illustrate chain migration, as prosperous (but often lonely) immigrants persuaded others to join them. Further, male Iberian colonists often married, or kept as mistresses, local women who had converted to Catholicism.

To make the royal investment in these colonies pay off, to profit the Iberian colonists, and to advance Catholicism, the crown, immigrants, and the Church all made a range of efforts to mobilize local people they called "Indians." To force the local populations to come to work, the state imposed a series of legal systems of labor demands. In each colony, the state and society attempted to establish fixed (and often legally enforced) hierarchies based on biological ancestry (i.e., the proportion of European "blood") and also the degree to which the person was Catholicized and Europeanized. This both reflected and tried to contain physical, cultural, and social mobility.

From early in the seventeenth century onward, the formal empires of Spain and Portugal were challenged by new kinds of informal global empires created by northern European states. These combined state power, new kinds of naval architecture, capitalism, and substantial emigration to white settler colonies, to transform the nature of intercontinental mobility and also empire. Atlantic-facing European empires in particular demanded larger and faster vessels and fleets. Increasingly, trained naval architects designed and shipyards constructed a variety of improved types of warships. The largest national warships carried well over 100 heavy-caliber guns on three (or even four) gun decks, displacing up to 5,000 tons and manned by a thousand seamen.

Individual ventures by armed northern European adventurers, merchants, and settlers had long been sailing to the Americas, Africa, Asia, and Australia with a range of legal sanctions by the English, French, Dutch, and other states. But these enterprises were risky, as well as potentially profitable, since many ships and men failed to return. Consequently, bands of merchants began to create commercial joint-stock corporations that sought profit by negotiating from their own governments overseas trade monopolies and colonies. Such corporations included the East India Companies of the English (founded 1600), Dutch (1602), Danes (1616), French (1660), and Swedes (1731) and the Dutch West India Company (1621) and the English Royal African Company (1660). These corporations spread out the risk over many vessels and voyages. They accumulated international capital for investment in ships and purchases.

These corporations also hired European merchants, military officers, and officials to trade in (and later conquer and administer) their many and often vast colonies. Marine architects, shipwrights, and shipowners designed larger armed Indiamen merchants ships out of the Dutch *fluitschip* model, with more efficient dockyards and maritime supply systems of equipment. Manning these ships were corps of experienced officers and regularly paid seamen (mostly Europeans but also substantial numbers of Asians, Africans, and Americans, especially on the return voyage to Europe).

Wherever profitable trade could be established without the cost of formal imperial governments and garrisons, informal empires persisted. The Portuguese, followed by other European empires, only held small but generally lucrative trading enclaves along the African and Chinese coasts. From these, European merchants dealt with local intermediaries. Some Asian empires, such as the Mughal empire (1526–1858), attempted vainly to limit European commerce but proved unable to control even its own imperial governors. Chinese emperors licensed selected Chinese merchants (organized into *hongs*) to have exclusive and controlled access to European merchants, with limited success.

More successful in blocking European imperialism was the Japanese empire under the Shogunate (1600–1867). Apprehending disruptions from Europeans, in 1635, the shogun had the (puppet) emperor issue the "Closed Country Edict," which decreed execution for any Japanese subject who attempted to leave (Emperor of Japan [1635] 1997: 221). Further, shoguns wanted to keep the sacred land of Japan pure by forcibly expelling all Europeans and suppressing Japanese converts to Christianity. But to control Japan's focused foreign trade of exporting silver, copper, and porcelain while importing Chinese silks and Indian cotton and sugar, shoguns from 1641 licensed a few Dutch East India Company merchants to stay on a rented artificial island in Nagasaki harbor. (Japan remained a closed empire until after 1852, when an American war fleet forced Japan to end years of isolationism.)

In particularly populous or rich areas where informal empire was threatened, European commercial corporations formed their own types of empires of direct rule. Even where these commercial corporations did not form white settler colonies, the cumulative number of Europeans could be substantial: in the seventeenth and eighteenth centuries, for example, the Dutch East India Company sent a million Europeans (many of them German emigrants) to Asia, especially to Indonesia.

Throughout this period, northern European states, including individuals and corporations chartered by the monarch, also established white settler colonies, especially in North America, South Africa, and Australia. Some of these settlers chose to immigrate for economic opportunity or to found their own religious communities. For instance, the English royal family paid off some personal debts by granting Pennsylvania in 1681 to William Penn (1644–1718), an English Quaker (member of the Society of Friends) (Figure 5.4). Penn then sold a 60-square kilometer tract to a German company in Frankfurt, which created Germantown, Pennsylvania.

FIGURE 5.4: William Penn. Held at the Los Angeles County Museum of Art, California. Public domain.

In 1683, this Frankfurt company hired Francis Daniel Pastorius (1651–1720), a university-educated German lawyer, poet, antislavery abolitionist, and beekeeper, to lead their settlement. Pastorius recalled the diversity of his fellow emigrants, including his nine servants:

> My [shipmates crossing the Atlantic] consisted of many sorts of people. There was a doctor of medicine with his wife and eight children, a French captain, a Low Dutch cake baker, an apothecary, a glassblower, a mason, a smith, a wheelwright, a cabinet-maker, a cooper, a hat-maker, a cobbler, a tailor, a gardener, farmers, seamstresses, etc., in all about eighty persons besides the crew. They were not only different in respect to age (for our oldest woman was sixty years of age and the youngest child only twelve weeks) and in respect to their occupations ... but were also of such different religions and behaviors that I might not unfittingly compare the ship that bore them hither with Noah's Ark, but that there were more unclean than clean (rational) animals to be found therein. In my household I have those who hold to the Roman, to the Lutheran, to the Calvinistic, to the Anabaptist, and to the Anglican church, and only one Quaker (Pastorius 1912: 392–9).

Many companies sought to profit by encouraging European immigration.

Many would-be European emigrants lacked enough money for the voyage. Some two-thirds of the Irish, English, Scots, French, and German immigrants to North America by the end of the eighteenth century went as indentured laborers (see Seth and Swingen in this volume). They borrowed their passage-costs and signed indentures, contracts that bound them to repay the advance by working for a specified number of years at low wages plus often minimal lodging and food. Many European immigrants, having served the term of their indenture, settled as free colonists or else chose to return to their original homeland. This system echoed the European guild system, however, many indentured laborers in America received little vocational training and their lives as manual laborers could be hard. Many did not survive the term of their indenture. Indenture to North America largely ended with the American Revolution (1776–83).

This migration pattern of temporary indentured servitude in America had a parallel in the transportation of European criminals sentenced to work there, often in lieu of execution. The British king authorized this sentence in 1718. Over the following half-century, the British transported 40,000 to 50,000 British convicts to North America, many dying during the passage.

In other European colonies, for instance British colonies in Australia, many of the European white immigrants came freely but others were compelled to move as prisoners. After the newly independent United States refused to take more British prisoners, the British crown started transporting them to Australia. In 1787, the First Fleet transported to south-eastern Australia over 500 male British convicts, about 200 female convicts, almost twenty of their children, and about 350 free persons. (By 1868, when the practice of criminal transportation ended, over 160,000 men and almost 25,000 women prisoners had emigrated this way.) Many more European immigrants voluntarily settled along Australia's coasts but also pushed expansive sheep ranches, farms, and mines inland, driving back aboriginal peoples and reducing their population by about ninety percent.

European politics and wars also globalized. European monarchs traded distant colonies. For instance, the negotiated dowry of Portuguese princess Catherine of Braganza, when she married English King Charles II in 1661, included Bombay (which he then rented to the English East India Company). More significantly, the Seven Years' War (1754–63) mobilized huge armies across almost all of Europe (except for the Ottoman empire and Dutch Republic) and raged in North America (where it was called the "French and Indian War" by the British and the "War of Conquest" by the French), India (where it mainly became a war between the French and the English East India Companies), the Caribbean, West Africa, and the Philippines. In the peace treaty of Paris (1763), European negotiators traded captured territories and the people living on them: the Spanish (temporarily) ceded Florida to the British and recovered Manila and Havana; the French recovered sugar-producing French Guadeloupe and three other Caribbean islands but ceded to the British all of the rest of the French Caribbean, Canada (except two small islands used by its Newfoundland fisheries), Louisiana east of the Mississippi River (except New Orleans town), and Senegal and two other west African outposts.

To different degrees, European overseas informal and formal empires also created new arenas of mobility for African, American, and Asian populations of all classes. Throughout this period, non-Europeans moved to Europe. Among the earliest were seamen, slaves or free servants and their wives. Over time, a growing number of non-European students, scholars, diplomats, and tourists also made this voyage. By the end of this period, tens of thousands of non-Europeans had arrived in Europe, some of whom made multiple trips. Some were sojourners but others immigrated permanently (Fryer 1984; Visram 2002; Fisher 2004).

European crews had high death and desertion rates on overseas voyages. From the earliest European voyages, many ship captains hired experienced, and relatively expensive, non-European seamen in order to man their ships on the return voyage to Europe. These seamen customarily remained in European ports, shipping home with the next outbound vessel to their homelands. But some of these men spent years or the rest of their lives in Europe, entering European society, usually by marrying with European women and becoming Christian (at least nominally).

Even before the seventeenth century, some of the most prestigious servants in Europe were male and female Africans, Americans, or Asians, free or slave. Elite Europeans commissioned paintings that showed these men and women adorning themselves or their households. By 1800, the number of these non-European servants, while still a tiny percentage of the population, had increased and they became more affordable even for middle-class European households.

Since most Europeans moving overseas were male, some established long-term relationships with non-European women and had children with them. Many of these European men abandoned their local wives and progeny, but some recognized their responsibilities to these families, providing for them in wills or endowments. A few brought them back to Europe where they entered the local society in various ways, according to the social class of the patriarch.

A small number of Europeanized, Catholic Africans, Americans, and Asians traveled to Europe as intermediaries-in-training: translators, or agents of conversion, especially for the Roman Catholic Church (Spence 1989). Even just considering Chinese Catholic converts: "Michael Alphonsius" Shen Fu-tsung arrived in 1682, met the kings of France and England, and taught Chinese language and culture at Oxford University, but died in 1691 during the voyage home. "Lionne Arcadio" Huang immigrated at age 23 in 1702 via London and Rome to Paris to translate and catalog Chinese books in the French Royal Library. In 1714, he married a Frenchwoman, Marie-Claude Regnier and had a daughter, but died in Paris soon thereafter. "Louis/Luigi" Fan Shouyi went at age 26 in 1708 to Rome as part of a diplomatic mission from the Chinese emperor to the pope, visiting Brazil and much of southern Europe on his way. He learned Latin and was ordained a priest. After his return to China in 1719, he personally informed the Qing emperor about Europe, its geography and curious customs. "John/Giovanni" Hu Ruowang converted to Catholicism, went in 1722 to France and Italy as a scribe of Chinese books, but never adapted to local customs and was confined in a lunatic asylum for twenty months. Finally, after four years in Europe, he returned to China.

One of the most numerous and destructive forced migrations directly caused by European colonialism was the brutal exportation of approximately twelve million Africans as slaves across the Atlantic (see Seth and Swingen in this volume). This kind of European chattel slavery differed significantly from the domestic slavery more customary in Africa or Asia. In the European form, slaves were private property, legally salable, with few or no human rights against abuse. Further, their children were also born into slavery (except in some instances where their European owner was their father or granted them freedom).

European commercial demand enhanced in Africa the monetary value of slaves as property and rerouted some of their longstanding forced migrations to the west African coast, instead of north across the Sahara or east across the Indian Ocean. Some entrepreneurial African communities along the west African coast profited as intermediaries collecting and transporting slaves from the interior to European coastal outposts and ships, from where they were forcibly exported to American markets. Portuguese slave ships predominated until 1640 but were thereafter surpassed by English ships in numbers of voyages and of slaves carried.

Up to a third of these unwilling emigrants died aboard or soon after sale in the Americas. Of the survivors, about five million were sold in Brazil, three million in British North America and the Caribbean and one-and-a-half million in Spanish America. French, British, Portuguese, and Dutch merchants sold another half million African and Asian slaves in the Indian Ocean region. Most slave-ship captains treated these enslaved African people like commodities—inhumanely transported and sold for the highest possible profit. Captains practiced either "tight packing" (which increased both the number of slaves crammed into the ship but also their death rate) or "loose packing" (which loaded fewer slaves but expected a higher proportion to survive the voyage) (Figure 5.5).

This Middle Passage, along which many European and American seamen and merchants brutally shipped African slaves in roughly 35,000 slave-ship voyages, formed the second leg of the Atlantic "triangular trade." On the first leg, from Europe to West Africa, European ships brought European manufactured weapons and other products and also cloth from India. On the third leg, European and

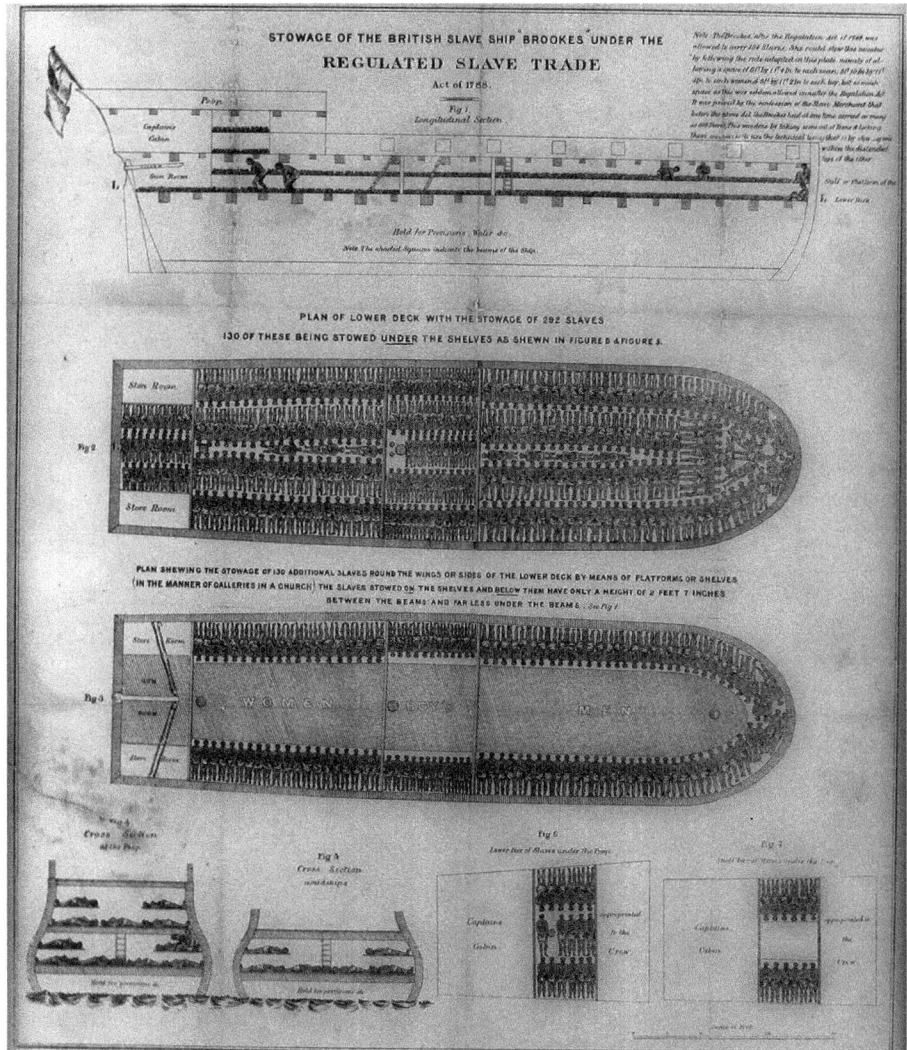

FIGURE 5.5: Stowage of the British slave ship *Brookes* under the regulated slave trade act of 1788. Public domain. Retrieved from the Library of Congress, http://www.loc.gov/pictures/item/98504459/.

American ships carried to Europe: rum produced from Caribbean and Brazilian sugar; tobacco, rice, and indigo from south-eastern North America; and other raw materials for Europe's burgeoning industries and consumers.

Even more than most other immigrants, enslaved Africans in the Americas had to struggle to retain their cultural identities. Most endured the disorientation of their vicious capture, hellish transportation to remote, overseas lands without realistic prospect of return home, degrading sale as objects, brutal life as manual laborers, often limited or no contact with Africans of their own ethnicity, and constant threat of resale away from whatever family or community they had managed to create. But many had sophisticated skills, including expertise in rice growing and drumming and we can see their cultural resilience in many of their arts, the Vodun religion, and periodic uprisings. However, European property laws meant that slaves and their children had few rights or realistic ways to obtain their freedom:

> ... we were unjustly dragged by the cruel hand of power from our dearest friends and some of us stolen from the bosoms of our tender Parents and from a Populous Pleasant and plentiful country and Brought hither to be made slaves for Life in a Christian land. Thus we are deprived of every thing that hath a tendency to make life even tolerable, the endearing ties of husband and wife, we are strangers too for we are no longer man and wife than our masters or mistresses think proper married or unmarried. Our children are also taken from us by force and sent many miles from us where we seldom or ever see them again, there to be made slaves of for Life which sometimes; is very short by Reason of Being dragged from their mother's Breast ("Slaves' Appeal" 1774).

Thus, African slaves in Boston described their forced emigration and current pitiful condition through a futile appeal in 1774 to the British Governor of Massachusetts for protection against their colonial America owners. Indeed, self-representation using the new medium of print became during the Enlightenment period a vital power that could enhance mobility.

WRITTEN EXPRESSIONS OF CULTURES OF MOBILITY

Enlightenment ideas about individual achievement and rational exploration of the world helped produce new genres of literature that themselves stimulated national cultures and also expanding European empires. Some scholars argue that the concept of the individual as historically minded and the European autobiographical travel-narrative reflected the creation of "modernity" in Europe alone (e.g., Weintraub 1975). Others (e.g., Subrahmanyam 2004; Green 2015) argue for multiple and independent origins of modernities or Enlightenments.

A growing number of European explorers publicized their discoveries and achievements. Instead of leaving them in manuscript form to circulate among acquaintances, as earlier, authors increasingly printed their works so that a wider range of readers could appreciate them (and their authors). Additionally, European compliers sought out and republished these accounts and also printed private manuscripts not intended by their authors to be published. In England, for example, editors like Richard Hakluyt (1552–1616) and Samuel Purchas (c. 1577–1626) started printing and selling vast compilations of travel narratives, first to celebrate English achievements and then also as comprehensive documentation of European exploration throughout the world. These publications thereby reinforced the national desire to explore and profit from distant lands; they inspired European soldiers, merchants, and colonial administrators to go out into the world for personal, national, and imperial gain.

Many commentators argue that the travel literature genre served as handmaiden to exploitative European colonialism and racism, as the European imperious traveler abroad and the Orientalist at home both gazed on the "othered" non-White subject and then enshrined his description as the sole truth about the non-West (e.g., Said 1978). Such travel narratives also made gender inherent in this distancing: mostly male Europeans surveilled and unveiled American, Asian, or African women and their effeminized menfolk.

Yet European authors each traveled with different companions and wrote for different readers. On the road and in writing, each identified with a distinct reference group: countrymen, people of the same Christian sect, or groups of indigenous people, including friends, attendants, and allies. Some went in the company of similar Europeans; others traveled alone except for local servants. How and with whom each author traveled clearly affected those experiences. These writings reflected the authors' diverse orientations but also intended audiences, all of whom were European of various types.

Within this genre, one type, informational travel narratives, were supposed to be chronological accounts of exploratory journeys, systematically describing unfamiliar landscapes and people, thus empowering the reader with a range of aesthetically pleasure-giving and usefully instructive accurate knowledge (Batten 1978). Another type, more romantic and autobiographical travel narratives, highlighted the achievements of the individual traveler-author, with a conventional structure of sad departure from home, exotic adventures, grateful return.

More than a memoir, an autobiography often reveals a self-awareness of how the author believed he or she was viewed by others. Lejune defines autobiography as "Retrospective prose narrative written by a real person concerning his own existence, where the focus is his individual life, in particular the story of his personality" (1989: 4; see also Olney 1980; Folkenflik 1993). Yet, the term "autobiography" only appeared in German in the late eighteenth century and in French and English in the early nineteenth century.

Elite and middle-class European men and, increasingly women, used novels to recount in fiction similar physical and moral journeys of individuals. During the eighteenth century, the protagonist did not usually display upward social mobility as much as restoration of his or her rightful class, which circumstances had temporarily and unjustly denied. Many novelists used the epistolary form fashionable for fiction and travel literature, which established a personal connection between the protagonist and the reader as fictive correspondent, enabling the author to write more intimately and confidently, to notionally address an (unnamed) friend, rather than a faceless world of unknown readers. England had produced nearly 1,000 epistolary novels by 1800, when approximately one out of every six works of fiction used it (Adams 1983; see also Day 1966). Famously, in order to critique European society, Montesquieu's 1721 novel *Persian Letters* created 150 letters between fictional Iranians moving through France.

During this period, most of the Americans, Asians, and Africans who went to Europe only orally recounted their travels. But, increasingly, some of the more educated among them used their own languages and their own literary genres to write descriptions and explanations about these new lands to the limited readership of their literate countrymen among whom their manuscripts circulated. Turkish, Arabic, Persian, and other non-European languages had established genres of chronological descriptions of journeys and adventures in distant lands, often including the author's own emotional responses to discoveries and encounters there (see Eickelman and Piscatori 1990; Alam and Subrahmanyam 2007).

Ocean-going ships within and among these European empires remained largely under European ownership and command. Further, printing presses and literacy did not spread as widely in Asia or Africa as in Europe. Hence, the power of mobility and the accumulation of knowledge asymmetrically favored Europeans. Nonetheless, some non-Europeans used the evolving European literary forms and commercial printing to address European readers, thereby attempting to prove their capacity to become cultured authors and to assert their own full humanity.

Over the late eighteenth century, a small but growing number of Africans and Asians (including both slaves and former slaves) used the writing of books and other literature in order to demonstrate to Europeans that they and their "race" had the capacity for intellectual accomplishment. This assertion remained particularly salient, since many European supporters of slavery defended that institution on the basis that non-Europeans lacked this very capacity. Some European abolitionists also presupposed that non-Europeans were unable to write for themselves. Like many early European women authors, virtually all early non-European writers therefore explicitly stated in their European language publications that they were indeed the authors in their own right. Most of these authors also emphasized their continuing racial identity with their still enslaved compatriots. Yet many of these works centered on the author's enslavement, stripping of identity, and renaming by the slave-owner, followed by eventual emancipation, with conversion to Christianity and Europeanization often as crucial points in this transformation of their personal identity (see Gates 1987; Edwards and Dabydeen 1991).

Indeed, movement to some parts of Europe also meant freedom, for instance after the 1772 ruling in the James Somerset case that forbade legal enforcement of slavery within Britain. This reinforced an increasingly popular belief that the air of Britain was too pure to support slavery, part of the abolition movement that culminated in the end of the international slave trade. Few slaves were able to liberate themselves and even fewer to write about their unwilling migrations. But those who did write aided the abolition movement by demonstrating their literacy and humanity to white Europeans and Americans.

The tempestuous life and writings of Olaudah Equiano (c. 1745–97) illustrate how European empires became arenas for the intercontinental movement of non-Europeans, both coercing forced migrations and opening limited opportunities for free mobility. Over his lifetime, he sailed multiple times across the Atlantic, as far as the Arctic and around the Mediterranean to Italy and the Ottoman port of Smyrna. He also stands among the most widely read ex-slave authors and an influential speaker and writer for abolition of the slave trade.

An Igbo born in the mid-eighteenth century, Olaudah Equiano movingly described enslavement and forced migration from the Biafra coast by Africans who were slavecatchers, responding to the heightened demand for chattel slaves created by Europeans. Equiano then detailed his own migrations as a slave in the Caribbean and North and South America, being repeatedly renamed by his owners until he accepted the name Gustavus Vassa, in ironic imitation of a Swedish monarch (Equiano [1789] 1794; see also Costanzo 1987; Carretta 2005). Saving diligently from his own trading, he purchased his freedom around age twenty-one in Montserrat, a British Caribbean colony: "I who had been a slave in the morning, trembling at the will of another, was become my own master, and completely free. . . . [T]he fair as well as black people immediately styled me by a new appellation, to me the most desirable in the world, which was Freeman" (Equiano [1789] 1794: 193). Nonetheless, as he migrated, he still had to struggle to escape re-enslavement. He settled in England in 1767.

In 1787, Equiano received the British Government's official appointment as "Commissary of Provisions and Stores for the Black Poor going to Sierra Leone" in West Africa. Especially following the American Revolution, many escaped or liberated slaves like him had immigrated to London. Britons of the Committee for the Relief of the Black Poor and the British government sponsored the emigration of more than 400 colonists to Africa (where most had never been) to start the colony of Sierra Leone as a place where former slaves could build their own community. Some British authorities wished to clear London's streets of homeless or other undesirable people, so, in addition to poor Blacks, some white British women and at least one Asian were also shipped to this colony. Creating Sierra Leone, however, displaced indigenous African communities. Further, due to corruption and inefficiencies by the British organizers, which led Equiano to protest and then be dismissed, the first settlement of 1787 did poorly. However, after new immigration by 1,200 free black people, mainly from Nova Scotia, Canada, this colony became permanent in 1792. (Sierra Leone became an independent nation in 1961.)

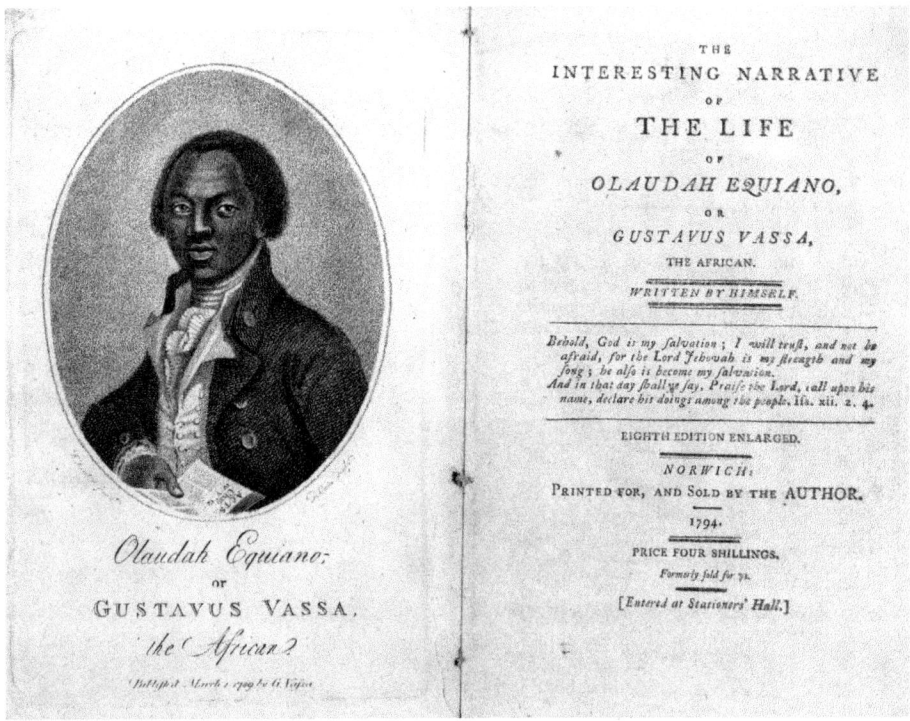

FIGURE 5.6: Title page of *The Interesting Narrative of the Life of Olaudah Equiano*, 1794. Public domain.

Calling himself "The Oppressed Ethiopean," Equiano worked tirelessly with other British abolitionists to shift public sentiment against slavery and to protect the "millions of my African countrymen, who groan under the lash of tyranny in the West Indies" (Equiano [1788] 1794: 352). He eventually converted to the Church of England and became a professional orator and author, publishing his autobiography in 1789: *The Interesting Narrative of the Life of Olaudah Equiano, or Gustavus Vassa, The African, Written by Himself* (Figure 5.6). In 1792, he married a white Englishwoman, Susan Cullen, with whom he had two daughters.

Over the period 1650–1800, within European empires in Europe and also overseas, many Europeans and non-Europeans developed new cultures about mobility and also the means to move overland and overseas—mobility for themselves, others, and their possessions. However, not all men and women sought or achieved the same level or types of mobility, physically or by class or in cultural categories like race. Further, European formal and informal empires both impelled this movement and created new arenas for it and also sought to control it.

CHAPTER SIX

Sexuality

MERRY E. WIESNER-HANKS

Imperial power is explicitly and implicitly linked with sexuality. Empires become empires through conquest, but they only *stay* empires by controlling and regulating sexual relations and the children that result from them, from the top of society to the bottom. Jane Burbank and Frederick Cooper have recently argued that across the millennia during which empires dominated the political landscape, they sustained their power by accommodating, creating, and manipulating differences among populations (Burbank and Cooper 2010). Control of sexuality, especially heterosexual procreative sexuality, was key to this, sometimes accomplished through laws and institutions, but more effectively by the fostering of internalized traditions and norms through which people were taught who was unthinkable as a marriage partner or unattractive as a sexual partner, as well as more general cultural values such as ideals of masculinity and femininity, or notions of proper family life and a moral society. Empires themselves were one force in these cultural constructions, but so too were families, clan and ethnic groups, religious leaders, writers and artists, and so on. Through words, pictures, and actions, socially defined categories of identity and difference such as race, nation, and class were created and maintained, although there were always boundary-crossers. These categories of difference, the restrictions that maintained them, and the possibilities for ignoring or overcoming them were gendered, with women's experience different from that of men.

This essay will examine four topics in which sexuality played a significant role in the cultural history of empires in the early modern period: hereditary dynasties; sexual politics and cultural power in courts and capitals; reformations of manners and morals; social discipline and sexual mixing in the colonial world. It is organized thematically rather than geographically because the similarities in Western empires on all of these topics are greater than the differences. This is particularly true for Christian empires, but on many issues there are strong parallels in the Ottoman empire as well.

HEREDITARY DYNASTIES

Other than the British Empire during the two decades of the Interregnum (1640–60) and the French empire after 1789, every empire in this era was ruled by a hereditary monarchy. Thus sexual relationships that produced children who could legitimately inherit were at the heart of power (Figure 6.1). This connection between politics and (hetero)sexuality in most of recorded history is so close that it has often been invisible to historians, but it was not to those who held power or hoped to gain it.

Claiming and holding land and other resources involved military conquest, but also shrewd marital strategies that built on those of previous centuries, a process that can be seen most dramatically with the Habsburgs (Ingrao 2000; Cruz and Stampino 2013; Curtis 2013). Emperor Charles V (r. 1519–56, Charles I in Spain) owed his vast empire—about half of Europe and the Spanish

FIGURE 6.1: King Louis XIV of France and the royal family in the personae of classical deities, *c.* 1670. Living room of the Oeil-de-Boeuf of the Grand Trianon of Versailles. Credit: Roger Viollet/Getty Images.

New World when he was elected Holy Roman emperor in 1519—to a series of dynastic marriages in the fifteenth century that gave rise to the saying: "Let others wage wars; you, happy Austria, marry" (*Bella gerant alii, tu felix Austria nube*). (The frequency with which the Habsburgs went to war makes this aphorism somewhat ironic.) Charles abdicated and split Habsburg holdings in 1556, but his successors continued to build up their power in their inherited family lands through marriage as well as warfare and alliances, creating a composite monarchy that stretched across much of the world.

The Spanish branch of the Habsburgs was successful to a point, but then reproductive failures intervened, exacerbated by inbreeding. All eight of the Spanish King Charles II's grandparents were descendants of Charles V's father Philip I, and his mother was also his father's niece. When he died childless and heirless in 1700, despite two dynastic marriages to young noble women chosen for their beauty and the fertility of their relatives, the ensuing War of the Spanish Succession (1701–13) eventually drew in all of western Europe's imperial powers. Fighting extended into their colonies, as the British attacked Spanish forts in Florida and the French attacked Portuguese Brazilian ports. At its root was sexual failure, as Charles II appears to have been impotent as well as childless.

The Austrian Habsburgs also had succession problems, with reproductive failure complicated by gender. Emperor Charles VI (r. 1711–40) had no sons, and imperial law officially prohibited the emperorship passing to a woman. Charles issued a Pragmatic Sanction, or imperial decree, allowing his eldest daughter to inherit, and persuaded a number of states within the empire and most other European countries to agree to this. At his death, however, several of these reneged on their promises and attacked Austria, claiming parts of the territories of his eldest daughter Maria Theresa (r. 1740–80) in what became known as the War of the Austrian Succession (1740–48). Her ineligibility was largely a pretext for what was a land grab on the part of Prussia, but all the major powers of Europe eventually lined up on one side or the other, bringing disputes over international trade and colonial holdings in as well and setting the stage for what was arguably the first "world war," the Seven Years' War (1755–63), fought in North America, the Caribbean, the Pacific, and India as well as Europe.

The War of the Bavarian Succession (1778–9), in which the Austrian Habsburgs were major players along with Prussia and Russia, was similarly sparked by the lack of legitimate heirs, this time on the part of the Wittelsbach rulers of Bavaria, and saw one contender scheming to find territories he could bequeath to his nine sons born out of wedlock to French actresses, along with two widows linked by marriage to other contenders secretly negotiating for them. All of these wars were "modern" wars, fought primarily over territory and trade by well-disciplined and well-trained standing armies using new military technology, but what set them off were failures in procreation, a very old reason to go to war.

Both failures and successes in procreation led to dynastic transitions that did not involve military conflict as well. In Britain, when the wife of the Catholic James II gave birth to a son, thus assuring a Catholic dynasty, a group of leaders in the House of Commons orchestrated a coup, making James's Protestant daughter Mary and her husband William, a Dutch prince and grandson of Charles I, joint rulers of England in the "Glorious Revolution" of 1688. They had no surviving children, and were succeeded by Mary's sister Anne (r. 1702–14), who also had no surviving children, despite seventeen pregnancies (Somerset 2013). At Anne's death, the crown passed, with Parliament's approval, to Anne's distant cousin George, the ruler of the small German principality of Hanover and her closest living Protestant relative. British writers and politicians remarked—often in pamphlets published anonymously—on the problems created by depending on women's wombs for political continuity, though this had in fact worked to enhance Parliamentary power *vis-à-vis* the monarchy in Britain.

In Russia, Michael Romanov, elected as tsar by the *Zemski sobor* in 1613, fathered four children who survived him, most importantly one son Alexei who inherited without conflict, as did Alexei's son Fyodor. When Fyodor died childless in 1682, the clear line of succession ended, however, and although Romanovs ruled Russia until the Russian Revolution, this included a royal mistress (Catherine I), a daughter born out of wedlock (Elizabeth), a shirt-tail relative from Germany who overthrew and possibly assassinated her husband (Catherine II, i.e., Catherine the Great), and an emperor who may have been the son of his mother's lover (Paul I). Although some of the stories of the sexual exploits of the Romanovs and their spouses are certainly legend, the history of the expanding Russian empire in this era is one in which the consequences of their marital and extramarital matches were dramatic (Dixon 2010).

Sexual connections to rulers were even more important in the Ottoman empire, which during the sixteenth and seventeenth centuries saw what became known as the Sultanate of Women, in which the mothers of sultans were often the rulers in fact, aided by grand viziers. Hadice Turhan Sultan (1627–83), the mother of Sultan Mehmet IV, for example, commissioned a mosque complex in the center of Istanbul and two fortresses at the entrance to the Dardenelles, designed to help the Ottoman empire ward off Venetian naval attacks. Turhan Sultan was thus key in building up both the actual power of the Ottoman empire and the public representation of that power (Peirce 1993; Thys-Senocak 2008).

The Ottoman empire was unique among Western empires in that from the mid-fifteenth century to the end of the Ottoman dynasty after the First World War, the sultans never formed alliances through marriage with foreign ruling families, though earlier they had often married rulers' daughters, including those of the Byzantine imperial family. Although there is no evidence about why this happened, daughters of Safavid rulers were most likely regarded as unacceptable because of their Shi'ite faith, and Sunni princes in Central Asia were too distant to be considered for dynastic alliances (Faroqhi 2015). Instead, the sultans relied on concubinage, primarily with formerly Christian captives, which brought new blood into the dynastic line (thus avoiding the inbreeding problems of the Habsburgs) and shut the dynasty off from powerful noble families within the empire who might have been contenders for power if their daughters had married heirs to the throne. The sultans further strengthened their control of viziers and other powerful men by giving them their daughters or harem concubines as wives, thus making them royal sons-in-law, but with no chance of inheritance.

By contrast, the dynasties ruling every Christian empire intermarried with one another and with the ruling houses of smaller powers, sometimes ignoring religious affiliation in their desire for an heir. These marriages were agents of cultural transfer, and created webs of alliance and connection that could have a very great impact (Palos and Sánchez 2016). Political historians make much of the reversal of longstanding alliances right before the Seven Years' War, which they term the "Diplomatic Revolution" of 1756. This saw Prussia and Britain form an alliance, to which France, Russia, and the Austrian Habsburgs responded with a triple alliance. The reasons for this shift are generally described as balance of power considerations and expansionary aims, but an important element is the fact that after 1688, monarchs in Britain came from the ruling houses of two medium-sized states in the Netherlands and Germany, so they had continental territories to defend. And the reason for *this* was successful or unsuccessful reproduction on the part of British monarchs, combined with marital choices that had made the rulers of continental states heirs to the British throne. It does not take much digging into imperial politics, war, or diplomacy in this era to find sexual relationships.

CULTURAL POWER AND SEXUAL POLITICS IN COURTS AND CAPITALS

Displays of power were essential to every hereditary dynasty, and these were especially concentrated at royal courts, which had both practical and symbolic functions. Courts were cultural, political, and economic centers in which rulers dispensed favors, offices, gifts, and rewards (Duindam 2011). They were thus centers of intense competition for power and prestige, as officials, advisors, courtiers, generals, wives, mistresses, and a host of others jostled, plotted, and campaigned with and against one another. Among the rewards were noble titles, which brought prestige, certain legal privileges, greater access to landed property, and in some places freedom from most taxes (Dewald 1996).

As empires expanded, trade increased in importance as a source of wealth, but it never replaced land, which was almost all in noble hands in eastern Europe and Russia and about one-half to two-thirds owned by nobles in western Europe.

The most common way to gain a noble title was to buy one, but the fastest way to climb in terms of title, status, and actual power was through gaining favor at court. Nobles and wealthy commoners hoping to become noble vied with each other to attend to the physical and emotional needs of the monarch, and they also sought positions at court for their adolescent children, especially if the young men or women were physically attractive, intelligent, and talented in music, conversation, or dance. Success at court called for deference, understanding of ceremony and protocol, discretion, charm, skill, and luck. For women—and for men with some monarchs—sexual attraction could also be a powerful tool, with royal mistresses and male favorites gaining wealth, influence, and the power to dispense favors of their own (Andrews and Kalpakli 2005; Walthall 2008). Jeanne-Antoinette Poisson, Madame de Pompadour (1721–64), for example, the third official mistress (called *maîtresse en titre*) to Louis XV of France, was also an important patron of the arts and a skilled courtier. Her role eventually included choosing younger sexual partners for the king (Lever 2002).

Courts were also sites of cultural production and consumption, of ceremonies and activities through which rulers demonstrated that they were not simply able military leaders and administrators, but also glorious, learned, and godly. In fact, the early modern world is often described as one of "theater-states" in which cultural events such as religious rites and musical performances were as important as military and political actions in maintaining power (Mulryne *et al.* 2004; Curran 2009). These activities were opportunities for rulers and those jockeying for power to display wealth and charm, escape boredom, engage in flirtation, and scout for marital prospects. They often involved ever-more complicated gestures and patterns of placement and movement, such as dance steps, place-settings at meals, and proper order for processions. Louis XIV's Versailles set the model for Christian courts, as diplomats and nobles spread French styles to Sweden, Russia, and the smaller German states, but the officials, servants, wives, and concubines who surrounded the sultan at the Ottoman court also followed complex protocol, particularly as the sultans rarely left their extensive palaces (Fuess and Hartung 2014).

Life at court was thus performative from dawn to deep in the night. Many events involved courtiers themselves, but some were professional performances of increasingly complex instrumental and vocal music. The grandest of these was opera, which emerged in Italy in the late sixteenth century, with serious stories and sweeping emotions involving larger-than-life classical heroes and heroines, and comic opera with characters that were normal people. Opera

FIGURE 6.2: Portrait of Mademoiselle Guimard, ballerina of the Paris Opera, by Frederic Schall (1752–1825). France, eighteenth century. Nantes, Musée des Beaux-Arts de Nantes. Credit: De Agostini Picture Library/Getty Images.

began at courts, but as its popularity grew, public opera houses were opened as well, the first at Venice in 1637, with Claudio Monteverdi as its resident composer (Snowman 2010). Parts for high voices in opera were sometimes sung by women, and sometimes by castrati, whose huge vocal range—often more than four octaves—and brilliant technique developed through years of training allowed them to sing both female roles and those of the male heroic lead. (Figure 6.2)

Courtly and public entertainments also included ballet with lavish costumes and scenery, as royal academies of dance and ballet schools were established in many European capitals, including the Russian Imperial Ballet of St. Petersburg. Ballet involved male and female performers, and spoken theater did as well. Women had always played women's parts on the European continent, and when the theaters in London opened again with the restoration of the monarchy in 1660, they generally did there, too. Throughout Europe, audiences flocked to satirical "comedies of manners" that both criticized and celebrated excessive behavior, full of beautiful young women, cuckolded husbands, and scheming mothers-in-law, character types that were exaggerated, but also familiar. Particular actors or actresses became wealthy celebrities, and sometimes the favorites of kings, another way that the fictional stories of romance, sex, and intrigue shown on stage linked with real life. In the Ottoman empire, shadow puppet theater depicting sexual activity and powerful women was extremely popular, despite attempts of moralists to restrict it, and musical training was common for female courtiers (Ze'evi 2006) (Figure 6.3).

The goings-on at courts were retold in thinly disguised form in ballet and opera, but they were also avidly reported in scurrilous pamphlets, often fictionalized and exaggerated but passed on as true. James II's son, it was claimed, was not his, but an imposter smuggled into the birthing room in a

FIGURE 6.3: Female musicians lead a concubine of the sultan into a room, miniature from Turkish Memories, Arabic manuscript, Cicogna Codex, Turkey seventeenth century. Credit: De Agostini Picture Library/Getty Images.

warming pan; James was forced to publish the testimonies of scores of eye-witnesses to squelch this rumor, though it never completely died. Marie Antoinette, the wife of Louis XVI, was accused in pamphlets of being insatiable and debauched in her sexual desires, engaging in incestuous and lesbian affairs, and killing children (Goodman 2003). This sexual demonization of Marie Antoinette, along with reports of her lavish spending and seeming unconcern for the people of France, contributed to growing hostility toward the monarchy in the 1780s.

The increasingly sumptuous houses of nobles and affluent commoners in both metropole and colonies also offered opportunities to display wealth and assess marriage prospects through a steady round of social activities. Marriage continued to be primarily socially endogamous, but trade and banking had made some families fabulously wealthy, allowing them to offer high dowries that made their daughters more attractive in the marriage market. They thus traded cash and the young woman's procreative powers for the social cachet and access to power that marrying into a noble family could bring. Conversely, wealthy commoners might well accept a lower dowry if the bride had a high noble pedigree.

Royal officials, nobles, bishops, and wealthy merchants transported European cultural life to the far-flung capitals of colonies as much as they could, and with these came the sexual themes that made opera, ballet, and theater popular in the metropole (Thornton 2012). For example, the second known opera composed and performed in the Americas, Manuel de Zumaya's three-act *Partenope*, involves Queen Partenope (the mythical founder of Naples), three princes who are seeking her hand in marriage, and the jilted lover of one of them, who happens to be a princess of Cyprus. The princess dresses as a man and challenges her faithless lover to a duel, but her identity is revealed when he demands they fight stripped to the waist. The opera was commissioned by the royal viceroy in Mexico City and performed to an enthusiastic audience at the viceroyal palace in 1711, in the middle of the War of the Spanish Succession, a real-life conflict that also involved Naples and other Mediterranean powers, princely intrigue, and sexual frustration.

Whether at a royal court in the metropole, the home of an affluent noble, or the palace of the viceroy in a colonial capital, cultural events required the proper dress, which in the eighteenth century came to mean styles that were new and fashionable as well as expensive. Global trade brought a huge variety of new goods, in what historians have termed the "commercial revolution" that led to today's consumer society. Merchants opened fancy boutiques with large windows, initiated marketing campaigns, and sought noble clients. In Paris, Rose Bertin, who began as a poor shop assistant, became the official purveyor of fashion to Queen Marie-Antoinette—her "minister of fashion" as one journalist sniffed—and sent her dresses even after the royal family was arrested (Crowston 2013). What was *en vogue* in Paris was news not only in the French empire, but in the other European empires as well, communicated through merchants' samples, pattern books, illustrations, and personal letters (Duplessis 2015). Fashionability thus joined money, status, and sexual allure as factors in determining one's place in the social scene and marriage market (Haulman 2014).

REFORMATIONS OF MANNERS AND MORALS

The highly performative nature of life at court and in wealthy households provides evidence for an idea initially developed by the German sociologist Norbert Elias in 1939, that the early modern period saw a "reformation of manners" in western Europe that then spread with European colonization (Elias [1939] 2000). He analyzed books of conduct designed for middle-class readers, which increasingly taught that basic bodily functions, such as blowing one's nose, eating, defecating, and sleeping, should be done in specific ways, with specialized objects such as handkerchiefs, forks, and night clothes. Good manners were an exterior matter involving increasing amounts of material goods, and also an interior matter of internalizing more controlled habits to develop feelings of shame, propriety, embarrassment, and modesty.

This reformation of manners was, in Elias's opinion, related to political, social, and economic changes. Centralizing states claimed a monopoly on the legitimate use of violence, and people had to settle conflicts in non-violent ways. Nobles demonstrated their superiority through "courtliness" or "courtesy" (common terms for good manners), rather than through military prowess. Middle-class urban residents sought to learn courtly manners as a demonstration of their improving status and increasing influence in a "civilizing process" that trickled down the social scale. Self-restraint became a marker of class status, with the "lower orders" those who still spat, fought, and drank in public. Sexual relations were also to occur away from public view, and the houses of middle-class and noble families were often rebuilt to include specialized bedchambers furnished with pillows and linens, with curtains that could be drawn for privacy (Chartier 1989).

Studies of the "civilizing process" since Elias have been based on many other types of sources along with books of conduct, including personal documents, court records, and material culture (Arditi 1998). This research has generally supported Elias's contention that self-restraint, formality, and discipline were becoming widespread ideals among middle- and upper-class Europeans, but there is disagreement about how fully or quickly these ideals were becoming reality, and whether the consequences were positive or negative. The French philosopher Michel Foucault, for example, has highlighted the negative effects of the "civilizing process," pointing to the establishment of workhouses for the poor or vagrants as examples of what he calls the "Great Confinement," in which those who upset notions of the proper public order were removed from public view (Foucault 1979). Other critics have pointed out that notions about what was civilized and what uncivilized shaped European ideas about race as well as social class. As they created empires, Europeans came to view themselves as "civilized" and superior to the "savages" in areas being colonized, not only because they were Christian, but also because of their "gentility" and more restrained deportment. Elias's harshest critics have accused him of sharing these ideas of European superiority, and have argued that many other cultures have strong restraints on public behavior. It is hard to find more refined and genteel courts or noble households, they note, than those of Tokugawa Japan or Ming China.

The reformation of manners as Elias and others since have portrayed it was a secular development, but it was closely linked with a larger and ultimately more significant reformation of behavior that grew out of the religious reformations of the sixteenth century, as church and state authorities first in Europe and then in European colonies sought to make people more moral, pious, and orderly (Hull 1996; Hsia 2005). Protestants and Catholics differed on certain aspects of sexuality and marriage, including clerical celibacy, the spiritual worth of virginity, and divorce, but they agreed on many more.

In both Europe and beyond, authorities established and supported institutions that attempted to control the activities of their adherents or subjects, and tried to instill attitudes that would encourage discipline and decorum, which they saw as marks of divine favor. In Protestant areas they created new institutions, such as marriage courts, consistories, and bodies of elders, and in Catholic areas they expanded the reach of existing bishops' courts and the Inquisition. Church officials began to keep registers of marriages, births, baptisms, and deaths, which could be used to prevent bigamous or incestuous marriages and sometimes to monitor sex out of wedlock. They restricted gambling and drinking, increased the punishments for adultery and fornication, forbade certain books and encouraged the reading of others, and prohibited popular celebrations such as Carnival that involved sexually suggestive elements (Figure 6.4). This process has been traced most fully in Protestant and Catholic areas, but Russian Orthodox authorities also outlawed bawdy traditions that undercut the solemnity of religious holidays or contained pagan elements, required a church ceremony as part of wedding celebrations, and began keeping records, which also allowed the state to determine men's status for military service (Levin 1989). The English historian Peter Burke has described the process of social discipline as a "triumph of Lent," and other historians have dubbed it the "criminalization of sin" (Burke 2009). Secular courts adopted procedures and punishments developed by religious bodies, imposing sentences which involved public confession and shaming rituals. As sins were made crimes, crimes were also made sins.

FIGURE 6.4: Bailiffs arrest a woman for selling sex, from A Harlot's Progress, 1732. Engraving by William Hogarth. Credit: Culture Club/Getty Images.

Sexual activities were at the center of social discipline, as the attitude toward sexuality that is often loosely termed "Puritan" was shared by religious reformers of all confessions (Wiesner-Hanks 2010). Authorities attempted to draw a sharp boundary between marriage and other types of sexual relationships, and to limit sexual activity to married people. They prohibited premarital sexuality, labelling it "fornication," and in some places even forbade flirting, as "lewd and lascivious conduct." In many places parental consent was required for marriage, with young people who married against their fathers' wishes subject to imprisonment. In Catholic and Eastern Orthodox areas, clerical concubinage and other types of sexual activity by clergy were more vigorously prosecuted. More women were executed for infanticide in early modern Europe than for any other crime except witchcraft, although this number decreased in the eighteenth century with the spread of notions of women's emotional fragility and more foundling homes available as an option for desperate mothers.

Control of language was an important part of social discipline, and individuals were punished for denying church doctrines about sex, reciting love charms, using sexual blasphemy, or defaming their neighbors with sexual slander. The most rigorous authorities hoped to shape thoughts and emotions along with words and actions, haranguing people in confession and sermons about lascivious thoughts and dreams at they tried to create internalized agents of control such as a sense of shame or guilt.

Selling sex for money was increasingly prohibited, and the licensed brothels that had existed in many cities since the Middle Ages were closed. Large cities such as Paris and Amsterdam organized police forces, which monitored taverns and streets, arresting women suspected of selling sex, and in London the Society for the Reformation of Manners, founded in 1690 as a private group with a paid staff, brought complaints regarding drunkenness, swearing, prostitution, and other moral offenses to the attention of authorities. Religious and civic leaders regarded prostitutes as worse than other criminals, for they seduced other citizens from the life of moral order and discipline that authorities regarded as essential to a godly community. Women who sold sex, and women who simply engaged in sex outside of marriage, were "whores," and portrayed extremely negatively in sermons, popular plays, illustrations, and ballads. Women charged with prostitution were generally so poor that punishment by fine was impossible, so they were imprisoned, punished corporally and then banished from the area; in England this banishment occasionally included deportation to the colonies. Imprisoning women for sexual crimes marks the first time in Europe that prison was used as a punishment rather than simply as a place to hold people until their trial or before deportation. Foucault's "Great Confinement" was clearly gendered, with women judged morally deviant imprisoned along with the mentally ill and vagrants.

Same-sex relations were even more deviant than whoredom in the minds of many clerics and jurists, and police in some cities watched men suspected of sodomy, using spies and informers. There were occasional crackdowns on "sodomites" that led to arrests, torture, imprisonment, and executions, though these were sporadic "moral panics," high points of concern with morality and sexual conduct, followed by periods of less intense scrutiny. Despite such repression, in the late seventeenth century homosexual subcultures began to develop in a few large cities, with special styles of dress, behavior, slang terms, and meeting places (Trumbach 1998).

Fornicators, whores, and sodomites were to be punished, in the minds of authorities, but creating a moral society also involved positive measures. Just as marriages that produced children were the basis of power in hereditary monarchies, they were also the basis of the envisioned godly social order, what Puritans in England and New England referred to as the "little commonwealth" on which the greater commonwealth rested (Figure 6.5). In addition, marriage was an opportunity to enhance the standing and wellbeing of one's family, so far too important a decision to leave up to the young people themselves. Family goals and individual desires might clash, and sometimes did, but young people and their parents also shared feelings and aims regarding marriage, such as the

FIGURE 6.5: A family group, with the patriarch smoking a pipe, early seventeenth century. Woodcut from the Roxburghe Ballads (early seventeenth century). Credit: Ann Ronan Pictures/Print Collector/Getty Images.

desire for social prestige, the hope for children, and the need for economic security and companionship. Such emotions helped create stable families, so were to be encouraged. Christian authors—first Protestant, then Catholic—frequently addressed the sexual and emotional elements of marriage, glorifying heterosexual married love and creating an ideal of domesticity and spousal affection and fidelity in sermons, treatises, and printed advice manuals (Karant-Nunn 2012).

Ideals of social discipline and institutions designed to enforce these have left many traces in the sources, but it is more difficult to assess their actual impact. The enforcement of most sexual laws was intermittant, and rarely applied to the upper classes, who continued to have extramarital affairs of all types, generally with little social sanction. (Though even here there were limits: royal mistresses had convenience marriages so that if they became pregnant there was a handy husband around to be listed as the father, and the only one of Catherine the Great's three children by her several noble lovers to be publicly recognized was the one born while her husband was still alive.) Particularly in rural areas, people refused to accept the idea that sex between engaged persons was wrong, for it did not upset the marital household as long as the wedding actually took place as planned; thus they continued to engage in it, defend it verbally, and hold fancy weddings despite the obvious pregnancy of the bride. Fornication was prohibited, but it was almost never prosecuted unless it resulted in the birth of a child. Brothels were closed, but prostitution continued; popular rituals celebrating or condemning sexual activity, such as Maypoles in England, charivaris in France, and masked dances in Siberia, were prohibited, but went on; clerical concubinage and solicitation were condemned and punished and probably declined, but did not disappear. Nowhere were religious authorities as successful as they hoped they would be, as the agents of control available to them or to secular authorities did not approach the policing possibilities available to modern states.

SOCIAL DISCIPLINE AND SEXUAL MIXTURE IN THE COLONIAL WORLD

When European Christians established empires, they took this moral reformation and the institutions to enforce it with them. In the Spanish empire of the Americas, for example, as missionaries preached and taught concepts central to Christianity to indigenous peoples, they attempted to persuade—or force—possible converts to adopt Christian practices of marriage, sexual morality, and day-to-day behavior. Once one was baptized, following loosely Christian patterns in terms of marriage and personal demeanor became a more important sign of conversion than understanding the Trinity or other aspects of Christian doctrine, in part because these were easily visible to one's neighbors. Those patterns might be quite different than in Europe, however, because where Christian practices conflicted with existing patterns or with the realities of life in colonial settings, they were often adopted selectively and modified in a process of creolization. What emerged were new forms that mixed local and imported practices (Sigal 2000).

Colonization brought together peoples who had long been separated from one another, but this was often perceived as a problem. In Europe as well as many other places around the world, "blood" had long been a common way of conceptualizing family, clan, social, religious, ethnic, and national identity. Thus there was "noble blood," "French blood," "Christian blood" (which after the Reformation became Protestant and Catholic blood), and so on, with membership in these groups created and maintained by intermarriage, and sexual relationships that crossed lines prohibited or viewed as aberrant. The most dramatic expression of this was in Spain, where "purity of blood"—having no Jewish or Muslim ancestors—became an obsession, but it was also true elsewhere. Thus in the earliest colonial empires of the Americas, the Spanish and Portuguese crowns hoped to keep various groups—Europeans, Africans, and indigenous peoples—apart, but the gender balance among both European and African immigrants made this impossible, and authorities quickly gave up. Relationships developed across every line, so that people as well as practices were mixed and creolized.

The response of colonial authorities to ethnic mixture was to create a complex system of categories for persons of mixed ancestry, who were called *castas*. By the eighteenth century, paintings produced primarily for Spanish purchasers fascinated by racial mixture frequently portrayed couples of differing ancestry and their offspring (Figure 6.6). In theory one's *casta* was based on place of birth, assumed geographic origin, and the status of one's mother, but in practice whether one was a "mestizo" or "mulatto" or "caboclo" or another category was to a large extent determined by how one looked, with lighter-

FIGURE 6.6: A casta painting showing a couple of differing ancestry and their child, 1774, by Andres de Islas (active *c.* 1753–75). Mexican painter. Museum of America, Madrid, Spain. Credit: PHAS/UIG via Getty Images.

skinned mixed-ancestry persons accorded a higher rank than darker ones, even if they were siblings (Carrera 2003). In most Spanish and Portuguese American colonies, about one-quarter of the population was *casta* by the end of the eighteenth century. (The majority of the population remained indigenous.) New laws passed after 1763 in the French Caribbean colonies set out a similar system. (Garraway 2005).

The social structure that developed in colonial Spanish and Portuguese America, including the Caribbean (and later in the French Caribbean), was a system based partly on skin color and physical appearance—what historians have called a "pigmentocracy"—but intricately linked to concepts of honor and virtue as derived from class and family status. Family honor was also based on perceived conformity to behavioral standards demanded by the reformations in manners and morals, especially for women. Thus one's social status—termed *calidad*—rested on a precarious balance of moral, physical, and class judgments that frequently shifted within the social hierarchy. Since one's ability to marry or inherit, enter a convent or the priesthood, or attend university relied on official determination of ancestral purity, in many areas families of property and status bought licenses to pass as descendants of Europeans, regardless of their ethnic ancestry, in what scholars have called a "racial drift" toward whiteness.

The granting of honorary whiteness and the difficulty of assigning people to *castas* points out just how subjective this entire system was, but it was the essential determinant of family life and sexual norms in Latin America. For members of the white European elite, the concern about bloodlines and skin color created a pattern of intermarriage within the extended family. These marriages were often between an older man and younger woman, which limited the number of potential spouses for women, and many never married. Most elite men married, and they often also had children by slaves or servants who were part of their household. Rural indigenous people also married most often within their own ethnic group, with the extended family exerting control over choice of spouses just as it did for elite whites. Catholic rules about consanguinity were officially relaxed for indigenous marriages, and marriage among kin remained a common practice, as did second marriages after divorce, although this was never officially allowed. For slaves, many persons of mixed ancestry, and poor people of all types, family and property considerations did not enter into marital considerations. Although marriage was the ideal, it cost money to pay clerical marriage fees and many poor people did not get married at all, though in many cases they did establish long-term unions regarded by their neighbors and friends as stable. Avoiding a Christian wedding also meant restrictions on divorce could be ignored.

Church courts and the Inquisition were important agents in the control of marriage and other aspects of sexuality in Spanish and Portuguese colonies, just as they were in Europe, but there were also new institutions created for the colonial situation, of which the most distinctive was the mission, in which indigenous people were settled by members of religious orders for conversion, taxpaying, and cultural assimilation. By the seventeenth century missions stretched from what is now northern California to Argentina, in some places serving as the only real evidence of Spanish power. Mission priests had great control over all aspects of people's lives and tried to impose monogamous marriage and patriarchal nuclear families (Gutiérrez 1991). European clergy were assisted by lay indigenous or mestizo *fiscales* who punished those found guilty of moral lapses, examined candidates for marriage and communion, and brought cases of alleged adultery, consanguinity, concubinage, bigamy, lascivious dancing, or other sexual crimes to the attention of the local priest.

None of these measures were successful in creating the type of disciplined society that Catholic reformers and missionaries sought, however. The number of births out of wedlock in Latin America remained startlingly high compared with most of Europe (although Spain did have the highest rate of out-of-wedlock births in Europe). During the period from 1640 to 1700 in central Mexico, one-third of the births to Spanish or creole (European-background born in the colonies) women were out of wedlock, along with two-thirds of those of mixed-race individuals (Twinam 1999). Although divorce was not allowed, annulments were common and desertion even more common, leading to bigamous unions in which men—and occasionally women—had one spouse in one part of the vast Spanish empire and another somewhere else. The Spanish crown attempted to limit prostitution by prohibiting unmarried women from immigrating on their own, but this was never enforced successfully and prostitution was actually not criminalized until the nineteenth century. Sodomy was in theory punishable by death to the mid-eighteenth century, but actual prosecutions were rare. In all of these matters, people distinguished between a *"vida práctica"* which people actually lived and religious and legal standards set so high that people could not follow them.

While Spanish and Portuguese authorities were developing hierarchies of classification, Dutch authorities were less systematic in their approach to ethnic mixing. For a brief period in the early seventeenth century, the directors of the Dutch United East India Company (Verenigde Oost-Indische Compagnie in Dutch, abbreviated as VOC), which ran the Dutch empire in the east, arranged for orphan girls to be brought from the Netherlands to marry company officials. Those who were willing to leave Europe were not the sort of respectable women the VOC had in mind, however, and the program was stopped. Instead, the VOC encouraged sexual relations and even marriage between European men and indigenous women as a means of making alliances, cementing colonial power, and increasing the population (Taylor 2009). This policy was opposed by some Dutch missionaries, but accepted by others, who hoped marriage with local women would not only win converts but give missionaries access to female religious rituals so that they could be overseen and suppressed. Dutch missionaries were willing to accommodate somewhat to local cultural practices, including allowing men and women to sit separately at church, as men and women did not normally eat together.

The pattern in the Dutch empire was repeated in those of other European nations in the Indian Ocean basin. The directors of the English East India Company generally approved of intermarriage in the seventeenth century; in 1687, they even decreed that any child resulting from the marriage of a soldier and native woman be paid a small grant on the day of its christening. There were limits to this acceptance of intermarriage, however. Rijkloff von Goens, VOC governor-general in the 1670s, supported mixed marriages, but then wanted the daughters of those marriages married to Dutchmen. By the second and third generation, many European men preferred women of mixed race rather than fully indigenous women as marital partners.

As more white women moved to the colonies in the eighteenth century, long-term interracial relationships became less acceptable as the European communities worried about what they termed "racial survival." Ideas about racial differences were often expressed in gendered and sexualized terms. In India, Englishmen were judged "manly" while Bengali men were seen as "effeminate," while in French Saint Domingue mixed-race men were foppish and beardless while mixed-race women, according to one European visitor, "combine the explosiveness of salt-peter with an exuberance of desire, that, scorning all, drives them to pursue, acquire and devour pleasure" (Burnard and Garrigus 2016: 26) (Figure 6.7).

Hesitation about intermarriage also came from the other side. In India, high-caste families were not interested in marrying their daughters to the type of European men usually found in the colonies. In much of West Africa, Portuguese men were not allowed to marry local women of free standing, as this would give them and their mixed-race children claims to land use and membership in the kin and age-grade associations that shaped political power structures. Instead, they married women of lesser standing, and their mixed-race sons generally continued in the trading occupation of their fathers. In some places women became the major traders, with large households, extensive networks of trade, and many servants and slaves. Because these wealthy female traders—termed *nharas* in Crioulo and *signares* in French—had connections with both the African and European worlds, they were valued as both economic and marriage partners by the French and English traders who moved into this area in the eighteenth century (Brooks 2003). In south-east Asia, temporary marriages in which women married men from outside their group in order to create connections and networks of obligations had long integrated Chinese merchants into local society. These ended if the man returned home, but they were marriage, not concubinage or something less formal (Andaya 2006). Such temporary marriages were less common with the much smaller number of European traders, so

FIGURE 6.7: A black woman and mixed-race woman of Santo Domingo, colour engraving from a drawing by Labrousse (active 1796), from Encyclopedia of voyages, by Jacques Grasset de Saint-Sauveur. Greater Antilles, eighteenth century. Paris, Bibliothèque des Arts Decoratifs (Library). Credit: DeAgostini/Getty Images.

European rule in south-east Asia did not disrupt existing family patterns to a great extent, and they continued to be shaped by existing traditions.

The same was largely true in French North America, especially in the interior fur-trading areas that supplied tens of millions of animal skins to Europe. As in the Dutch VOC colonies, the French crown briefly experimented with importing wives from France for the young men who were the majority of early colonists, but their numbers were never high enough to have a significant effect on the population. French officials then advocated a policy of *Francisation* (literally "Frenchification"), through which Native Americans would be "made French" by intermarriage and cultural assimilation. In a few cases, this policy had exactly the effect that the government hoped it would: couples married in

Christian ceremonies and native women adopted the clothing, work patterns, and language of French women. In other cases, women blended cultures through the clothing, household goods, and other objects they chose to make or purchase (White 2012). More often, however, marriages, if they occurred at all, were "in the custom of the land" (*à la façon du pays*) rather than Christian ceremonies, and French men adopted what officials regarded as "savage" customs. Official opinion changed, and prohibition of intermarriage became official policy. Despite such laws, however, European men and Native American women continued to engage in sexual relations in much of French North America and, in areas where intermarriage worked to the benefit of the local people, to marry, often in ceremonies formalized by Native American rituals rather than Christian ones (Sleeper-Smith 2001; Havard 2003; Belmessous 2013). The same pattern developed in Siberia, where by the seventeenth century Russian fur trappers and traders often remained permanently, marrying women from among the indigenous Komi or other local peoples.

Marriage was, of course, only one type of interracial sexual relationship, and perhaps the least common in most European colonies. Spanish, Portuguese, VOC, and church officials sporadically tried to control extramarital sex, prostitution, and concubinage with fines and threats of deportation, but such prohibitions were generally ineffective, and at times counterproductive. In VOC colonies, for example, marriages could only be solemnized when a pastor visited, which in remote areas might be once every several years. This encouraged people to maintain traditional patterns of marriage, in which cohabitation and sexual relations began with the exchange of gifts, rather than a church wedding. In Lutheran Tranquebar, a tiny colony on the south-east coast of India that was part of the Danish empire, children of European men and local women born out of wedlock were denied baptism, but they were simply taken down the road and baptized in Portuguese Catholic churches, clearly not the intent of the Danish authorities.

Although the Dutch and English East India Companies and authorities in New France tolerated or even encouraged intermarriage in the seventeenth century, Dutch and British colonies in North America forbade it from the beginning, with laws that first regulated sexual relations between Europeans and Africans and then extended to Native Americans. In 1638, the Dutch colony of New Amsterdam forbade fornication between "Christians" and "Negroes," and in 1662 the Virginia Assembly set double the normal fine for fornication involving people from these two groups. In the very same sentence, the Virginia law declares that "children got by any Englishman upon a negro woman . . . shall be held bond or free only according to the condition of the mother." The law makes no distinction for married couples, so reverses normal English practice, in which the legal status of children born in a marriage followed the father, and contrasts with Islamic law, in which the children of free fathers were free. Thus laws about mixing in North America were determined by slavery from the very beginning. A 1691 Virginia law closed any marriage loophole, flatly forbidding marriage between an "English or other white man or woman", and a "negroe, mulatto, or Indian man or woman," with a punishment of banishment. In this law skin color has replaced religion as the defining feature of classification for everyone. Though such laws were usually gender-neutral, what lawmakers were most worried about was, as the preamble to the Virginia law states: "negroes, mulattoes, and Indians intermarrying with English, or other white women" and the resultant "abominable mixture and spurious issue" (Wiesner-Hanks 2010: 289–90). Such laws were passed in all the southern colonies in North America and also in Pennsylvania and Massachusetts between 1700 and 1750.

The declining numbers of indigenous women because of violence and disease, combined with a relatively large number of women among European settlers, were more effective deterrents to marriage or other types of sexual relations between Europeans and Native Americans than laws. Thus especially in the northern colonies, regulating sexuality and other aspects of social discipline largely involved immigrants and people of European descent and generally followed a pattern similar to that sketched above for Europe, but with a wider range (Godbeer 2002). In a few settlements, religious authorities attempted to create disciplined moral and sexual utopias where God's law, as they interpreted it, would be the basis of all social and legal institutions. These included Puritan towns in Massachusetts, Moravian communities in Pennsylvania, and small groups elsewhere that experimented with distinctive sexual patterns and family forms. For brief periods such places may have been the most sexually disciplined communities in the Christian world, but their isolation was difficult to maintain for long, and those who objected to discipline went elsewhere. In general, however, opportunities for Christian discipline were less rather than more intense than those in Europe. Christian authorities were generally few in number and widely scattered, so their ability to shape actual behavior was more limited than it was in Europe, and the opportunities for neighborly surveillance were minimal. Men and women often bounced from one port or one city and sometimes one spouse to another as they created new imperial economies, tied into networks created by family, trade, friendship, and godparentage, but also able to evade those networks (Romney 2015; Poska 2016).

Most people of African descent in North America were enslaved until the middle of the nineteenth century. Only in New England were marriages between slaves legally recognized, although, as in Latin America, long-term family relationships developed among enslaved people, though these could be easily broken up by the decision of a slave owner. White men's fathering of children with their slaves was not recognized legally and rarely spoken about publicly, though this was so common over generations that by the nineteenth century a large part of the North American slave population was mixed. In contrast to the hierarchy of categories found in Spanish, Portuguese, and French colonies, however, the British North American colonies and later the United States developed a dichotomous system, in which in theory one drop of "black blood" made one black, though in practice lighter-skinned mixed-ancestry individuals may have passed over without notice into the white world.

Slavery is not simply a method of organizing labor, but also a method through which a labor force can be reproduced. In Africa, the Muslim world, and southeast Asia, enslaved women were often part of households, as secondary wives, concubines, or servants. They thus increased the wealth and power of their owner/husband through their work and their children, although under Islamic law those children would be legally free, as the legal status of children followed that of their father. This was not the case in the slave societies of the Americas, where children inherited their "condition of servitude," as the law described it, from their mothers. In some parts of the Americas, especially Brazil, conditions were so brutal that slaves died quickly and slave owners simply bought new slaves. In North America, "natural increase" came to be more important than continued importation in increasing the slave population; of the millions of people who were taken from Africa to be slaves in the New World, only five percent went to North America. Evidence from Africa, the Caribbean, and North America suggests that enslaved women sometimes took steps to control their fertility, limiting childbirth through plants and other products that lessened fertility. Childbearing, along with agricultural labor, remained a central part of most enslaved women's lives, however, though the number of children who survived to adulthood varied greatly (Morgan 2004).

In the Ottoman empire, the most important category of difference was religious allegiance rather than skin color or condition of servitude, but this line was sometimes crossed for marriage. Orthodox Christian women sometimes converted to Islam in order to marry Muslim men, occasionally divorcing Christian husbands to do so. They had to swear in a Muslim court that they had done so of their own volition, and that their husbands had refused conversion (Jennings 1992). Courts also handled cases of women's sexual indiscretion (termed *zina*), which in Sharia law merited harsh corporal punishment or even execution, but in actuality were more often punished by non-violent means, such as removal from the community (Semerdijan 2016). On other sexual and marriage matters as well, law was moderated by sensitivities to people's practical needs (Tucker 2000). Muslims living within the Russian empire were also under the jurisdiction of Muslim courts for marriage, family, and sexual matters, for the Russian way of handling difference was to let their subjects keep their own laws, customs, religious beliefs, and in many places institutions rather than require cultural uniformity. The same generally applied to Catholic and Protestant subjects acquired as Russia spread west and annexed part of Poland. Although there was some missionary work among pagan Siberian and steppe peoples and some attempts to convert Polish Catholics and Uniates to Orthodoxy, in general Russia accepted religious pluralism, a policy formalized in Catherine the Great's 1773 decree declaring "toleration of all confessions."

CONCLUSION

As empires were created and expanded in the early modern period, sexual regimes accompanied political regimes as a means of controlling people and manipulating differences. At the top of society, those regimes were essentially the same, for the political regimes of hereditary dynasties *were* sexual regimes, or perhaps better said, procreative (or sometimes non-procreative) regimes. Dynastic entanglements created webs of alliance that led to war and shaped imperial boundaries. Among nobles and wealthy social-climbing commoners, although non-marital sexual relationships could facilitate advancement and provide good plot lines for stories, marriage was a far more important means of cementing alliances and solidifying fortunes, as it was for middle-status people as well. Marriage was also a religious matter and thus under the jurisdiction of religious authorities, who viewed morality and stable male-headed families as marks of divine favor and sought to maintain them. This was true in every Western empire, Ottoman as well as European Christian, but it was not true in other empires or smaller polities around the world, in which the making and unmaking of marriages involved families, clans, and sometimes political authorities, but not priests or pastors. Not surprisingly, imperial sexual regimes and religious mores were more readily accepted if they fit with indigenous patterns or were blended with them, just as in Europe the moral aims of religious reformers were more enforceable when they supported existing traditions.

Across Western empires, reforming authorities despaired over people's inability or unwillingness to live up to the standards they wished to impose, however, and by the mid-eighteenth century they decided that draconian punishments for most sexual crimes were ineffective. New ideas were also beginning to develop about the sexual natures of women and men, the importance of personal and familial privacy, and the proper boundaries between religion and the state. All of these ideas would shape the development of "modern" sexuality and create a world where religion played a lesser role in its definition and regulation than it had in the early modern period. The contemporary world has not shaken this earlier history as much as some theorists of sexuality have posited, however, for sex scandals continue to topple political leaders, moral panics lead to changes in laws and their enforcement, and the global spread of both Christianity and Islam carry their ideals and practices far beyond the borders of what were Western empires in 1800.

CHAPTER SEVEN

Resistance

KARWAN FATAH-BLACK

INTRODUCTION

All acts that hinder the expansion, consolidation, or working of empire are forms of resistance. Such a broad definition brings to light a wide variety of man-made obstacles to empire, including *competition* from rival empires, unwillingness to be governed as *subjects*, and insubordination by *agents* in the service of the empire. These types of resistance did not have the same importance for all empires throughout history. The centralized and intertwined nature of the maritime empires of the Atlantic world in the Enlightenment era reflects a specific dependence on shipping, technology transfer, connected markets and inter-imperial commodity chains, which created a set of geographical and organizational challenges that made these empires uniquely vulnerable to certain types of resistance. These inter-imperial connections enabled the circulation and transfer of repertoires of resistance across the world.

The Western empires under discussion here did not primarily seek a tax base, or even the inflow of commodities, but rather attempted to wrest political (military) control from their European neighbors (Burbank and Cooper 2010: 153). For comparison, we can look at their land-based, exclusively agricultural, expansive, and more decentralized counterparts in Eurasia. While the Eurasian empires, such as the Russian, Persian, Mongol or Chinese, feared tax revolts and secessions, resistance in the Western maritime empires can be found in places of intense capital concentration. There, ships, overseas mines, forts, and plantations were vulnerable to resistance. An uprising by sailors, dockworkers, soldiers, mineworkers, or plantation laborers easily crippled military and economic logistics. Intense competition led Western maritime empires to develop in relation to one another, transferring the technologies and tactics for expansion across hostile boundaries. Instead of the open and undefined margins that characterize the landed empires of Eurasia, we find that Western maritime empires shared many points of contact and porous borderlands.

The Spanish and Portuguese had long ruled over a rather neatly delineated world, which saw little competition from their northern European neighbors. From the late sixteenth century, cracks were beginning to show, and slowly but surely the overseas empires became a chaotic marchland in which territories were won and lost in rapid succession by all those competing (Bailyn 2005: 69–81). In the wake of the seventeenth-century crisis there followed a long-drawn-out search for a new inter-imperial equilibrium. This violent period, with its specific forms of resistance—often related to military endeavors—was followed by a short period of stability after the Peace of Utrecht (1714). This allowed for investment in plantations, inaugurating the "production" phase in the Atlantic world. The location of violence and resistance was transferred from the battlefield to the workplace. While international relations became ostensibly less violent, with smaller armies mobilized by the maritime empires than in the seventeenth century, production intensified, and so did resistance on the plantations, aboard ships, and in other areas of the economy. The end of the eighteenth century saw the fusing of war and resistance in the rise of the revolutionary armies of the age of revolution.

While competition made the empires more synchronous, their success was distributed unevenly. The Iberians remained a considerable, although decline-ridden, presence. The Dutch quickly fell from grace at the end of the eighteenth century and became unable to hold their ground even at home. This was in contrast to the intensely resisted rise of both the French and British empires, which at that point had not reached their zenith. The wave of revolutions that touched all empires in the closing decades of the period under discussion produced a variety of outcomes. Those outcomes greatly depended on how well each empire's institutions were able to absorb, repress, and deflect revolutionary unrest. Mass resistance by slaves in the revolutionary period prompted an uneasiness with colonial slavery and created growing doubts about the human cost of empire.

This chapter will focus primarily on internal resistance within the empires. However, the relevance of inter-imperial competition to resistance is too important to gloss over. Uprisings and insubordination within an empire always influenced relations between empires. And, on occasion, instances of resistance were inter-imperial in nature. Inter-imperial competition shaped the definitions of loyalty and attempts at control and suppression that were organized in response. By the end of the eighteenth century, inciting devastating slave rebellions became part and parcel of inter-imperial rivalry; and fear of these rebellions became a means for rulers who sought to demand loyalty from their agents and subjects.

The history of resistance is always an entwined history. The flight that regularly followed the suppression of resistance movements often crossed imperial borders (van Rossum and Kamp 2016). Here we can also see inter-imperial cooperation against resistance. Faced with the Saint Domingue slave revolt, British conservative MP Edmund Burke hoped to form an alliance between the British state and the French plantation aristocracy on the island (O'Neill 2016: 90). In part, cooperation between the empires can be explained as a form of a solidarity between rulers against a "hydra" of lower-class rebels and maroons (Linebaugh and Rediker 2000). An added dynamic was the activities of inter-imperial agents who had clout in multiple empires and who were pooling resources from multiple polities to protect their interests. This is well illustrated by the role of the British merchant Gedney Clarke in the suppression of the Berbice slave revolt of 1763 (Smith 2003). When Dutch forces were unable to retake control of Berbice (as support troops drawn from Suriname mutinied), Clarke was able to muster a relief force that helped to re-enslave the men and women who had overrun the Dutch colonists. After the recovery of the colony it was simply returned into Dutch hands (Figure 7.1).

The overseas empires were culturally and ethnically diverse. This diversity is important to consider, since this often meant that colonies were home to a variety of competing legal jurisdictions and multiple definitions of subjecthood

FIGURE 7.1: Engraving Print Depicting Scene of Surinam: The Slave Rebellion by D.K. Bonatti. Credit: Historical Picture Archive/CORBIS/Corbis via Getty Images.

could apply to those residing in the colonies. People and polities in the borderlands of empire could refuse to be cooperative or carve out a space for communitarian autonomy within an empire and in doing so subvert imperial designs. Resistance was not always a question of an indigenous population rising up against imperial agents and settlers, as the borderland settlers themselves regularly became adverse to imperial meddling. When the defiance of these settlers "becomes open, habitual and successful, the empire comes to an end" (Parry 1974: 13). The line between an enterprising agent of empire and a renegade was surprisingly thin in the early modern empires.

Resistance in its most extreme form could result in territorial secession from the empire or marronage by captives in the empire. We also find more indirect forms of resistance that challenge imperial hierarchies, for example, smuggling within the empire or across its borders. The uncontrolled movement of goods contributed to the development of colonial counter-economies and the development of cultures that challenged imperial hegemony. Resistance also took the form of more general threats to social hierarchies within the empire. Transgression of sexual or gender norms as well as racial categories in colonies, on board ships, or in fortresses, could be perceived as threats to the imperial order. Bans on fraternization between slaves and soldiers, and on sexual relations between black men and white women, were widespread. Transgressions were not necessarily perceived as a threat by the imperial centers alone. Local governors and their councils in colonial localities were often far more eager to prevent an "explosive combination of workers" by segregating them along racial, ethnic, or religious lines (Linebaugh and Rediker 2000: 197).

All Western empires faced open challenges to imperial hierarchy in the period between 1650 and 1800. In their dependence on maritime connections in the age of sail, these simultaneously developing empires faced obstacles that were greatly determined by the time and effort it took to direct actions across the empire. Resistance, on the other hand, remained much more localized. It is only at the end of the period—a time commonly referred to as the "Age of Revolutions"—that we see waves of resistance spreading across geographies and challenging the Western empires virtually simultaneously. This challenge to hierarchies was, however, rarely anti-imperial in nature. While hierarchies of race and imperial hierarchies were challenged, this did not lead to the formulation of anti-imperialist rhetoric beyond a purely economic critique of the profitability of colonial ventures.

RESISTANCE IN THE ORIGINS OF EMPIRES

The grand imperial ambitions of the Renaissance often developed from what started as a series of *ad hoc* attempts by European powers to move the theater of war away from their homeland. The Portuguese sought to relieve internal pressures by sending out military expeditions in search of territorial expansion and simultaneously serving merchant interests (Subrahmanyam 1993: 35–7). For the British and Dutch, the assault on the Spanish empire was directly the result of a search for the weak spot in their enemy's defenses, both economically and militarily. These assaults laid the foundations for their later empires. The foundations for the Dutch overseas empire were laid when they began contesting Habsburg rule in the Seventeen Provinces (Israel 1990, 60–74). When the revolt began to turn sour, the northern provinces shifted the attention of their foe away from the Low Countries by undertaking a daring assault on Portuguese Brazil. Similarly, the British under Queen Elizabeth were seeing Catholic encroachment on their nearby coasts. The piratical expeditions by Drake successfully helped divert attention to overseas theaters. The French seem to have been the exception here. With their country embroiled in internal strife, the attempts at overseas settlement in the early seventeenth century seem to be no more than an afterthought instead of a conscious offensive or diversionary tactics. French colonial initiatives rested more fully on local enterprise and self-organized merchant networks (Marzagalli 1999).

The Dutch and English resistance to the Spanish empire galvanized a rudimentary anti-imperialism. Although arguably a tax revolt in its initial stages and later a civil war within the provinces, the Dutch Revolt did develop characteristics that are reminiscent of the revolts that plagued many of the Western empires in this period. Comparison with the resistance of indigenous Americans, such as the recently suppressed kingdom under Tupac Amaru, was not lost on contemporaries. By the time the seven northerly provinces united in the Union of Utrecht (1579) and began to form a more durable solidarity against their king we see its leader, William of Orange, beginning to fashion himself as a victim of Spanish imperialist terror analogous to the destruction of the Indies in the Americas. In his *Apologie* (defence) (1580), William of Orange repeatedly made reference to atrocities against the indigenous Americans, and with the Act of Abjuration (1581) the provinces formally declared themselves no longer under the authority of the Spanish king. Forming an empire of their own was not the foregone conclusion from the revolt. At the time, the crisis of Spain was seen by some as an echo of the fall of Rome, itself interpreted as the result of its colonial expansion (Weststeijn 2012).

The English, who also had had longstanding relations with the Spanish king, saw a deterioration of their relationship with Spain in much the same way as the Dutch had. The two Protestant nations found themselves on the same side as the Ottomans, recognizing their shared opposition to the Spanish king and his Roman Catholic faith. Many of the naval exploits against the Spanish, including the defeat of the Armada, contained elements of Anglo-Dutch cooperation. The same is true for the early naval attacks on Spanish positions in the Low Countries, by groups known as the "sea beggars." Especially in the overseas context, the difference between "Dutch" and "English" was often not all that relevant. Many initiatives were undertaken using expertise and capital from multiple cities across the permeable boundaries of northern Europe. In many places, the resistance to empire would lead to the development of Dutch and British imperial aspirations. The revolting states and kingdoms were thus set on a path to become empires in their own right.

The war with the Spanish in the Low Countries resulted in many atrocities on both sides, especially in the southern Low Countries. Relevant for the formation of the empire was the fall of Antwerp in 1585. Fleeing from the south to the north, many people with merchant connections and an understanding of trade in the Spanish and Portuguese overseas empires moved to the northern provinces. Here they resettled and continued or restructured their business in colonial and other overseas trade to service the northern European and Baltic markets for these products (Israel 1990). Their knowledge, however, had now to be utilized in the context of a hostile empire and the context of war. This did not deter those settlers, who likely acted on a knowledge of the weakness of the overseas systems of control. Smuggling into overseas possessions of the Spanish became a significant and condoned contribution to the resistance strategy of the northern provinces.

Smuggling was a pervasive form of anti-imperial resistance against the Habsburgs, both from inside and outside the imperial realm (Figure 7.2). This had much to do with the overstretched nature of this empire, which made it possible, and sometimes even necessary, to evade metropolitan control. In neglected settlement colonies, the loyalty of the settlers was uncertain at best. This could result in smuggling arrangements by neglected Spanish settlements with Dutch and English interlopers, as happened on the Guiana coast and Tobago (Lorimer 1993). In Brazil, the independence of the nominally Portuguese sugar traders meant that they illicitly connected with their Dutch, French, and British counterparts in their search for access to European markets. Among the Portuguese, visions of an imperial expansion and one led by private traders were often at odds with each other (Disney 2009: 173). Private traders had few qualms in setting up their own connections to Africa and smuggling from as far as Bengal to Africa and onward to Brazil. Resisting imperial authority in this way, they began to decenter the Portuguese empire from within (Burbank and Cooper 2010: 158; Machado 2014).

From the outside, smuggling could be a deliberate strategy to resist the Habsburg empire and evade its restrictions on trade. Out of this resistance, however, grew new polities with their own trade connections and settlements, facing their own internal resistance. Private merchants on occasion led armed incursions into the Spanish empire. The most impressive of these were probably the assaults under the auspices of the Antwerp-born merchant Balthazar de Moucheron, who not only engaged in trading ventures to Asia and Russia, but also fitted out a fleet to capture the island of Principe from the Portuguese. The

FIGURE 7.2: Smugglers coming ashore, c. 1750. Credit: Rischgitz/Getty Images.

States General first promoted and later sought to take control of these private initiatives. De Moucheron for one was side-tracked by the formation of the Dutch East India Company. Antwerp refugees can be found at the beginning of many of these early overseas assaults and designs for the forming of an overseas empire. Willem Usselinx, also an Antwerp refugee, tried on many occasions to found a Dutch West India Company that would develop overseas settlements that could disrupt the workings of the Spanish empire and "eclipse the [Spanish] king's treasures" (Usselinx 1622). The Dutch resistance to Spanish rule neatly transitioned to the conquest of overseas territories, and with that the formation of the empire.

Refugees could have very explicit religious and sometimes vengeful motivations for assaulting the empires from which they fled. The nascent empires of the Dutch and British were also all too happy to see religious dissenters and fanatics leave the homeland to settle in the violent overseas frontiers. A general dissatisfaction with the religious direction of England, and specifically the fear of a return of Catholic practices, famously motivated the Puritans to leave. Once overseas, interaction with other religious communities could be a threat to the empire. This was visible in the case of Catholic/Portuguese resistance to Dutch rule in Brazil. In Brazil, the Dutch were never fully able to control the colony's economic life and deal with the persistence of the Catholic faith (Antunes *et al.* 2015). The deviations away from Catholicism toward Islam or Hinduism by Portuguese settlers overseas were met by violent waves of inquisitorial repression and Jesuit missionary work. The *arrenegados* as they were called, could slip from the imperial hierarchy, and decide to not only switch sides, but faiths as well (Subrahmanyam 1993).

RESISTANCE IN THE COMPETITION BETWEEN EMPIRES

The maritime empires were born out of fierce intra-European competition and this competition played a large role in their subsequent expansion. The Dutch empire started as a direct challenge to the Iberians. Once established, it clashed violently with its other European competitors. Such competition was a great motivation for fostering resistance movements in competing empires. Competition between the empires was felt not only in direct military confrontations but permeated all forms of resistance that the empires encountered. Perceived weaknesses of rivals were exploited in many different ways. Escaped slaves in Brazil formed powerful settlements that were a military force to be reckoned with, and the same goes for the maroons in Jamaica, Haiti, and Guyana. Bringing these forces on board in any foreign invasion scheme could have devastating effects on the balance of power. This was demonstrated during the slave revolt on Saint Domingue, when the revolt cleared the ground for intervention by the Spanish, who found in the revolt's leader a valuable ally (James 1963). The slave armies were supplied weapons and uniforms from the Spanish side of the island in an attempt by the Spanish authorities to take over the French part. When the British became involved, they also tried to lure the slaves to their side (Klooster 2009: 104–5). Also on revolutionary Guadeloupe the royalist planters actively courted British intervention, while the opposing republicans tried to find common cause with rebellious slaves who could be motivated to form a formidable army (Dubois 2006: 238).

Uncooperative borderlands and territorial secessions were a common phenomenon across empires. Borderlands that were unable to be incorporated highlighted the limits to imperial expansion for all to see. Some areas successfully resisted attempts by different empires to bring them into the imperial fold. The onward expansion of the Portuguese can be contrasted with the decline of the Spanish. They gradually abandoned areas that they were unable or uninterested to control during the crisis that plagued their empire in the seventeenth century. Breakaways from empires were more problematic for imperial authority than unconquered borderlands inhabited by indigenous or maroon societies. Internal dissatisfaction and resistance on the margins of empires could be employed to provoke outright defection to the enemy by colonists and colonial forces. Plantation owners and traders of indigenous goods as well as those exploiting saltpans and mines had more to lose in a spirited defense than by letting a rival empire take over the colony. This resulted on several occasions in colonists inviting foreign powers to invade. In Dutch-ruled Curaçao, opposing factions of the local elite invited both the French and British to invade the island. Those who feared the French revolutionary ideals and the inspiration that the enslaved and other non-white people drew from them sought British intervention (Fatah-Black 2013).

One reason for inviting hostile takeovers might be that changing sides would create substantial problems for creditors seeking to recover debts from colonists now under a new jurisdiction. The rebellion by the Portuguese Brazilians against Dutch rule in Brazil which began in the early 1640s—only ten years after the Dutch had established their colony there by conquering Portuguese-controlled territories on Brazil's north-eastern Atlantic coast—is a case in point (Figure 7.3). Important in this respect is that the colonists did not rise up immediately or universally after Dutch conquest (Klooster 2016: 77–83). Although the Dutch proclaimed freedom of religion in their Brazilian conquests, the peace agreements in the captaincies became increasingly offensive to Catholic planters, while opening the door for their Jewish counterparts. Meanwhile, the Dutch were never able to attract enough colonists to the colony to seriously begin creating a substantial religiously loyal colonial population. This inability to attract loyal settlers was not the only problem that beset the Dutch in the colony. A second challenge was finding men who were able and willing to serve in the military. Although many set sail across the ocean, often having arrived from Germany and other European countries, their numbers and their loyalty could not be relied upon to hold enemy forces at bay. In fact,

FIGURE 7.3: Dutch ships fight Portuguese carracks in long-running trade dispute. Credit: Richard Schlecht/National Geographic/Getty Images.

desertion among the soldiers serving in Brazil was so rampant that the Portuguese were able to muster eight full companies of deserters to fight against the Dutch (Klooster 2013: 336).

The large armies deployed in the inter-imperial conflicts of the early seventeenth century faced insubordination, mutiny, and desertion. Indigenous allies of the Dutch in Brazil came to make up for a lack of soldiers, and the hopes of the Dutch West India Company to find an ally in the common Iberian enemy triggered multiple attempts to recruit indigenous Brazilians to their cause. And they initially did so with success. Without the indigenous forces the Dutch would probably not have been able to conquer the slaving forts on the African coast (Lam 2013). However, these transatlantic military operations came at a cost. Heavy losses among the indigenous Brazilian fighters triggered opposition back in Brazil. The erstwhile allies began to become more and more suspicious of the Dutch West India Company, and their loyalty became uncertain (Meuwese 2012: 163–90). With the onset of the Portuguese rebellion against the Dutch, some groups of indigenous Brazilians soon made common cause against the Dutch. This was not a unique pattern, as we can see in a similar case in Chile. The expedition under the leadership of Hendrik Brouwer in 1643 was intent on attacking Spanish-controlled mines on the southern tip of South America. Although the Dutch were initially able to gain indigenous allies, desertion of their own troops as well as deteriorating relations with the indigenous peoples made clear that Chile would have to remain outside the scope of Dutch imperial ambitions (Brouwer and Heijer 2015).

Forced to choose between two competing European empires, the ever-present and resilient indigenous populations might opt for resistance over accommodation. In the seventeenth century, the effects of such resistance were invariably devastating for the empires. Nowhere was this more clear than on the Guiana coast, which is littered with failed attempts at settlement. It is a chronic problem for the historian that few such failures leave enough sources to be studied. Close examination of material on settlement attempts by the Dutch on the Guiana coast reveals that there were at least fourteen failed and subsequently forgotten attempts at settlement there. The settlements on the Guiana coast were so feeble, however, that even non-cooperation by the indigenous population meant that colonists would perish even before the next ship arrived (Heijer 2005).

Fears of abandonment by the metropolis or its inability to adequately supply the colony and defend its property were also widespread in the more developed colonies. In Suriname, which quickly developed into a productive plantation colony after 1651, the colonists were very reluctant to side fully with either the Dutch or the English. When a small fleet from Zeeland sailed up the Suriname River in 1667, the English governor mounted only a half-hearted defense. Soon after this conquest, the colony under Dutch rule ran into trouble. The Dutch, seeking to stir up resistance from indigenous groups by claiming that the English had abducted indigenous people when departing the colony, soon faced an outright rebellion (Enthoven 1996).

More important than the ambivalent allegiance of colonists was the persistent presence of non-conformist religious subjects within empires. Local administration was forced to pursue a balancing act between enforcing loyalty and conformity on one hand, and attracting or keeping colonists by allowing for religious toleration on the other. When alternative identities were not "exotic" or "indigenous" but rather connected to imperial rivals, there seems to have been greater enmity. The presence of Catholic subjects posed a challenge to the legitimacy of imperial authority for the Dutch, for example. Especially where the Dutch and the English were not actively converting their (enslaved) subjects overseas, the presence of Catholics in colonies, and the activities of Catholic orders, could contribute to enmity between the imperial state, local authority, and overseas subjects (Rupert 2012: 148–9). However, it has to be said that empires were far less susceptible to fear of counter-identities than nation-states would become after the eighteenth century.

In the later eighteenth century, there were many instances in which rulers decided to make common cause across imperial boundaries against rebellions. Faced with revolts and attacks by indigenous forces, colonial authorities could quite easily set aside the conflicts that raged in the metropolitan context and offer mutual aid in crushing uprisings. The Berbice slave revolt of 1763 is a case in point. Initially, the Dutch tried to handle the revolt themselves. Troops were sent in from Suriname, marching overland to Berbice. However, the mistreatment of the troops, and their fears of what they would face was so great that they decided to desert. The carrier-slaves in the company had already begun deserting, but the soldiers attempted to flee as well. Ironically, when they encountered the rebels and attempted to form an alliance, a good number of them were executed by the rebelling slaves. The failure of the Suriname expedition prolonged the stand-off between the liberated territories governed by Cuffy (or Coffij) and the former slaves and the Dutch colonial power which had been forced to retreat entirely (Kars 2009). Help came from the side of the English, importantly including a private initiative from Gedney Clarke.

One can ask if the distinctions made between empires along national lines obscure more than they clarify. The slave ships of many different empires encountered each other along the West African coast looking for places to purchase enslaved Africans. This chapter has so far looked at how resistance was a hindrance to the workings and expansion of the empires at the political level. This approach runs the danger of glossing over the desperation that was behind many undirected acts of resistance. Plantations, fortresses, and ships were the site of regular mutinies and revolts, many of which have gone unnoticed by historians and, to some degree, in the archive itself. Inter-imperial cooperation between slaving vessels surfaces occasionally in the archives of slave trade companies. An example of this kind of cooperation has come to light as a result of research into the mass-suicide by enslaved Africans on board the ship *Neptunus* in October 1785. The rebelling Africans on board the Dutch ship had managed to break free from the hold and seized control of the ship. Threatening to blow up the powder chamber, the European crew and assailing free Africans retreated. On hearing about the predicament of the *Neptunus*, a nearby British slaver came to the aid of the Dutch—or possibly it came to plunder it after suppressing the revolt. We will never be certain since the rebels on board decided, in a last dramatic stance, to blow the ship up (Paesie 2016).

Inter-imperial rivalry often played a role in aggravating the effects of resistance (Figure 7.4). Rival empires on occasion made direct attempts at

FIGURE 7.4: Toussaint Louverture, former black slave who went over to the French after the first proclamation of the abolition of slavery. Credit: Photo12/UIG/Getty Images.

inciting disobedience and (slave) rebellions and flight to disrupt competing empires (Rupert 2012: 95–6). The Spanish refusal to extradite slave refugees from Protestant colonies slowly but surely gave the empire an abolitionist reputation. It was an ironic turning of the tables: resistance against the Spanish empire had been central to the building of the other Western empires; however, during the wave of rebellions in the 1730s and 1740s, the Spanish empire had become a beacon of hope for those in slavery (Linebaugh and Rediker 2000: 205). Insurrectionists on occasion stated that they hoped for a Spanish invasion of the land. During the insurrection in New York in 1741, rumors of a Spanish invasion filled the rebels with hope. In the war with the maroons on Jamaica, the maroons had made an agreement with the Spanish that they would hand over the island after they had taken it, as long as the Spanish would guarantee their freedom (Linebaugh and Rediker 2000: 195).

RESISTANCE IN THE TRANSFORMATION OF THE EMPIRES

The end of the period under discussion was marked by the reconfiguration of the Western empires. There was a temporary weakening of the trans-oceanic ties while European states descended into war and revolution. A wave of independence wars erupted across the Atlantic world—importantly that of Saint Domingue, later the Haitian empire, from France and the American War of Independence (1776–84) in which thirteen colonies left the British empire to form the United States—as well as the numerous independence wars that broke out in Spanish territories around 1810, including those of Argentina, Chile, Bolivia, and Colombia. While the authority of imperial powers weakened, the control of colonial elites over their societies strengthened and exchange between the (former) colonies proved intensive. The concept of "liberty" became a rallying cry for people across Western empires, regardless of the European power they (had) belonged to.

The creole class of planters, merchants, and artisans, and on occasion also the enslaved were able to break imperial control over their societies. Such fissures in the power structures and intra-elite rivalries created opportunities for movements from below. While these were mostly unable to usher in the egalitarian world to which some aspired, the age of revolution arguably fundamentally transformed the imperial landscape. The upsurge of resistance was met by imperial repression. In the last quarter of the eighteenth century, the suppression of subversive ideas became a priority for the Portuguese empire. This included campaigns against freemasonry, which was seen as a channel for disseminating subversive ideas (Disney 2009: 319–22).

The age of revolution saw the development of a common imagery of resistance across the empires. Songs, dress, and even skin color became signifiers of revolt and independence. The aftermath of the Saint Domingue slave revolt of 1791 and the French Revolution added new energy to the possibilities of inciting of rebellion across imperial boundaries in attempts to weaken competitors. The revolt had a devastating effect on the Atlantic world and it began to transform what was understood to be the difference between white and black. Conservatives opposed to the principles of the French Revolution began to include references to the revolt on Saint Domingue as further arguments against liberty. Edmund Burke remarked in the British Parliament that while the "West India colonies" had been "happy and flourishing" [sic], the idea of the rights of man had opened "Pandora's box" (O'Neill 2016: 88). It had engendered a vicious violence between white and black in which "every man seemed to thirst for the blood of his neighbor" (O'Neill 2016: 88). Black people escaping their subordinate status came to be seen as harbingers of a violent collapse of society. Meanwhile, everywhere across the Atlantic, enslaved black people also began to change their understanding of freedom. In Virginia, people of African descent invoked "Frenchness" as a metaphor for the new meaning of freedom (Sidbury 1997). The news from Saint Domingue was that a slave army was defeating the whites and ending slavery. It was news that could not be contained, and traveled rapidly with black mariners across the Atlantic (Scott 1996).

The Saint Domingue revolt had a clear knock-on effect, moving from one colony to the next. The story of Victor Hugues on Guadeloupe in that regard is exemplary here. The (temporary) abolition of slavery by the French in 1794 was in part inspired by a need to quell the uprisings in the colonies, as well as recruiting the newly freed Africans to their armies (Dubois 1999). In Guadeloupe, Hugues was successful in building a French Caribbean navy that was combating the English and swaying the allegiance of the Dutch on Curaçao. The arrival of Guadeloupian ships with black crews and captains in the port of Willemstad had a tremendous impact on the colony as the stories of their exploits will have had around the Caribbean. The sailors marched with sabers and French flags through the streets of Willemstad and insubordination by local people of color, both free and enslaved soon followed. This culminated in the Curaçao slave revolt of 1795. The leader of the Curacao slave rebellion argued openly that since the French had abolished slavery, and the Netherlands had been occupied by France, that they too should now be free (Fatah-Black 2013).

With the inspiration of the Saint Domingue revolt also traveled the imagery, symbolism, and repertoires of revolt. A visiting priest in the rebel encampment on Curaçao heard the singing of French songs among the rebels; and during the revolt the colonists had found a "Jacobin cap" (likely a Phrygian or Liberty cap) and a saber prominently placed on the altar of a local chapel. The origin of the Phrygian cap on the island of Curaçao is unknown, although its meaning was by then well understood across the Western empires. The imagery of the cap in the context of resistance against imperial rule first appeared in North America as part of the resistance against the Stamp Act (repealed in 1766). It gained more acceptance as a symbol of liberty during the War of Independence. The liberty cap and its meaning merged with that of the somewhat similar cap worn during the revolution in France (Korshak 1987). In France its meaning was initially contested, but in the long run the red cap with a forward-facing bend became a symbol of liberty across the empire (Wrigley 1997). Although its color (white, blue, or red) and shape were far from uniform at the time, the Phrygian shape of the cap came to grace the flag of independent Haiti as the crest on the country's coat of arms. It also adorned the American seal from the 1780s onward, and not much later it had become a near-universal symbol of independence in the Latin-American nations that broke away from the Spanish empire. It was incorporated in the early coats of arms of independent Argentina and several of its provinces, and in the coats of arms of Bolivia, Columbia, and other Latin American nations. Also, the short-lived Federated Republic of Central America incorporated the cap in its national seal. Understood as the symbol of independence from empire, Cuba much later would come to include the cap in its coat of arms, signaling a commonality with the independence movements that had torn apart the Spanish empire a century earlier.

Not only symbols and news, but also agents traveled the Atlantic spreading the feverish anticipation of freedom. With the express purpose to incite rebellions, agents were sent to provide arms and inspiration for revolts. Isaac Sasportas, a Jewish merchant accused of inciting slave revolts appears regularly in histories of the Atlantic in the age of revolution. He has been accused of preparing to incite a slave revolt on Curaçao, possibly a slave revolt in Charleston, and was finally executed for attempting to incite a slave revolt on Jamaica (Loker 1981; Sidbury 1997; Jordaan 2011). Rumors of such "outside agitators" were easily used by those in power to serve as a pretext for repression. Although the Curaçao slave revolt of 1795 was crushed, and the old governing elite deposed in 1796, the local Thermidorian-style governor Johan Rudolph Lauffer sought to firmly establish his power. The rumor of Sasportas inciting a new revolt allowed Lauffer to invite a British invasion force to take control of the island, while leaving him in power (Jordaan 2011). Slave rebellion after "Saint Domingue" had become integral to inter-imperial competition in the Atlantic world.

The destabilization of colonial slave society on Saint Domingue was in large part due to the fight for civil reform led by free people of color on the island. This group had risen to economic prominence by smuggling products, mainly indigo, from its plantations and they now demanded that their legal status catch up with their elevated position (Garrigus 1993). In the age of revolution, smuggling proved to be important for undermining imperial authority. Smuggling often preceded open rebellion against imperial authority and could even prepare the minds and stomachs for independence. Large-scale smuggling undermined not only imperial finance, but also authority. Condoning smuggling, or sanctioning it as legal private trade did much to keep together empires, although the detrimental effects began to show in the long run. Smugglers effectively brought down the Spanish empire in South America, where smugglers took center stage in the collapse of imperial authority and the formation of new elites and states. Smuggling also played a great role in the conflicts that raged within the British Empire, contributing greatly to its loss of thirteen colonies (McCusker 1989) (Figure 7.5).

FIGURE 7.5: The Bostonians Paying the Exciseman, or Tarring and Feathering, 1774. Lithograph by Snooks. Credit: The New York Historical Society/Getty Images.

The illicit movement of goods was also a sign of something else: that colonial elites were increasingly able to control economic processes. They were more able to control production and extract more and more wealth from the land and labor force. The mid-eighteenth century saw a spectacular rise in slavery and slave-based agricultural production. A rapidly increasing number of enslaved Africans were deported from Africa and with the depletion of the continent, their average age dropped. While the elites creolized, the workforce de-creolized, with ever greater proportions of the enslaved population being newly imported from Africa. The British Caribbean could be seen as an exception to this trend, since although the same economic and demographic trends were apparent, revolts were less salient. In the French, Dutch, and Iberian colonies, the period not only saw the growth in the size of slave populations, but also in the size of the workforces on individual plantations. Incidents of generalized revolt became more regular as the eighteenth century progressed. Tacky's War on Jamaica in 1760, in which the rebels attempted to take over the island, and the Berbice slave revolt of 1763, in which they successfully took control of the entire colony were the largest in a wave of rebellions that swept the Caribbean at the time (Linebaugh and Rediker 2000: 224–6).

No sooner had this wave of revolts died down than a new upsurge in the number and scale of revolts threatened the Western empires. The closing decades of the century would see an increase in the number of revolts, rebellions, and conspiracies among the enslaved. These were neither wholly separate from nor completely dependent on the revolts led by free citizens against the strictures of empire. Slave revolts could be taken as a sign that imperial authority was crumbling, with local elites responding by taking matters into their own hands. When, on Guadeloupe, a group of slaves revolted and killed the owners of several plantations, they marched toward the nearest military fortress. There they declared that they had uncovered a royalist plot, had executed the conspirators, and proceeded to the fortress to profess their loyalty (Dubois 2006). But in the seminal secession of the era, the American War of Independence, slaves fought on both sides, without revolts contributing to the development of the struggle.

It was not only the slave revolt on French Saint Domingue that sent shockwaves around the Atlantic. The influence of the revolt was felt in the British Empire and stretched to the other empires as well. The Minas Conspiracy (1788–9) was directly inspired by the unfolding of the independence of the thirteen colonies in North America at a time when the goldmining industry in the captaincy entered a crisis (Maxwell 2004: 53). Ten years later, the Bahia Conspiracy (1798) was a lower-class affair. The greater leeway afforded by the Bahian governor to its merchants and planters had put pressure on the lives of the poor. The year before the conspiracy, food riots had broken out. Race and regional background were used to block people from advancing in society, creating further disaffection. Together this created a fertile ground for revolt, along lines that became familiar in the age of revolution, adding to this the goal of the "extermination for all time of the heavy yoke of European domination" (Ramos 1976).

CONCLUSION

Resistance against the Spanish empire was dynamic and creative. Attempts to break into the Spanish empire by several European powers were the first and essential steps toward building up their own empires. The successful attack of Spanish dominance was aided by the long period of crisis that plagued the Spanish in the first half of the seventeenth century. These assaults on Spanish dominance were often military in character. A second form of resistance were attempts to break down the exclusive relationship between Spain and its colonies. In the context of empires predicated on shipping and trade, smuggling turned out to be an effective form of resistance. Smuggling was also a creative force, resulting in new economic ties, as well as providing an economic basis for new polities to arise.

The new economic basis of the Western empires also made them more vulnerable to resistance. Ships, plantations, mines, and cities offered plenty of opportunities for rebels to damage infrastructure. Arson proved to be an effective weapon to resist the functioning of colonial societies. It also meant that inciting rebellion could strategically weaken enemies. Provoking uprisings or desertion by slaves, sailors, or soldiers became an effective strategy. The fear of abandonment and neglect by imperial authorities not only made slaves and workers susceptible to agitation, but also colonists could simply chose to hand a colony over to a competing empire. The dynamism and creative force of resistance was again witnessed at the end of the eighteenth century, when a wave of resistance against empire was at the basis of a long list of new nations.

During the eighteenth century, the culture of resistance in the Western empires was increasingly shaped by a fear on the part of the authorities about secessions from those empires, the promotion of free trade, and the fear of slave revolts. Imperial provinces asserting their autonomy became a real threat in the last quarter of the eighteenth century. The liberal ideologies regarding trade policies that often accompanied these successions became perceived as threats by metropolitan authorities and were combatted by the promotion of anti-Enlightenment. The unwillingness to be governed from overseas could, however, no longer be contained by the imperial centers. Those colonies in particular that were not dependent on slave trading for their economic survival took the plunge and broke away from their motherlands. Slave-dependent colonies were more reluctant to open intra-elite conflicts, especially after the revolts on Saint Domingue that would ultimately lead to the independence of Haiti.

CHAPTER EIGHT

Race

VANITA SETH

Race is not an object of nature that science is called upon to classify and study, but rather a socially and historically contingent way of organizing human difference—a product of political imperatives and relations of power motivated by the legitimizing demands of European expansion, slavery, and colonialism. In other words, historicizing race requires locating its organizing discourse within the history of early modern European colonial expansion, empire-building, and the slave trade.

While empire-building is often viewed through the lens of war, expansion, pillage, economic might, and military technology, of equal importance are the multiple forms of cultural legitimation that conquering states appeal to in defense of territorial and political expansion. Religion, food, clothing, environment, class, and later, skin color were all markers of difference that defined colonial peoples and slaves as inferior and thereby justifiably subject to colonial rule. It is in an effort to both identify and account for the appeal of these multiple registers of organizing human difference in the period 1650–1800 that is the focus of this paper.

DATING RACISM: THE ORIGINS DEBATE

Against the backdrop of a growing scientific consensus which has refuted the biological purchase of race, scholars from diverse disciplines within the humanities and social sciences have turned to historical sources in an effort to define race and racism, identify their point of origin, and offer causal explanations for why race (rather than, for example, religious or ethnic diversity) came to be such a pervasive measure of human difference. For at least

FIGURE 8.1: Antique colored illustrations: Ethnicities: American Indian, Mongolian, Caucasian, Ethiopian, Malay. Credit: ilbusca via Getty Images.

three decades, scholars have been engaged in what can best be described as the "Origins Debate." The primary node of contention has centered around the dating of racism—did racial difference figure in ancient Greek and Roman thought, was it appealed to in the European Middle Ages or Renaissance, in the early modern period (roughly 1650 to the late eighteenth century), or alternatively, is race as a marker of difference, a distinctive feature of modernity (from the nineteenth century on)? What is uncontroversial is that no equivalent concept such as "race" existed in ancient Greek and Latin—rather, it entered many European languages in the Middle Ages (1200–1500) and carried a variety of meanings: blood, lineage, breed (particularly in references to horses), and descent (Hannaford 1996: 5).

Whereas most scholars emphasize the need to distinguish racism from other forms of prejudice such as xenophobia and ethnocentrism, how expansive or restrictive their definition of racism is will inevitably inform their historical dating of its origins. Thus for Benjamin Isaac, who argues that racial thinking dates back to antiquity, racism is defined as:

> an attitude towards individuals or groups of people which posits a direct and linear connection between physical and mental qualities. It therefore attributes to those individuals or groups of people collective traits, physical, mental and moral, which are constant and unalterable by human will, because they are caused by hereditary factors or external influences, such as climate or geography (Isaac 2004: 23).

In contrast, Ivan Hannaford's work *Race* insists on the modern origins of racial thinking and thus included in his five-point definition is the premise

> that human beings are independent of ethical, moral, religious, and mythological laws or rules and are subject to the laws of nature . . .; that descent is about the transmission of biological characteristics, once 'blood', now 'genes' . . . [and] that races may be distinguished hierarchically so as to allow recognition of peoples by 'type' (Hannaford 1996: 57–8).

Notably, while Isaac's definition precludes any reference to biological determinism, it is precisely racial science that is at the core of Hannaford's understanding of race. And while Isaac's definition extends racism to include environmental explanations for difference, Hannaford's contention is that appeals to race presuppose that which is physiologically immutable and irreversible. Given the extensive use of climatic explanations in ancient Greek and Roman accounts of human difference, it is not surprising that Isaac would "find" racism in antiquity. That Hannaford's definition of racism privileges biological determinism and the normative classification of bodies, equally ensures that race is an idea of nineteenth-century provenance.

Rather than beginning with an abstract definition of race and then determining what does, or does not, fit into its definitional container, one of the questions this chapter pursues is: how was human variety represented during the period 1650–1800? The time period is not arbitrary. Despite the fact that it was in the late fifteenth and early sixteenth centuries that European explorers discovered the sea routes to the New World and Asia, and established trading ports off the coast of Africa, it took at least a century, according to Henry Elliot (1992), before the magnitude of these voyages and explorations fully entered European consciousness (see also Hunter [1964] 2000). From the middle of the seventeenth century and after, however, travel stories, philosophical writings, artistic works, and literary texts were exposing Europeans to a myriad of physiological, religious, and cultural differences that purportedly distinguished Europeans from the inhabitants of the New World, Africa, and Asia (Figure 8.2). Once such knowledge began to proliferate in Britain and the Continent, there emerged a multiplicity of explanations offered to account for human differences. Were these representations the precursor to modern racism or do they testify to the absence of racial categories?

FIGURE 8.2: Explorers on the Shores of the Saint Lawrence River, seventeenth century. Credit: duncan1890 via Getty Images.

But 1650–1800 is notable for another reason. Often celebrated for its philosophical and political defense of the rights of man, the privileging of the individual, and the sanctity of human freedom against Divine rule, arbitrary power, and political despotism, this is also the age when the transatlantic slave trade was both consolidated and reached its apex. The debate concerning the origin of race in Europe comes to be equally contentious in accounting for its role in the emergence of New World slavery. Was slavery born of a racism that preceded it, or was racial thinking the outgrowth of African enslavement?

Despite the contentious scholarly debates regarding the origins of race, what is uncontroversial is the fact that from at least the mid-nineteenth century to evoke human difference across cultures was first and foremost to speak of racial physiognomy. Biological differences predicated on skin color, facial angles, cranial size, and sexual organs were the scientific grounds for extrapolating on the moral and intellectual inferiority of New World aboriginals, Asians, and Africans. In contrast, what strikes even the cursory reader of European accounts of difference in the late seventeenth and eighteenth centuries is the seeming absence of any coherent, hegemonic principles for translating human variety.

REPRESENTING DIFFERENCE IN THE AGE OF ENLIGHTENMENT

Many European countries were not unfamiliar with cultural and physiognomic diversity even within their own populations. Seventeenth- and eighteenth-century Spain and Portugal were famously diverse due in part to their crusading wars with the Ottoman empire, a long history of slave trading (which included populations from the Mediterranean, northern Africa, and the near East), and ambassadorial relations with some African kingdoms (Lowe 2007: 101–28). And when, in 1492, the Spanish crown expelled Jews and Moors from their territory, sixteenth- and seventeenth-century Holland saw an influx of Sephardic Jews escaping the Inquisition in Spain and Portugal as well as approximately 150,000 Flemings and 75,000 Huguenots escaping religious persecution in France (Blakely 1993: 9). As to "black" Africans, Blakely argues that their presence became a constant feature in Dutch religious art from the fifteenth century. Indeed, "[t]he Adoration of the Magi, featured in thousands of works, was the single most popular religious theme featuring 'blacks' in sixteenth and seventeenth century European art" (1993: 84). By the middle of the seventeenth century, Philip Morgan argues, "blacks" were already a visible presence in parts of England. By the mid-eighteenth century, there were approximately ten to fifteen thousand people of African descent in London alone—the largest urban concentration of "blacks" in the British Empire outside of Africa despite the fact that they only made up about two percent of the population (1991: 159). And, of course, the Turks/Moors (the distinction is by no means clear) were an essential ingredient in the making of the "idea" of a European (Christian) self. The Moor was a figure of genuine fear in some cases, an exotic subject of art in others, a common literary villain, and at times, a crucial, albeit awkward ally. Finally, it is important to note that when accounting for human variety, European representations were not limited to non-Europeans. Hunter (2000: 45), for example, reproduces an early seventeenth-century English verse that neatly captures some of the prevailing stereotypes:

The Dutchman for a drunkard
The Dane for golden locks
The Irishman for usquebaugh [whisky]
The Frenchmen for the [pox].

How difference—physiognomic, religious, and cultural—was engaged in different parts of Europe was not uniform and yet, it would seem that whatever positive or pejorative representations were formed to convey alterity were not, for the most part, perceived as innate or immutable.

Indeed, as Roxann Wheeler argues in the seventeenth- and eighteenth-century British context, "a color binary of 'black' and 'white' does not help to elucidate British reactions to other Europeans, Moors, West Africans or native Caribbean's, or indeed, their representations of them" (2000: 50). Ernst van den Boogaart makes a similar observation in reference to the Dutch, arguing that "heathenism and not blackness was the core attribute of the African" (1982: 39), while for Rebecca Earle, Spanish colonialists in the New World "viewed both Indian and European bodies as mutable and porous, open to the influence of many external factors, including, critically, food" (2010: 713).

And yet, there is no question that hierarchies did exist, that descriptions by Europeans of Africans, Asians, and Amerindians were often pejorative, that "blackness" did, at times, connote inferiority—that, in short, many European writers presumed upon their own superiority *vis-à-vis* the non-European world. The mechanism by which such differences were identified and articulated is what is distinctive compared with the nineteenth century. It was not the body that was the primary or even significant referent for identifying difference. Human variety, whether derided or admired, was instead rendered commensurable through the fluid and malleable prism of climate, environment, dress, diet, class, religion, customs, and "civility."

While the French philosopher Montesquieu may have produced the most exhaustive compendium on the correlation between environmental conditions and human differences in the eighteenth century, such theories were not novel. As Clarence Glacken (1976) has demonstrated, environmental explanations for human variety were already well rehearsed in ancient Greek and Roman texts—the central characteristics of which were revived in the seventeenth and eighteenth centuries. Thus in 1733 John Arbuthnot suggested that: "It seems agreeable to Reason and Experience that the Air operates sensibly in forming the Constitution of Mankind, the Specialities of Features, Complexion, Temper, and consequently the Manners of Mankind, which are found to vary much in different Countries and Climates" (quoted in Wahrman 2004: 88). A similar argument was followed by the German author Johann Joachim Winckelmann, who observed in 1763 that "The mouth swollen and raised, such as the Negroes have in common with the monkeys of their country is a superfluous excrescence, a swelling caused by the heat of the climate, as our lips are inflated by heat, or by an abundance of bitter humours" (quoted in Bindman 2002: 89). But perhaps the most definitive proof of the effect of climate was demonstrated by Jews, who were "Fair in Britain and Germany, brown in France and in Turkey, swarthy in Portugal and in Spain, olive in Syria and in Chaldea, tawny or copper-colored in Arabia and Egypt" (quoted in Wahrman 2004: 89).

It was the very malleability that such explanations afforded which ensured that physiognomy was often regarded as reversible. Indeed, the French naturalist, the Comte de Buffon, was adamant that if one transported an African to Paris, the French diet and climate would, after a few generations, produce "white" progeny (Roger 1997: 179). In yet other instances, eighteenth-century commentators reported on the metamorphosis of individuals within their lifespan. The prestigious *Philosophical Transactions* of the Royal Society reported "An Account of the Remarkable Alteration of Colour in a Negro Woman" who became as "white" as "a fair European," though by far the most famous case was that of Henry Moss, an African American man, "whose dark skin turned white in his early middle age" (quoted in Melish 2001: 225). And, of course, the reverse was also possible as many anxious European accounts of "going native" demonstrate. Rebecca Earle, for example, documents the sixteenth- and seventeenth-century concerns of Spanish colonial writers who agreed that "those who come from other climates through [eating] foods generate new blood, which produces new humors, [and] the new humors [create] new abilities and conditions." The danger of course, was that Spaniards might turn into "timid, beardless Indians" (quoted in Earle 2010: 693). Wahrman recounts similar concerns among the English where, as one author asserted, it was well established that "white" captives of indigenous Americans acquired "a great resemblance to the savages, not only in their manners, but in their colour and the expression of the countenance" (2004: 86).

But climate was only one of many conditions that informed European explanations for difference. Indeed, as Wheeler argues, efforts to account for human variety relied even more on cultural signifiers: "Embodied in dress, manners, and language, the concepts of Christianity, and civility, and rank were not simply abstract categories of difference; they constituted visible distinctions that are difficult for us to recover" (2000: 7). Jorge Esguerra (1999) and Emilia da Costa (1985) both point to the importance of astrology to Spanish and Portuguese accounts of difference. Far from being censored by the Church, Esguerra notes that, "as the science that studied the influence of stars over temperaments and complexions, astrology was in fact officially sanctioned" (1999: 50). Boogaart argues that Dutch accounts of Africans in the seventeenth century repeatedly appealed to notions of African savagery in opposition to Dutch civility: "[The Africans] eat as indecently and greedily as pigs . . . they do not use cutlery to put their food in their mouths . . ." (quoted 1982: 47). Rebecca Earle (2010) has emphasized the importance of Hippocratic-Galenic medical physiology—most notably humoral theories and the importance of food—in Spanish efforts to account for the different complexions and temperaments of Amerindians. The French writer Louis-Alexandre Deverite appears to concur, for in his 1786 treatise he attributed the lack of body hair and beards on Amerindian men to be the consequence of "the simplicity of their nourishment and the non-usage of salt"—the effect of which was a lack of sexual appetite (quoted in Jaenen 1982: 51). His fellow countryman, the eighteenth-century philosopher Denis Diderot, explained in his *Encyclopedie*, that "color depends a lot on climate, but not entirely. There are different causes which must influence color, and even the form of features; among these are food and custom" (quoted in Earle 2016: 440). Included among such reported customs was the propensity of Greenlanders to use whale oil as fuel, the effects of which was the darkening of their skin as a consequence of the smoke (Kidd 2006: 103), and the Amerindian practice of oiling their skin with the fat of bears, thus giving it a red tinge (Wahrman 2004: 96).

Equally, if not more importantly, class and religion were crucial to the normative logic and organizing framework of distinguishing human beings. David Davis, who argues for the premodern origins of race, nevertheless emphasizes the correlation between skin color and class. European serfs, slaves, and peasants—in short, those populations engaged in outdoor manual labor and thus exposed to the sun—were often deemed to be dark and thus savage. "It would be hard," Davis argues, "to overemphasize the importance of this linkage between low social class and the physical markers of menial labor" (2006: 51). Colin Kidd similarly acknowledges the frequent use of animal descriptors in describing Africans but notes that such adjectives were equally employed to describe the Irish and the poor in England (2006: 77). Norbert Elias (1982) has provided the most detailed history of civility and manners as first and foremost an effort by the French and German aristocracies to distinguish themselves from the middle and lower classes. It is only in the later part of the eighteenth century, he suggests, that such distinctions come to be displaced onto populations outside of Europe.

But perhaps the most illustrative example of the intersection between class and human variation can be seen in the significance accorded to lineage. The etymological correlation between race, lineage, and (somewhat later) blood in many European languages since the Middle Ages, has led some scholars to defend the premodern origins of race (Eliav-Felden *et al.* 2009). For Guillaume Aubert, it is the innate, inheritable quality presumed in appeals to lineage that leads him to argue that race emerged as a defining feature of French intellectual thought in the eighteenth century. Prior to that, the idea of race in early modern France was still informed by notions of social status and rank. Indeed, the aristocratic appeal to race-as-lineage was renewed with some urgency when the privileges accorded the nobility were seen to be under threat. When, in 1604, the king was petitioned to recognize that nobility consisted of "well purified blood" (quoted in Aubert 2004: 444), it was the conflation of race with aristocratic birthright that was being evoked (449; also see Bouille 1985: 221–41). It is the correlation between race, lineage, blood, and inheritance that metamorphosed, Aubert argues, into a discourse of racial difference in French colonial policy—assertions of racial purity displaced noble lineage. And yet, as Rebecca Earle documents, such assertions of descent and claims to racial purity in the Spanish Americas were hopelessly frustrated, given that racial intermixing was the norm: the familial portraits in eighteenth-century Mexican casta paintings reflect the profound ambiguity and instability inherent in physiognomic representations (2016: 427–66).

Finally, we cannot underestimate the centrality of religious thought during this period. Infidel, heathen, pagan, and heretic were common descriptors denoting the inferiority of everyone from the Muslims of North Africa and the Middle East, the Jews within Europe, the pagans of the Americas, the heathens of Africa and Asia, and Catholic or Lutheran heretics. As Chaplin argues, "if lineage and sex indicated where Europeans belonged within their own societies, religion (like climate and language) showed where they belonged in relation to the rest of the world" (2002: 158). For Chaplin, the centrality of religion in distinguishing populations was, like climate, custom, and language, further proof of the fact that difference in the seventeenth and eighteenth centuries was posited as mutable, fluid, and reversible. For other scholars—most notably those who defend the medieval origins of race—it was through an appeal to Christian theology that assertions of African inferiority found expression. Whereas Noah's sons Japhet and Shem populated Europe and Asia respectively, Noah's cursed son Ham was the progenitor of Africans. The "blackness" of the Africans it followed, was a mark of his enslavement and testimony to his servile status (Fenton 1996: 8). It should be noted, however, that the ubiquity of this argument has come to be challenged. In the most detailed refutation of this thesis, Benjamin Braude has demonstrated not only that the association of Ham with Africa fails to comply with the Old Testament and thus represents a serious misinterpretation of the biblical text, but also details the absence of a racialized depiction of Ham through much of the Medieval and early modern period

(1997: 103–42). Indeed, both Colin Kidd and Braude argue that artistic depictions of Ham as "black" only emerge in the nineteenth and twentieth centuries (Braude 1997: 121; Kidd 2006: 75).

The sons of Noah have, however, another significance within early modern European debates on human difference. As central as religion was to distinguishing populations, Christian theology was also crucial to the doctrine of human unity. Despite the wide variety of explanations for human difference, however ethnocentric and prejudicial were European representations of Africans and Amerindians, the foundational premise that underwrote most of these accounts rested on the belief in monogenesis—that human origin was singular and drew its common descent from Adam and Eve. It is precisely for this reason Colin Kidd argues, that accounting for human diversity was overwhelmingly "a theological problem": "Throughout much of the early modern period theologians were concerned to reconcile the ethnological diversity of the world—whether in terms of color and other physical differences, language and religion—with the common origins of humanity set out in Scripture and agreed to belong to a timespan of around six thousand years" (2004: 262).

But it was not only theologians that sought to reconcile the Bible with the fact of human variety. Legal scholars, naturalists, philosophers, philologists, and ethnologists all addressed the question of human variation within the presumptive restraints of man's shared biblical origin. Indeed, almost from the moment of European explorations in the sixteenth century, the challenge that the Americas posed to biblical history was the source of endless debates concerning the origin of the New World populations. If Noah's sons—Shem, Ham, and Japhet and their progeny—were said to have populated the known continents of Africa, Asia, and Europe, no ancestral source was accorded the Amerindians in the Old Testament. Thus began elaborate genealogies—Vikings, Ethiopians, Chinese, south-east Asians, Tartars, Carthaginians, and the Welsh were among some twenty contenders identified as the original ancestors of indigenous Americans (Ryan 1981: 533; Grafton 1992: 210; Kidd 2004: 265). The question they all sought to engage across multiple fields was: how to account for the sheer scale of human difference within the scriptural constraints of human unity, of monogenesis?

ACCOUNTING FOR HUMAN DIFFERENCE: THE PRESENCE AND ABSENCE OF RACE

If many of the examples provided thus far attest to the fact that physiognomy was not the primary signifier of difference, they also demonstrate the presumption of European superiority that informed much of seventeenth- and eighteenth-century writings on the non-West. Whether through reference to climate, class, customs, civility, or religion, there was, with some notable exceptions, a shared belief in the inferiority of Africans and New World Aboriginals.

What is striking about these examples is not the absence of ethnocentrism and prejudice, but the implied mutability and transient quality accorded the human body: change the external variables of climate, diet, or religion and in principle the heathen is converted, the pagan is saved, the "black" body "whitened," and, more anxiously, the European turns native. But if the porousness of the body was the underwriting assumption of many European accounts of human variety in the seventeenth and eighteenth centuries, these coexisted with conflicting representations that appear to preempt the biological racism we have come to identify with the nineteenth century. In perhaps the most (in)famous footnote in English philosophy, David Hume (1711–76) in his 1748 essay "Of national characters" wrote that, "I am apt to suspect the negroes, and in general all the other species of men (for there are four or five different kinds) to be naturally inferior to the whites" (quoted in Kidd 2006: 94).

Hume was not the only eighteenth-century philosopher to pronounce on the innate inferiority of Africans. Indeed, the French philosopher Voltaire (1694–1788) is equally renowned for his musings on African origins, suggesting in *Candide* that African women copulate with monkeys ([1759] 1969: 43) and while the German philosopher Immanuel Kant (1724–1804) was perhaps less crude, he was no less adamant that Africans constituted an inferior race ([1777] 2000: 8–22). To these preeminent figures in the western philosophical canon can be added lesser names such as the Scottish philosopher and judge, Lord Kames (1696–1782) and Jamaican slave-owner, Edward Long (1784–1813)—both of whom appealed to innate racial differences in their defense of slavery.

The point is not that such appeals to innate, hereditary differences were absent in the eighteenth century, but rather that they constitute one strain—and a minority one at that—through which human variation found explanatory purchase. What I have sought to demonstrate in my discussion of European representations of difference through the course of the seventeenth and eighteenth centuries are the multiple registers through which human variation was identified, represented, and normatively evaluated. While the examples can be multiplied, the more interesting question is why such a plethora of possibilities had explanatory power when, through the course of the nineteenth century, accounts of human difference largely coalesced around biological theories of racial hierarchy? I want to tentatively identify four overlapping explanations for the seemingly incoherent, chaotic, and contradictory theories proffered by European writers to account for human variation from 1650 to 1800.

First, we need to be cognizant of the fact that much of the language employed to designate difference in the seventeenth and eighteenth centuries conveyed meanings that no longer resonate with contemporary understandings. In other words, language itself mitigated against coherent, stable signifiers of difference while simultaneously enabling/generating the multiplicity of meanings through which the unfamiliar was rendered commensurable. We have already noted the fact that race retained its medieval association with breed and lineage and, when applied to humans, was commonly recognized as a marker of class, rank, and status. Similarly, skin color, something as "self-evident" and binary as "black" and "white," has long resisted conceptual integrity. It is for this reason that I have placed such term as "black" and "white" in inverted commas throughout this chapter—it signifies the inherent instability, slipperiness, and porous nature of these seemingly "natural" referents.

Indeed, Wheeler's contention that "whiteness" often conveyed Christianity rather than color, is further supported by the work of G.K. Hunter and Daniel Vitkus in their discussion of the Moor. A common ethnographic descriptor employed in European early modern texts, "[t]he word 'Moor,'" Hunter argues, "was very vague ethnographically ... but it was not vague in its antithetical relationship to the European norm of the civilized 'white' Christian" ([1964] 2000: 56). The "Moor" was not, Vitkus argues, "identified with a specific, historically accurate racial category; rather he is a hybrid who might be associated ... with a whole set of related terms—*Moor, Turk, Ottomite, Saracen, Mahometan, Egyptian, Judean, Indian*—all constructed and positioned in opposition to Christian faith and virtue" (1997: 159–60, original emphasis). In other words, we should be cautious in identifying the "Moor" as a racialized figure, rather "The Moor, like the Jew, ... is seen in primarily religious terms" (Hunter [1964] 2000: 56). While Hunter and Vitkus are engaging specifically with the age of Shakespeare, the ambiguity of the term "Moor" continued into the eighteenth century and though "Moors were not as Other as they once had been," it was their religious identification and the acknowledged power of the Ottoman empire that signified their difference (Wheeler 2000: 56). But we should not presume that even the correlation between "whiteness" and Christianity was entirely stable. The racial nomenclature that we have inherited from the nineteenth century was absent in seventeenth- and eighteenth-century European descriptions of China and Japan where, as Rotem Kowner argues, on the rare occasions where complexion was mentioned, the Chinese and Japanese were identified as "white." It was not skin color or physiognomy that excited European commentary but their different customs and, notably, their religion (2004: 751–78).

What all the above examples alert us to is the need to guard against anachronistic readings of early modern representations of difference. The very ambiguity, slipperiness, and multivariate usage of such terms as race, lineage, "white," "black," and "Moor" capture how porous and fluid were seventeenth- and eighteenth-century conceptions of alterity.

Secondly, it is important to remember that prior to late nineteenth-century anthropology, European accounts of cultural difference did not demand empirical observations or ethnographic study. Indeed, while traders, merchants, and travelers offered eyewitness testimonies of their experiences with Amerindians, Africans, and Asians, equally important were works of European philosophers and naturalists, many of whom had never left the Continent and Britain. The point was not to "know" the other so much as to define the self. Custom, diet, religion, geography, status, civility, trade, and environment not only constituted the multiple ways through which difference was organized but it also had the effect of defining what it meant to be European. Non-European societies functioned as reflecting mirrors held up for the purpose of either critiquing or elevating one's own society. For the eighteenth-century philosophers Jean-Jacques Rousseau (1712–78) and Denis Diderot (1713–84), the Amerindians and Tahitians respectively were noble savages who, living in accordance with nature, free from the hypocritical constraints of civilization and lacking the hypocrisy, vanity, and guile that marred European society, provided the ethno-philosophical vehicle for their inverted social criticism (Seth 2010: 207). But the reverse was also possible.

Whereas Rousseau and Diderot projected an uncorrupted human nature onto New World inhabitants, Buffon insisted that nature itself was the very reason for the inferiority of indigenous Americans. For Buffon, the "newness" of the New World resided not only in its recent "discovery" but in its "newness" as a continent. For this reason, Buffon argued, the Americas—its environment, fauna, flora, and peoples—were developmentally "immature": a region crawling with insects, infested with snakes, home to small animals (the puma was nothing more than an undeveloped lion), dotted with miniature mountains, and populated by inhabitants who were "small and feeble" (quoted in Jaenen 1982: 49; also see Gerbi 1973). But if for Buffon the Americas represented immaturity, for the Dutch naturalist Cornelius de Pauw (1739–99) it was the reverse: far from being "new," the Americas were exceedingly old and in decline. It was degeneration, not immaturity that accounted for the unfavorable environment and savagery of the inhabitants (Jaenen 1982: 50; Gerbi 1973).

Whether young and immature or old and degenerate, the conclusion was the same: through the foil of the Americas, the superiority of Europe—its climate, topography, fauna, flora, and people—was brought into relief. The presumed alterity of the indigenous peoples of America, Africa, and Asia was of value not in and of itself, but was rather the source of rich illustrative material mobilized in the interests of European philosophy along the axis of political conservatism and social critique.

Third, for all the contested, conflicting, and varied accounts of human difference reflected in mid-seventeenth- and eighteenth-century texts, one striking feature that they share (with only a few notable exceptions) is the scriptural premise of humanity's common descent—a shared lineage that traces its history back to Adam and Eve. If Voltaire and arguably Hume defended polygenesis—the blasphemous theory that human variety could only be accounted for with reference to multiple origins—the very novelty and controversy such a position represented only attests to the continued power and authority of Christian theology in the early modern period. As Colin Kidd argues, for seventeenth- and eighteenth-century European thinkers, "scripture dictated that beneath the world's ethnic diversity there was a web of family relationships" (2006: 58). In other words, early modern representations of difference presumed, as their philosophical point of departure, the fact of human sameness. Thus, despite the differences that inform the philosophical works of the seventeenth- and eighteenth-century philosophers Thomas Hobbes (1588–1679), John Locke (1632–1704), and Jean-Jacques Rousseau, they all build their respective accounts of the origins of political society on the foundations of a universal human nature—exemplified by New World inhabitants (Seth 2010: 61–118). And even though neither Buffon nor de Pauw shared Rousseau's romantic account of noble savages, their natural philosophy similarly rested upon a monogenetic understanding of human history. The same can be said for the authors of taxonomies—although Bernier, Linneaus, and Blumenbach cataloged human variety within a hierarchical and normative order, it was an order contained within a singular and unifying theory of man's shared origins. In other words, it was precisely human unity that made alterity a source of endless debate and fascination for seventeenth- and eighteenth-century European thought; Christian theology both enabled the recognition of human variety while simultaneously divesting such differences of any scriptural authority (Kidd 2006).

Finally, despite the seeming absence of a coherent interpretive framework there did, in fact, exist an internally regulated and organized system of reasoning that underwrote seventeenth- and eighteenth-century representations of the Amerindians, Asians, and Africans (Seth 2010: 190–209). A crucial condition of early modern European thought was the pliable, mutable, and porous nature of bodies (Seth 2010: 173–226). The foundational premise that human bodies were malleable ensured that seventeenth- and eighteenth-century accounts of gender and race were necessarily fluid and unstable. It is for this reason that, in 1726, the case of Mary Toft was something of a popular sensation in London. The wife of a poor cloth worker, Toft claimed to have given birth to a rabbit—indeed, by the conclusion of the controversy she had given birth to some seventeen rabbits. While her hoax was finally uncovered, the plausibility of her story was not rejected outright, for it was in keeping with long-established medical knowledge that a mother's imagination could imprint itself on her unborn child. Toft accounted for her unusual condition by recounting her fright when a rabbit suddenly jumped in her path during her pregnancy. The resultant shock produced rabbits rather than a human child. Significantly, it was not only the credulity of the public that was tested—some of the most notable medical practitioners in London, the king's surgeon included, testified to the truth of her rabbit-births (Todd 1995: 1–37). While we are inclined today to interpret the Toft case as a reflection of the superstition and irrationality of an earlier age, the plausibility of rabbit-births was entirely in keeping with the premise that bodies are inherently unstable. As with reproduction, so too with race: the unfamiliar bodies encountered by Europeans in the Americas, Africa, and Asia were not presumed to be fixed, but rather, as we have seen, the multiplicity of theories that sought to account for physiognomic differences attested to the malleability of bodies. The seventeenth- and eighteenth-century body was not the fixed, measurable, transparent, and passive entity that it was later to become (Seth 2010: 190–209).

TRANSATLANTIC SLAVERY AND RACE

But if it is the case that early modern representations of human variety did not produce a metanarrative of racialized difference, how, then, do we account for African slavery? Slavery, of course, did not begin with the forced removal of Africans—it has a long history stretching back to antiquity. Nor should we assume that slavery was confined to European powers—the "Barbary" slave trade references the north African Barbary coast where, from the sixteenth century Morocco as well as the Ottoman provinces of Algeria and Tunisia conducted slave raids off the coast of European Mediterranean; slaves were also traded across the Sahara (Davis 2003; El Hamel 2013). Finally, the European slave trade was not limited to the Americas—Indian Ocean slavery coexisted with that of the transatlantic trade (Arasaratnam 1995: 195–208; Vink 2003: 131–77).

It is, however, the very scale of transatlantic slavery—the wholesale, forced removal and migration of some six and half million Africans during the eighteenth century alone (Eltis 2001: 43)—that focuses my discussion on what Paul Gilroy (1993) referred to as the "Black Atlantic." Portugal, Spain, France, Holland, and England were all engaged in the lucrative trade of human cargo and Africa was the primary source for the vast majority of slaves shipped to New World colonies. The largest forced migration in recorded history witnessed, between 1500 and 1870, some twelve million Africans transported to the New World. Another one and half million never made it to the shores of the Americas, dying during the "middle passage" between the African coast and the New World (Blackburn 1997b: 3) (Figure 8.3).

In the early years of the conquest and colonization of the Americas, the status of free "blacks" as well as African slaves was relatively fluid. In differing degrees and varying from colony to colony, manumission was possible, free "blacks" could own property, serve on juries and possess firearms, and racial intermarriage was not prohibited (Handlin and Handlin 1950; Breen and Innes

FIGURE 8.3: Point of No Return Monument detail, infamous gateway of slavery, Route of Slaves (Route des Esclaves), Ouidah, Benin. Credit: Gallo Images.

1980). But the barbarous and oftentimes sadistic cruelty meted out to African slaves (the separation of families, rape and sexual exploitation, the whippings, facial brandings, plantation labor, savage punishments, and the power over life and death—treatment that was to be sanctioned and enshrined in a cascade of slave laws in the late seventeenth and eighteenth centuries)—has rightly come to define the horrors of modern chattel slavery in the New World. Moreover, the defense of African enslavement in the last hundred years of the slave trade was built upon racial theories that distinguished Africans as biologically, morally, and intellectually inferior. None of these facts are in dispute. But did racial differentiation provide the intellectual, political, and economic scaffolding of African enslavement from its infancy in the sixteenth and seventeenth centuries? (Figure 8.4).

Not surprisingly, the debate concerning the origins of race has been equally contentious and controversial in the contemporary scholarship on modern slavery. While the literature itself is complex and varied (Vaughan 1995: 136–74), the source of conflict can be succinctly identified as follows: was the transatlantic slave trade born of a racism that preceded it, or was racial thinking the outgrowth and consequence of the slave trade? Scholars agree that, for a multitude of reasons, slavery as it existed in the ancient and medieval Old World was radically different from its modern counterpart (Blackburn 1997a). Most significantly for our purposes, slave status was not defined through a

FIGURE 8.4: Vintage engraving of a Plantation Master with whip at the Slave market, while a man begs not to be separated from his son and daughter. From the antislavery story De planter brunel en zijne slaven asa en neno, by Henderikus Christophorus Schetsberg, Netherlands. 1858. Credit: duncan1890 via Getty Images.

racial logic. The very etymology of the English word "slave" (as well as its European counterparts) has its roots in *"Slav"*—denoting people of Slavic descent (Davis 2006: 49). Moreover, Davis cites the figure of "well over a million western Europeans from Italy, Spain, Portugal, Holland and Britain" who were enslaved by Muslim conquerors between 1550 and the early nineteenth century (2006: 78).

There is surprisingly limited sustained conversation between scholars on the origins of race in Europe and the significance of race in the early history of modern slavery (Boulukos 2008: 1–37). Nevertheless, given the transatlantic slave trade began in the sixteenth century, it is reasonable to conclude that if racism is posited as a causal factor in the emergence of modern slavery, then the organizing of human populations through racial categories was already a feature of premodern European thought. While the literature in defense of such a position is extensive, some works are particularly worth noting.

As early as 1959 Carl Degler argued that in contrast to the English experience, race was not a determining factor in the Spanish and Portuguese slave trade because of the influence of the Catholic Church, the continuation of Roman slave laws wherein "the legal status of the slave was [already] fixed before the Negro came to America" (1959: 52), and because the Iberian peninsula boasted a long history of exposure and "contact . . . with darker-skinned peoples" (1959: 50, 52). If these conditions mitigated against the privileging of race in the early years of the Spanish and Portuguese slave trade, the very absence of such historical constraints promised an altogether different slave experience in the English colonies where "the status of the Negro . . . was worked out within a framework of discrimination" ensuring "that from the outset, . . . the Negro was treated as an inferior to the white man, servant or free" (1959: 52).

Winthrop Jordan's majestic and influential work *White Over Black* (1968), similarly distinguishes between the early Iberian and English slave settlements. For Jordan, it is the confluence of a lack of contact and thus unfamiliarity with Africans as well as a long cultural history of pejorative associations with the concept of "blackness" that ensured the predominance of racial prejudice within the English colonies. As early as the sixteenth century Jordan argues, "'white' and 'black' connoted purity and filthiness, virginity and sin, virtue and baseness, beauty and ugliness, beneficence and evil, God and the devil" (1968: 7). Such long standing attitudes congealed in the body of the African slave: "It was important, if incalculably so, that English discovery of black Africans came at a time when the accepted standard of ideal beauty was a fair complexion of rose and white. Negroes not only failed to fit this ideal but seemed the very picture of perverse negation" (1968: 9).

Scholars who are otherwise sympathetic to Jordan's thesis that racial prejudice preceded and sanctioned African slavery, are nevertheless cautious in presuming a direct correlation between the abstraction of color and its attendant cultural associations, and actual bodies. David Davis, for example, argues that "it would be simplistic to assume that the negative associations evoked by the abstract absence of color were automatically applied to specific people who happened to have black or near black skin" (2006: 57). And yet, of the four preconditions Davis offers for premodern anti-black racism, he concedes that such cultural associations did contribute to the European disdain of Africans.

Given that much of the literature on New World slavery has been heavily skewed toward British involvement in the slave trade, James Sweet's focus on Portugal and Spain provides an important addition to the debate. Parting company with both Degler and Jordan, Sweet maintains that far from offering a contrast to racially encoded slave systems within the English colonies, the roots of slavery's racial logic was first established, as early as the fifteenth century, on the Iberian peninsula (1997: 144). Influenced by the Islamic slave trade and the already racist association between sub-Saharan Africans and slavery within the Islamic world, Portuguese and Spanish traders were predisposed, Sweet argues, to identifying "blacks" as inherently inferior. While Sweet acknowledges that "the Portuguese showed no clear preference for either white or black slaves" prior to the mid-fifteenth century, he nevertheless insists that "the subordination of blacks due to racial and cultural factors had long been a feature of Portuguese life" (1997: 156). Indeed, while Muslims may have "created a plethora of racist ideas" it was "the Iberians who, in conjunction with a rising demand for slave labor, turned these ideas into a coherent ideology" (1997: 162). They did so, moreover, long before their active participation in New World chattel slavery. "Iberian racism," Sweet concludes, "was a necessary precondition for the system of human bondage that would develop in the Americas during the sixteenth century and beyond" (1997: 166).

There are a number of reasons why a host of scholars on the transatlantic slave trade have challenged the thesis that New World slavery was the outgrowth of preexisting racial ideas within Europe. For these scholars, race, far from being a prelude to slavery, was the consequence of its entrenchment. In his influential work *Capitalism and Slavery*, Eric Williams argued that "Slavery was not born of racism: rather, racism was the consequence of slavery" (1980: 7). Williams, a Marxist historian, was not alone in arguing that the choice of Africans for transportation as slaves to the New World colonies was not born out of a racial logic, but an economic imperative. Robin Blackburn maintains that the turn to a wholesale reliance on African slaves in the New World "was made on economic grounds by merchants and planters who found out, by trial and error, that a construction of the economic based on racial exploitation served their purposes well" (1997b: 315), while Seymour Drescher insists that "Capitalism provided the principal motives and ideological underpinnings of British Atlantic slavery" (1987: 20). The grounds for identifying an economic rather than racial explanation for slavery rests in part on the fact that African slave labor coexisted with indigenous slavery and European indentured servitude. As Edmund Morgan argues in the context of seventeenth-century Virginia, "before 1660, it might have been difficult to distinguish racial prejudice from class prejudice" (2003: 327). In other words, we cannot presume that racial distinctions were the presumptive logic that underwrote and defined economic relations in the early years of North American settlement. Indeed, the prohibitive expense of

African slaves (between 1767 and 1775 in Maryland and Virginia, African slaves were priced at triple the cost of Irish or English convicts [Eltis 2000: 66]) ensured that until the latter part of the seventeenth century, Indian slaves and European indentured servants were the preferred source of labor on plantations, mines, and as domestic workers. The Spanish, Portuguese, and, to a lesser extent, the French and English all relied on indigenous slaves; indeed, despite a 1681 decree banning the enslavement of indigenous peoples in the Spanish-American colonies, it is estimated that as late as the mid-nineteenth century at least 2,000 Indians were still enslaved in New Mexico (Guasco 2008: 71). In Portuguese Brazil, the plantation economy in 1600 was still dominated by Indian rather than African slaves (Curtin 1990: 53). Similarly, in the British Carolinas some 30,000 to 50,000 Indians were enslaved before 1715 (that is, one in four of the slave population was Indian [Guasco 2008: 73]), while in French Canada, Amerindians provided the overwhelming source of slave labor (Eltis 2000: 63).

But it was "white" indentured servitude that defined the dominant source of labor in the British New World colonies in the seventeenth century—and, to a lesser degree, in the French Americas (Eltis 2000: 195; Guasco 2008: 73–4). Guasco estimates that of a population of 120,000 emigrants in Chesapeake in the seventeenth century, about 90,000 were indentured servants (2008: 74; also see Tomlins 2001: 5–43). Indeed, as late as 1770 convict arrivals outnumber slaves by at least two to one (the only exception to this trend being the decades of the 1730s and 1740s [Eltis 2000: 69]). In Barbados in 1655, approximately 12,000 Irish Catholics, political prisoners, orphans, convicts, and the homeless in Britain were forcibly removed to work on plantations in Barbados (Donoghue 2010: 960). Guasco calculates that through the course of the seventeenth century some 50,000 to 75,000 white indentured servants were transported to the British Caribbean. By the eighteenth century, some 150,000 Europeans (including Irish, Germans, and Scots) came to the New World in bondage (2008: 74–5).

Unfree "white" labor took multiple forms. To supply the English colony of Virginia, migrants in Europe would sell their labor for anywhere between four to seven years, "literally condemning themselves to bondage, in exchange for a passage to the Americas" (Guasco 2008: 73). French colonial policies were similar: of the total European population in early seventeenth-century French Antilles, a quarter were European indentured servants and slaves (Curtin 1990: 84). But in many other instances, unfree "white" labor in the colonies was provided by the forced deportation of political prisoners, convicts, orphans, and the homeless. Indeed, as demand for labor on expanding tobacco and sugar plantations increased in the mid-seventeenth century, a lucrative market of kidnapping and forced transportation of immigrants followed suit, as too did a new vocabulary: "New words such as 'spiriting', 'Barbadosed' and 'kidnapping' entered the English language, denoting the fraudulent and violent practices by which people from Britain and Ireland were lured or forced away from their own communities and coerced into colonial bond slavery" (Donoghue 2010: 951).

Some scholars have also suggested that the treatment of indentured servants was not significantly different from that of African and Indian slaves in the early years of settlement (Handlin and Handlin 1950: 199–222; Curtin 1990: 197; Fields 1990: 102–4; Morgan 1991: 169–73; Guasco 2008: 75; Donoghue 2010: 952). While indentured servitude did not entail lifetime bondage, the high mortality rate suggests that many bonded laborers died before the conclusion of a seven-year term (Fields 1990: 103–4; Morgan 2004: 297; Guasco 2008: 75). Indentured servants from Britain and Ireland were bought, sold, whipped, beaten, branded, weighed on scales, auctioned, resold to pay for their master's debts, starved, and at times killed with impunity (Breen and Innes 1980: 62–7; Fields 1990: 102; Guasco 2008: 75; Donoghue 2010: 952). Philip Morgan argues that "Irishmen, in particular, were viewed with almost as much contempt as Africans" in the late seventeenth and eighteenth century (1991: 197).

In dramatizing the treatment of indentured servants, none of these scholars seek to diminish the horrors of the African slave trade. Their combined work does, however, seek to emphasize the absence of a congealed racial logic where class stratification and property relations within an emerging capitalist economy played a more profound and prominent role in the early years of colonial settlement. Social differentiation and hierarchical relations, Breen and Innes conclude in their study of seventeenth-century Northampton County, Virginia, were not primarily "affected by the color of a man's skin, but by his economic status" (1980: 111).

Those scholars for whom capitalist imperatives rather than racial prejudice provided the crucial impetus for the origins of the African slave trade, have also privileged shifting economic conditions for the wholesale transition to African slavery in the late seventeenth century and the racial theories that were increasingly mounted in its defense. In this context, the Bacon Rebellion of 1676 is commonly identified as a pivotal turning point in labor relations within the British mainland and islands. An insurrection for control of the Virginia colony was the result of an alliance between disgruntled freedmen, indentured servants, and African slaves who proceeded to burn the capital, plunder the property of Governor Blakely and his loyalists, and temporarily force them into hiding. Similar, albeit less dramatic, cooperation between slaves and servants was also evident in the British Caribbean. In 1661 Bermuda, a planned revolt involving Irish servants and African slaves was discovered, and in Barbados "the first recorded instance of a maroon group (in 1665) was a multiracial coalition of Irish servants and slaves" (Morgan 1991: 196). But of course, it is the slave revolution that brought independence to Haiti in 1804 that shook New World European slave colonies to the core. The years 1788 to 1804 saw confused and shifting alliances between a "white" colonial aristocracy, a "white" petit bourgeoisie consisting of small planters, clerks, shopkeepers, and skilled workers, a French-mulatto population (some of whom were themselves wealthy slave owners), freedmen, and an enslaved African population (James 1963; Geggus 1989: 1290–1308; Curtin 1990: 158–69). The potential volatility of such class disparities and the alliances they made possible was finally realized in the first successful slave rebellion in recorded history.

While the French proved unsuccessful in quashing Haitian independence, the danger of such class alliances had, through the course of the seventeenth century, already been registered in other European colonies inciting an array of new laws that effectively institutionalized, systematized, and entrenched African slavery. In 1664, Maryland formalized legal codes establishing slavery for life, regulated "white"–"black" sexual relations and introduced manumission restrictions. In 1675, the Nevis legislature passed a law prohibiting servant and slaves to "company" or drink together (Morgan 1991: 196). In French Louisiana, the 1724 Code Noir saw the introduction of a systematic codification of laws that, among other things, forbade slaves of different masters from congregating, banned the selling or trading of commodities, and forbade slaves from possessing firearms. Significantly, as with the 1664 Maryland law, the Code Noir expressly forbade sexual relations between freemen (Europeans, free "blacks," and "coloreds") and African slaves. For much of the colony's history, "social relations were more fluid and social hierarchy less established" but it was exactly this social fluidity that, Jennifer Spear argues, "made it even more imperative to regulate sexual relations, marriage and reproduction" (2003: 91). For both Spear and Barbara Fields, it is through the codification, regulation, and implementation of laws that sharply delineated and distinguished slave status from all other forms of labor that the discourse of race came to define New World slavery. As Fields argues in reference to the Maryland law, "*Race* does not explain that law. Rather, the law shows society in the act of inventing race" (990: 107, original emphasis).

It would, however, be simplistic to suggest that the fear of potential alliances between slaves, servants, and indentured workers alone led to the entrenchment and racialization of slave laws. Other factors, such as a decline in European immigration to the Americas, the devastation of indigenous populations, the massive increase in the transatlantic African slave trade, the subsequent reduction in price for purchasing human cargo, the expansion of the plantation system, and resistance to a growing anti-abolitionist movement, all collectively informed what was to become the defining feature of New World slavery: its complete and unabashed defense of racial difference.

What is clear is that appeals to racial theories had a purchase in the New World colonies long before racial science became an orthodoxy in nineteenth-century Europe. Indeed, the more immediate and urgent need—economic, political, and social—of New World planters, merchants, and free "whites" to defend slavery has led some scholars to argue that racial and racist theories find their first sustained and systematic expression in distant colonies far removed from the metropole (Belmessous 2005; Seth, forthcoming) If, following Ann Stoler, the colonies were "laboratories of modernity" (1995: 15), then the slave systems of the New World provided the petri-dish for European racial science.

ACKNOWLEDGMENT

The author would like to thank Catherine Jones, Gregory O'Malley, Suman Seth, and Mark Weller whose expertise I availed of for references and guidance on this paper.

FURTHER READING

Acemoglu, Daron, Simon Johnson, and James Robinson (2005), "The Rise of Europe: Atlantic Trade, Institutional Change, and Economic Growth," *American Economic Review*, 95 (3): 546–79.
Acomb, Frances (1950), *Anglophobia in France: 1763–1789*, Durham, NC: Duke University Press.
Adelman, Jeremy (2006), *Sovereignty and Revolution in the Iberian Atlantic*, Princeton, NJ: Princeton University Press.
Aksan, Virginia (2013), *Ottoman Wars, 1700–1870: An Empire Besieged*, London: Routledge.
Aksan, Virginia (2015), "The Ottoman Army," in *European Armies of the French Revolution*, ed. Frederick C. Schneid, 245–72, Norman, OK: University of Oklahoma Press.
Aldridge, Alfred (1971), *The Ibero-American Enlightenment*, Champaign, IL: University of Illinois Press.
Analyse des papiers anglois (1787–8), Paris: Lejay fils.
Andaya, Barbara (2006), *The Flaming Womb: Repositioning Women in Early Modern Southeast Asia*, Honolulu, HI: University of Hawai'i Press.
Anderson, Virginia DeJohn (1994), "King Philip's Herds: Indians, Colonists, and the Problem of Livestock in Early New England," *William and Mary Quarterly*, 51 (4): 601–24.
Andrews, Walter G. and Mehmet Kalpakli (2005), *The Age of Beloveds: Love and the Beloved in Early Modern Ottoman and European Culture and Society*, Durham, NC: Duke University Press.
Antunes, Cátia, Erik Odegard, and Joris van den Tol (2015), "The Networks of Dutch Brazil: Rise, Entanglement and Fall of a Colonial Dream," in *Exploring the Dutch Empire: Agents, Networks and Institutions, 1600–1800*, ed. Cátia Antunes and Jos Gommans, 77–94, London: Bloomsbury Academic.
Arditi, Jorge (1998), *A Genealogy of Manners: Transformations of Social Relations in France and England from the Fourteenth to the Eighteenth Century*, Chicago, IL: University of Chicago Press.

Arasaratnam, Sinnappah (1995), "Slave Trade in the Indian Ocean in the Seventeenth Century," in *Mariners, Merchants and Oceans: Studies in Maritime History*, ed. K.S. Mathews, 195–208, New Delhi: Manohar.

Aslanian, Sebouh David (2011), *From the Indian Ocean to the Mediterranean: The Global Trade Networks of Armenian Merchants from New Julfa*, Berkeley, CA: University of California Press.

Aubert, Guillaume (2004), "'The Blood of France': Race and Purity of Blood in the French-Atlantic World," *William and Mary Quarterly*, 61 (3): 439–78.

Babeau, Albert (1890), *La vie militaire sous l'ancien Régime*, Paris: Firmin-Didot.

Bailyn, Bernard (2005), *Atlantic History: Concept and Contours*, Cambridge, MA: Harvard University Press.

Baker, Keith (1987), "Politics and Public Opinion Under the Old Regime: Some Reflections," in *Press and Politics in Pre-Revolutionary France*, ed. Jack Censer and Jeremy Popkin, 205–46, Berkeley, CA: University of California Press.

Ballantyne, Tony (2012), *Webs of Empire: Locating New Zealand's Colonial Past*, Wellington: Bridget Williams Books.

Bamford, Paul (1956), *Forests and French Sea Power: 1660–1789*, Toronto: University of Toronto Press.

Bayly, C.A. (1989), *Imperial Meridian: The British Empire and The World: 1780–1830*, London: Addison-Wesley Longman.

Bell, David A. (2007), *The First Total War*, Boston, MA: Houghton Mifflin.

Belmessous, Saliha (2005), "Assimilation and Racialism in Seventeenth- and Eightennth-Century French Colonial Policy," *American Historical Review*, 110 (2): 322–49.

Belmessous, Saliha (2013), *Assimilation and Empire: Uniformity in French and British Colonies, 1541–1954*, Part I, New York: Oxford University Press.

Berg, Maxine (1991), "Women's Work and the Industrial Revolution," in *ReFresh: Recent Findings in Economic and Social History*, 12: 1–4, http://www.ehs.org.uk/dotAsset/03e09441-1fde-4aac-812a-79f18507fcc4.pdf, accessed December 20, 2016.

Biggs, David Andrew (2012), *Quagmire: Nation-Building and Nature in the Mekong Delta*, Seattle, WA: University of Washington Press.

Bindman, David (2002), *Ape to Apollo*, London: Reaktion Books.

Blackburn, Robin (1997a), "The Old World Background to European Colonial Slavery," *William and Mary Quarterly*, 54 (1): 65–102.

Blackburn, Robin (1997b), *The Making of New World Slavery*, London: Verso.

Blakely, Allison (1993), *Blacks in the Dutch World*, Bloomington, IN: Indiana University Press.

Blanning, T.C.W. (1986), *The Origins of the French Revolutionary Wars*, New York: Longman.

Bleichmar, Daniela (2012), *Visible Empire: Botanical Expeditions and Visual Culture in the Hispanic Enlightenment*, Chicago, IL: University Of Chicago Press.

Boogaart, Ernst van den (1982), "Colour Prejudice and the Yardstick of Civility: The Initial Dutch Confrontation with Black Africans, 1590–1635," in *Racism and Colonialism*, ed. Robert Ross, 33–54, Dordrecht: Springer.

Bouille, Pierre H. (1985), "In Defense of Slavery: Eighteenth-Century Opposition to Abolition and the Origins of a Racist Ideology in France," in *History from Below: Studies in Popular Protest and Popular Ideology in Honor of George Rudé*, ed. Fredrick Krantz, 221–41, Montreal: Concordia University Press.

Boulukos, George (2008), *The Grateful Slave*, Cambridge: Cambridge University Press.

Bouton, Cynthia (1993), *The Flour War: Gender, Class and Community in Late Ancien Régime French Society*, University Park, PA: Pennsylvania State University Press.
Bradley James and Dale Van Kley, eds (2001), *Religion and Politics in Enlightenment Europe*, Notre Dame, IN: University of Notre Dame Press.
Branca, Sonia (1999), "Dictionnaires et sens social du mot 'Guerre' aux XVIIe et XVIIIe siècles," in *L'Armée au XVIIIe siècle (1715–1789)*, ed. Geneviève Goubier-Robert, 67–79, Aix-en-Provence: Publications de l'Université de Provence.
Braude, Benjamin (1997), "The Sons of Noah," *William and Mary Quarterly*, 54 (1): 103–42.
Braudel, Fernand (1996), *The Mediterranean and the Mediterranean World in the Age of Philip II*, Berkeley, CA: University of California Press.
Breen, T.H. and Stephen Innes (1980), *Myne Owne Ground*, New York: Oxford University Press.
Brooke, John L (2014), *Climate Change and the Course of Global History: A Rough Journey*, New York: Cambridge University Press.
Brooks, George E. (2003), *Eurafricans in Western Africa: Commerce, Social Status, Gender, and Religious Observance from the Sixteenth to the Eighteenth Century*, Athens, OH: Ohio University Press.
Brouwer, Hendrick and Henk den Heijer (2015), *Goud en indianen: het journaal van Hendrick Brouwers expeditie naar Chili in 1643*, Zutphen: Walburg Pers.
Brumwell, Stephen (2002), *Redcoats: The British Soldier and the War in the Americas, 1755–1763*, Cambridge: Cambridge University Press.
Bryant, Gerald (1978), "Officers of the East India Company's Army in the Days of Clive and Hastings," *Journal of Imperial and Commonwealth History*, 6: 203–27.
Burbank, Jane and Frederick Cooper (2010), *Empires in World History: Power and the Politics of Difference*, Princeton, NJ: Princeton University Press.
Burke, Peter (2009), *Popular Culture in Early Modern Europe*, 3rd edn, London: Routledge.
Burnard, Trevor and John Garrigus (2016), *The Plantation Machine: Atlantic Capitalism in French Saint-Domingue and British Jamaica*, Philadelphia, PA: University of Pennsylvania Press.
Butterwick, Richard, Simon Davies, and Gabriel Sánchez Espinosa, eds (2008), *Peripheries of the Enlightenment*, Oxford: Voltaire Foundation.
Calaresu, Melissa, Filippo de Vivo, and Joan-Pau Rubiés (2010), *Exploring Cultural History: Essays in Honour of Peter Burke*, Burlington, VT: Ashgate.
Cañizares-Esguerra, Jorge (2006), *Nature, Empire, and Nation: Explorations of the History of Science in the Iberian World*, Palo Alto, CA: Stanford University Press.
Carrera, Magal M. (2003), *Imagining Identity in New Spain: Pace, Lineage, and the Colonial Body in Portraiture and Casta Paintings*, Austin, TX: University of Texas Press.
Chakrabarty, Dipesh (2000), *Provincializing Europe: Postcolonial Thought and Historical Difference*, Princeton NJ: Princeton University Press.
Chaplin, Joyce, E. (2002), "Race," in *The British Atlantic World 1500–1800*, ed. David Armitage, 154–72, Basingstoke: Palgrave Macmillan.
Chartier, Roger, ed. (1989), *A History of Private Life, Vol. III: Passions of the Renaissance*, trans. Arthur Goldhammer, Cambridge, MA: Harvard University Press.
Chaumont, Chevalier de, Abbé de Choisy ([1685] 1997), *Aspects of the Embassy to Siam, 1685*, trans. Michael Smithies, Chiang Mai: Silkworm Books.
Cheney, Paul (2010), *Revolutionary Commerce: Globalization and the French Monarchy*, Cambridge, MA: Harvard University Press.

Cohen, William B. (1980), *The French Encounter with Africans: White Response to Blacks, 1530–1880*, Bloomington, IN: Indiana University Press.
Colbert, Jean-Baptiste ([1679] 1861) "Letter to M. Rouillé," and "Letter to T. Morant," in *Lettres, instructions, et mémoires de Colbert publiés d'après les orders de l'empereur*, Paris: Imprimerie imperial.
Coller, Ian (2014), "Rousseau's Turban: Entangled Encounters of Europe and Islam in the Age of Enlightenment," *Historical Reflections*, 40 (2): 56–77.
Colley, Linda (2007), *The Ordeal of Elizabeth Marsh: A Woman in World History*, New York: Pantheon.
Collins, James B. (1995), *The State in Early Modern France*, Cambridge: Cambridge University Press.
Conway, Stephen (2014), "The Eighteenth-Century British Army as a European Institution," in *Britain's Soldiers: Rethinking War and Society, 1715–1815*, ed. Kevin Linch and Matthew McCormack, 17–38, Liverpool: Liverpool University Press.
Cook, Harold J. (2008), *Matters of Exchange: Commerce, Medicine, and Science in the Dutch Golden Age*, New Haven, CT: Yale University Press.
Corvisier, André (1964), *L'Armée française de la fin du XVIIème siècle au ministère de Choiseul. Le soldat*, Paris: Presses universitaire de France.
Crosby, Alfred W. (1972), *The Columbian Exchange; Biological and Cultural Consequences of 1492*, Westport, CT: Greenwood Publishing.
Crosby, Alfred W. (1986), *Ecological Imperialism: The Biological Expansion of Europe, 900–1900*, New York: Cambridge University Press.
Crosby, Alfred W. (2006), *Children of the Sun: A History of Humanity's Unappeasable Appetite for Energy*, New York: W.W. Norton.
Crouch, Christiane (2014), *Nobility Lost: French and Canadian Martial Cultures, Indians, and the End of New France*, Ithaca, NY: Cornell University Press.
Crowston, Clare Haru (2013), *Credit, Fashion, Sex: Economies of Regard in Old Regime France*, Durham, NC: Duke University Press.
Cruz, Anne J. and Maria Galli Stampino, eds (2013), *Early Modern Habsburg Women: Transnational Contexts, Cultural Conflicts, Dynastic Continuities*, Burlington, VT: Ashgate.
Curran, Kevin (2009), *Marriage, Performance, and Politics at the Jacobean Court*, London, Routledge.
Curtin, Philip D. (1990), *The Rise and Fall of the Plantation Complex*, Cambridge: Cambridge University Press.
Curtin, Philip D. (1998), *The Rise and Fall of the Plantation Complex: Essays in Atlantic History*, 2nd edn, New York: Cambridge University Press.
Curtis, Benjamin (2013), *The Habsburgs: History of a Dynasty*, London: Bloomsbury.
Da Costa, Emila Viotti (1985), "The Portuguese-African Slave Trade: A Lesson in Colonialism," *Latin American Perspectives*, 12 (1): 42–61.
Daumalin, Xavier, Nicole Girard, and Olivier Raveux, eds (2003), *Du Savon à la Puce: L'Industrie marseillaise du XVIIe siècle à nos jours*, Marseille: Jeanne Laffitte.
Davis, David Brion (2006), *Inhuman Bondage*, Oxford: Oxford University Press.
Davis, Natalie Zemon (1997), *Women on the Margins: Three Seventeenth-Century Lives*, Cambridge, MA: Harvard University Press.
Davis, Robert C. (2003), *Christian Slaves, Muslim Masters*, Basingstoke: Palgrave Macmillan.
Degler, Carl N. (1959), "Slavery and the Genesis of American Race Prejudice," *Comparative Studies in Society and History*, 2 (1): 49–66.

de Vries, Jan (2008), *The Industrious Revolution: Consumer Behavior and the Household Economy, 1650 to the Present*, Cambridge: Cambridge University Press.

de Vries, Jan and A.M. van der Woude (1997), *The First Modern Economy: Success, Failure, and Perseverance of the Dutch Economy, 1500–1815*, New York: Cambridge University Press.

Dew, Nicholas (2009), *Orientalism in Louis XIV's France*, Oxford: Oxford University Press.

Dewald, Jonathan (1996), *The European Nobility 1400–1800*, Cambridge: Cambridge University Press.

Diderot, Denis ([1769] 2016), "Regrets on Parting with My Old Dressing Gown," trans. Kate Tunstall and Katie Scott, *Oxford Art Journal*, 39 (2): 175–84.

Diderot, Denis and Jean le Rond d'Alembert, eds (1751–65), *Encyclopédie, ou Dictionnaire raisonné des sciences, des arts et des métiers*, Paris: Briasson.

Disney, A. (2009), *A History of Portugal and the Portuguese Empire: From Beginnings to 1807, Vol. 2: The Portuguese Empire*, New York: Cambridge University Press.

Dixon, Simon (2010), *Catherine the Great*, London, Ecco.

Donahue-Wallace, Kelly (2017), *Jerónimo Antonio Gil and the Idea of the Spanish Enlightenment*, Albuquerque, NM: University of New Mexico Press.

Donavan, Ken (2006), "Germans in Louisbourg, 1713–1758," *The Huissier*, September 13.

Donoghue, John (2010), "'Out of the Land of Bondage': The English Revolution and the Atlantic Origins of Abolition," *American Historical Review*, 115 (4): 943–74.

Drayton, Richard (2000), *Nature's Government: Science, Imperial Britain, and the "Improvement" of the World*, New Haven, CT: Yale University Press.

Drescher, Seymour (1977), *Econocide: British Slavery in the Era of Abolition*, Pittsburgh, PA: University of Pittsburgh Press.

Drescher, Seymour (1987), *Capitalism and Antislavery*, New York: Oxford University Press.

Dubois, Laurent (1999), "'The Price of Liberty': Victor Hugues and the Administration of Freedom in Guadeloupe, 1794–1798," *William and Mary Quarterly*, 56 (2): 363–92.

Dubois, Laurent (2006), "Citizen Soldiers: Emancipation and Military Service in the Revolutionary French Caribbean," in *Arming Slaves*, ed. Christopher Leslie Brown and Philip D. Morgan, 233–51, New Haven, CT: Yale University Press.

Duindam, Jeroen (2011), *Royal Courts in Dynastic States and Empires: A Global Perspective*, Leiden: Brill.

Dupâquier, Jacques (1970), "French Population in the 17th and 18th Centuries," in *Essays in French Economic History*, ed. Rondo Cameron, 150–69, Homewood, IL: Richard D. Irwin.

Duplessis, Robert (2015), *The Material Atlantic: Clothing, Commerce, and Colonization in the Atlantic World*, Cambridge: Cambridge University Press.

Dursteler, Eric (2006), *Venetians in Constantinople: Nation, Identity and Coexistence in the Early Modern Mediterranean*, Baltimore, MD: Johns Hopkins University Press.

Duruy, Albert (1888), *L'armée royale en 1789*, Paris: Lévy.

Earle, Rebecca (2010), "'If You Eat Their Food . . .': Diets and Bodies in Early Spanish Americas," *American Historical Review*, 115 (3): 688–713.

Earle, Rebecca (2016), "The Pleasure of Taxonomy: Casta Paintings, Classification and Colonialism," *William and Mary Quarterly*, 73 (1): 427–66.

Eldem, Edhem (1999), *French Trade in Istanbul in the Eighteenth Century*, Leiden: Brill.

El Hamel, Chouki (2013), *Black Morocco: A History of Slavery, Race, and Islam*, Cambridge: Cambridge University Press.
Elias, Norbert (1982), *The Civilizing Process, Vol. I: The History of Manners*, New York: Pantheon.
Elias, Norbert ([1939] 2000), *The Civilizing Process*, trans. Edmund Jephcott, Oxford: Oxford University Press.
Eliav-Felden, Miriam, Benjamin Isaac, and Joseph Ziegler (2009), *The Origins of Racism in the West*, Cambridge: Cambridge University Press.
Elliot, Henry (1992), *The Old World and the New, 1492–1650*, Cambridge: Cambridge University Press.
Eltis, David (2000), *The Rise of African Slavery in the Americas*, Cambridge: Cambridge University Press.
Eltis, David (2001), "The Volume and Structure of the Transatlantic Slave Trade: A Reassessment," *William and Mary Quarterly*, 58 (1): 17–46.
Eltis, David and Stanley L. Engerman (2000), "The Importance of Slavery and the Slave Trade to Industrializing Britain," *Journal of Economic History*, 60 (1): 123–44.
Elvin, Mark (2006), *The Retreat of the Elephants: An Environmental History of China*, New Haven, CT: Yale University Press.
Enthoven, Victor (1996), "Suriname and Zeeland: Fifteen Years of Dutch Misery on the Wild Coast, 1667–1682," in *International Conference on Shipping, Factories and Colonization*, ed. J. Everaert and J. Parmentier, 249–60, Brussels: Académie Royale des Sciences d'Outre-Mer.
Erginbaş, Vefa (2013), "Enlightenment in the Ottoman Context: İbrahim Müteferrika and His Intellectual Landscape," in *Historical Aspects of Printing and Publishing in Languages of the Middle East*, ed. Geoffrey Roper, 53–100, Leiden: Brill.
Esguerra, Jorge Cañizares (1999), "New World New Stars: Patriotic Astrology and the Invention of Indian and Creole Bodies in Colonial Spanish America, 1600–1650," *American Historical Review*, 104 (1): 33–68.
Fara, Patricia (2004), *Sex, Botany and Empire: The Story of Carl Linnaeus and Joseph Banks*, Thriplow: Icon Books.
Faroqhi, Suraiya (2015), "The Ottoman Empire and the Islamic World," in *Empires and Encounters 1350–1750*, ed. Wolfgang Reinhard, 221–388, Cambridge, MA: Harvard University Press.
Fatah-Black, Karwan (2013), "Orangism, Patriotism, and Slavery in Curaçao, 1795–1796," *International Review of Social History*, 58 (suppl. 21): 35–60.
Fedman, David Abraham (2015), "The Saw and the Seed: Japanese Forestry in Colonial Korea, 1895–1945," PhD dissertation, Stanford University.
Fénélon, François (1850), *Oeuvres complètes de Fénélon, archevèque de Cambrai*, Paris: Leroux et Jouby.
Fenton, James (1996), "A Short History of Anti-Hamitism," *New York Review of Books*, February 15: 8.
Fernández-Armesto, Felipe (2008), *The World: A Brief History*, Vol. 1, Upper Saddle River, NJ: Prentice-Hall.
Fieffé, Eugène (1854), *Histoire des troupes étrangères au service de France*, Paris: Librairie militaire.
Fields, Barbara Jeanne (1990), "Slavery, Race and Ideology in the United States of America," *New Left Review*, 181: 95–118.
Floor, Willem (1979), "Dutch Painters in Iran during the First Half of the 17th Century," *Persica*, 8: 145–61.

Foucault, Michel (1979), *Discipline and Punish: The Birth of the Prison*, trans. Alan Sheridan, New York: Vintage.
Foucault, Michel (1984), "What is Enlightenment?," in *The Foucault Reader*, ed. Paul Rabinow, 32–50, New York: Pantheon Books.
Fuess, Albrecht and Jan-Peter Hartung, eds (2014), *Court Cultures in the Muslim World: Seventh to Nineteenth Centuries*, London: Routledge.
Gainot, Bernard (2007), *Les officiers de couleur dans les armées de la République et de l'Empire (1792–1815)*, Paris: Editions Karthala.
Gammage, Bill (2013), *The Biggest Estate on Earth: How Aborigines Made Australia*, Sydney: Allen & Unwin.
Garraway, Doris Lorraine (2005), *The Libertine Colony: Creolization in the Early French Caribbean*, Durham, NC: Duke University Press.
Garrigus, J. (1993), "Blue and Brown: Contraband Indigo and the Rise of a Free Colored Planter Class in French Saint-Domingue," *The Americas*, 50 (2): 233–63.
Geggus, David (1989), "Racial Equality, Slavery, and Colonial Secession During the Constituent Assembly," *American Historical Review*, 94 (5): 1290–1308.
Gerbi, Antonelle (1973), *The Dispute of the New World*, trans. Jeremy Moyle, Pittsburgh, PA: University of Pittsburgh Press.
Gerritsen, Anne and Giorgio Riello (2016), "The Global Lives of Things: Material Culture in the First Global Age," in *The Global Lives of Things: The Material Culture of Connections in the Early Modern World*, ed. Anne Gerritsen and Giorgio Riello, 1–28, London: Routledge.
Gilroy, Paul (1993), *The Black Atlantic: Modernity and Double Consciousness*, Cambridge, MA: Harvard University Press.
Glacken, Clarence (1976), *Traces on the Rhodian Shore*, Berkeley, CA: University of California Press.
Glamann, Kristof ([1958] 1981), *Dutch-Asiatic Trade, 1620–1740*, Copenhagen: Danish Science Press.
Godbeer, Richard (2002), *Sexual Revolution in Early America*, Baltimore, MD: Johns Hopkins University Press.
Gommans, Jos (2015), "Merchants among Kings: Dutch Diplomatic Encounters in Asia," in *Asia in Amsterdam: The Culture of Luxury in the Golden Age*, ed. Karina Corrigan, Jan van Campen, and Femke Diercks, 32–9, New Haven, CT: Yale University Press.
Goodman, Dena (1994), *The Republic of Letters: A Cultural History of the French Enlightenment*, Ithaca, NY: Cornell University Press.
Goodman, Dena, ed. (2003), *Marie Antoinette: Writings on the Body of a Queen*, London: Routledge.
Gosselink, Martine (2015), "The Dutch East Indian Company in Asia," in *Asia in Amsterdam: The Culture of Luxury in the Golden Age*, ed. Karina Corrigan, Jan van Campen, and Femke Diercks, 21–31, New Haven, CT: Yale University Press.
Goucher, Candice (2013), *Congotay! Congotay! A Global History of Caribbean Food*, Armonk, NY: Routledge.
Grafton, Anthony (1992), *New Worlds, Ancient Texts*, Cambridge, MA: Harvard University Press.
Greenfield, Amy Butler (2009), *A Perfect Red: Empire, Espionage, and the Quest for the Color of Desire*, New York: Harper Collins.
Grove, Richard H. (1995), *Green Imperialism: Colonial Expansion, Tropical Island Edens and the Origins of Environmentalism, 1600–1860*, New York: Cambridge University Press.

Guasco, Michael (2008), "From Servitude to Slavery," in *The Atlantic World, 1450–2000*, ed. Toyin Falola and Kevin D. Roberts, 69–95, Bloomington, IN: Indiana University Press.

Guinier, Arnaud (2014), *L'Honneur du soldat: Ethique martiale et discipline guerrière dans la France des Lumières*, Ceyzérieu: Éditions Champ-Vallon.

Guiomar, Jean-Yves (2004), *L'invention de la guerre totale, XVIIIe–XXe siècle*, Paris: Félin.

Gutiérrez, Ramón A. (1991), *When Jesus Came, the Corn Mothers Went Away: Marriage, Sexuality, and Power in New Mexico 1500–1846*, Stanford, CA: Stanford University Press.

Hamilton, Douglas (2005), *Scotland, The Caribbean and the Atlantic World, 1750–1820*, Manchester: Manchester University Press.

Hancock, David (1995), *Citizens of the World*, Cambridge: Cambridge University Press.

Handlin, Oscar and Mary F. Handlin (1950), "Origins of the Southern Labor System," *William and Mary Quarterly*, 7 (2): 199–222.

Hannaford, Ivan (1996), *Race*, Baltimore, MD: Johns Hopkins University Press.

Hansen, Viveka and Lars Hansen (2007), *The Linnaeus Apostles: Global Science and Adventure*, Whitby: IK Foundation.

Haulman, Kate (2014), *The Politics of Fashion in Eighteenth-Century America*, Chapel Hill, NC: University of North Carolina Press.

Havard, Gilles (2003), *Empire et métissage: Indiens et Français dans le Pays d'an Haut 1660–1715*, Sillery: Septentrion.

Havard, Gilles and Cécile Vidal (2008), *Histoire de l'Amérique française*, Paris: Flammarion.

Haythornthwaite, Philip J. and William Younghusband (1994), *The Austrian Army 1740–80: Infantry*, Oxford: Osprey.

Hazard, Paul ([1935] 2013), *The Crisis of the European Mind, 1680–1715*, New York: New York Review of Books.

Heijer, Henk den (2005), "'Over warme en koude landen': Mislukte Nederlandse volksplantingen op de Wilde Kust in de zeventiende eeuw," *De Zeventiende Eeuw*, 21 (1): 79–90.

Hersh, Jonathan and Hans-Joachim Voth (2009), "Sweet Diversity: Colonial Goods and the Rise of European Living Standards after 1492," SSRN Scholarly Paper ID 1402322, Rochester, NY: Social Science Research Network, https://papers.ssrn.com/abstract=1402322.

Hertzberg, Arthur (1990), *The French Enlightenment and the Jews*, New York: Columbia University Press.

Hesse, Carla (2001), *The Other Enlightenment: How French Women Became Modern*, Princeton, NJ: Princeton University Press.

Hobbes, Thomas ([1651] 2008), *Leviathan*, Oxford: Oxford University Press.

Hobsbawm, Eric (1954), "The Crisis of the Seventeenth Century," *Past and Present*, 5/6.

Hotz, Robert Lee (1995), "Scientists Say Race Has No Biological Basis," *Los Angeles Times*, February 20, http://articles.latimes.com/1995-02-20/news/mn-34098_1_biological-basis, accessed February 28, 2017.

Howse, Robert (2006), "Montesquieu on Commerce, Conquest, War, and Peace," *Brooklyn Journal of International Law*, 31: 693–708.

Hsia, R. Po-Chia (2005), *The World of Catholic Renewal, 1540–1770*, 2nd edn, Cambridge: Cambridge University Press.

Hui, Wang (2014), *China from Empire to Nation-State*, Cambridge, MA: Harvard University Press.

Hull, Isabel V. (1996), *Sexuality, State, and Civil Society in Germany, 1700–1815*, Ithaca, NY: Cornell University Press.

Hunt, Lynn and Margaret C. Jacob (2010), *The Book that Changed Europe: Picart & Bernard's Religious Ceremonies of the World*, Cambridge, MA: Harvard University Press.

Hunter, G.K. ([1964] 2000), "Elizabethans and Foreigners," in *Shakespeare and Race*, ed. Catherine M.S. Alexander and Stanley Wells, 37–63, Cambridge: Cambridge University Press.

Ingrao, Charles (2000), *The Hapsburg Monarchy, 1618–1815*, 2nd edn, Cambridge: Cambridge University Press.

Iqbal, Iftekhar (2006), "Towards an Environmental History of East Bengal: Paradigms and Praxis," *Journal of the Asiatic Society of Bangladesh*, 50 (1/2), https://www.academia.edu/10065850/Towards_an_Environmental_History_of_East_Bengal_Paradigms_and_Praxis.

Isaac, Benjamin (2004), *The Invention of Racism in Classical Antiquity*, Princeton, NJ: Princeton University Press.

Israel, Jonathan (1990), *Dutch Primacy in World Trade, 1585–1740*, Oxford: Oxford University Press.

Israel, Jonathan I. (2001), *Radical Enlightenment: Philosophy and the Making of Modernity 1650–1750*, Oxford: Oxford University Press.

Jacob, Margaret C. (1981), *The Radical Enlightenment: Pantheists, Freemasons and Republicans*, London: George Allen & Unwin.

Jacobs, E.M. (1991), *In Pursuit of Pepper and Tea: The Story of the Dutch East India Company*, Amsterdam: Netherlands Maritime Museum.

Jaenen, Cornelius J. (1982), "'Les Sauvages Ameriquains': Persistence into the Eighteenth Century of Traditional French Concepts and Constructs of Comprehending Amerindians," *Ethnohistory*, 29 (1): 43–56.

James, C.L.R. (1963), *The Black Jacobins: Toussaint L'Ouverture and the San Domingo Revolution*, 2nd revised edn, New York: Vintage Books.

Jennings, Ronald C. (1992), *Christians and Muslims in Ottoman Cyprus and the Mediterranean World, 1571–1640*, New York: New York University Press.

Johnson, David (2012), *Imagining the Cape Colony: History, Literature, and the South African Nation*, Edinburgh: Edinburgh University Press.

Jones, Colin (1995), "The Military Revolution and the Professionalisation of the French Army Under the Ancien Régime," in *The Military Revolution Debate: Readings on the Military Transformation of Early Modern Europe*, ed. Clifford Rogers, 149–68, Boulder, CO: Westview Press.

Jones, Ryan Tucker (2014), *Empire of Extinction: Russians and the North Pacific's Strange Beasts of the Sea, 1741–1867*, New York: Oxford University Press.

Jordaan, Han (2011), "Patriots, Privateers and International Politics: The Myth of the Conspiracy of Jean Baptiste Tierce Cadet," in *Curaçao in the Age of Revolutions, 1795–1800*, ed. Wim Klooster and Gert Oostindie, 141–70, Caribbean Series. Leiden: KITLV Press.

Jordan, Winthrop D. (1968), *White Over Black*, Chapel Hill, NC: University of North Carolina Press.

Jourdan, Annie (2008), *La Révolution batave entre la France et l'Amérique (1795–1806)*, Rennes: Presses universitaires de Rennes.

Kant, Immanuel ([1777] 2000), "Of the Different Human Races," in *The Idea of Race*, ed. Robert Bernasconi and Tommy L. Lott, 8–22, Indianapolis, IN: Hackett.

Kant, Immanuel (1795), *Zum ewigen Frieden. Ein philosophischer Entwurf*, Königsberg: Nicolovius.

Karant-Nunn, Susan C. (2012), *The Reformation of Feeling: Shaping the Religious Emotions in Early Modern Germany*, Oxford: Oxford University Press.

Kars, Marjoleine (2009), "Policing and Transgressing Borders: Soldiers and Cross-Cultural Relations in the Berbice Slave Rebellion, 1763–1764," Paper read at the conference on *Multiculturalism, Religion and Legal Status in the Dutch Colonial World, 1600–1960*, University of Maryland Baltimore County, Baltimore, Maryland.

Karténian, Rémy (2000), "Apparences baroques et production textile à Marseille, 1600–1750," *Revue Marseille*, 192: 85–92.

Kessler, Amalia (2004), "A 'Question of Name': Merchant-Court Jurisdiction and the Origins of the Noblesse Commerçante," in *A Vast and Useful Art: The Gustave Gimon Collection on French Political Economy*, ed. Mary-Jane Parrine, 49–65, Stanford, CA: Stanford University Library.

Khazeni, Arash (2014), *Sky Blue Stone: The Turquoise Trade in World History*, Berkeley, CA: University of California Press.

Kidd, Colin (2004), "Ethnicity in the British Atlantic World, 1688–1830," in *A New Imperial History*, ed. Kathleen Wilson, 260–77, Cambridge: Cambridge University Press.

Kidd, Colin (2006), *The Forging of Races*, Cambridge: Cambridge University Press.

Klooster, Wim (2009), *Revolutions in the Atlantic World: A Comparative History*, New York: New York University Press.

Klooster, Wim (2013), "Marteling, muiterij en beeldenstorm: militair geweld in de Nederlandse Atlantische wereld, 1624–1654," in *Geweld in de West: een militaire geschiedenis van de Nederlandse Atlantische wereld, 1600–1800*, ed. Victor Enthoven, Henk den Heijer, and Han Jordaan, 313–43, Leiden: Brill.

Klooster, Wim (2016), *The Dutch Moment: War, Trade, and Settlement in the Seventeenth-Century Atlantic World*, Leiden: Leiden University Press.

Korshak, Yvonne (1987), "The Liberty Cap as a Revolutionary Symbol in America and France," *Smithsonian Studies in American Art*, 1 (2): 53–69.

Kowner, Rotem (2004), "Skin as Metaphor: Early European Racial Views on Japan 1548–1853," *Ethnohistory*, 51 (4): 751–78.

Kwass, Michael (2013), "The Global Underground: Smuggling, Rebellion, and the Origins of the French Revolution," in *The French Revolution in Global Perspective*, ed. Susan Desan, Lynn Hunt, and William Max Nelson, 15–31, Ithaca, NY: Cornell University Press.

Kwass, Michael (2014), *Contraband: Louis Mandrin and the Making of a Global Underground*, Cambridge, MA: Harvard University Press.

Lam, Jan Dirksz (2013), *Expeditie naar de Goudkust: het journaal van Jan Dircksz Lam over de Nederlandse aanval op Elmina, 1624–1626*, ed. Henk den Heijer, Zutphen: Walburg Pers.

Lehner, Ulrich L. (2016), *The Catholic Enlightenment: The Forgotten History of a Global Movement*, Oxford: Oxford University Press.

Lemire, Beverly (2009), "Revising the Historical Narrative: India, Europe and the Cotton Trade, c. 1300–1800," in *The Spinning World: A Global History of Cotton Textiles, 1200–1850*, ed. Giorgio Riello and Prasannan Parthasarathi, 205–26, Oxford: Oxford University Press.

Les Eaux et Forêts du 12e au 20e siècle (1987), Histoire de L'administration Française, Paris: Editions du Centre national de la recherche scientifique.
Lever, Evelyne (2002), *Madame de Pompadour: A Life*, London: Farrar, Straus & Giroux.
Levin, Eve (1989), *Sex and Society in the World of the Orthodox Slavs, 900–1700*, Ithaca, NY: Cornell University Press.
Lieberman, Victor (2003), *Strange Parallels: Southeast Asia in Global Context, c. 800–1830*, New York: Cambridge University Press.
Linebaugh, Peter and Marcus Rediker (2000), *The Many-Headed Hydra: Sailors, Slaves, Commoners, and the Hidden History of the Revolutionary Atlantic*, Boston, MA: Beacon Press.
Locher, Fabien and Grégory Quenet (2009), "L'histoire environnementale: origines, enjeux et perspectives d'un nouveau chantier," *Revue d'histoire moderne et contemporaine*, 56 (4): 7–38.
Loker, Zvi (1981), "An Eighteenth-Century Plan to Invade Jamaica; Isaac Yeshurun Sasportas—French Patriot or Jewish Radical Idealist?," *Transactions & Miscellanies (Jewish Historical Society of England)*, 28: 132–44.
Lorimer, Joyce (1993), "The Failure of the English Guiana Ventures 1595–1667 and James I's Foreign Policy," *Journal of Imperial and Commonwealth History*, 21 (1): 1–30.
Louis XIV (1664), *Declarations du Roy portant établissement d'une Compagnie pour le Commerce des Indes Orientales*, Paris, 1664.
Lowe, Kate (2007), "Representing Africa: Ambassadors and Princes from Christian Africa to Renaissance Italy and Portugal 1402–1608," *Transactions of the Royal Historical Society*, 17: 101–28.
Lynn, John (1997), *Giant of the Grand Siècle: The French Army, 1610–1715*, Cambridge: Cambridge University Press.
Machado, Pedro (2014), *Ocean of Trade: South Asian Merchants, Africa and the Indian Ocean, c. 1750–1850*, Cambridge: Cambridge University Press.
Malthus, T.R. ([1798] 1958), *An Essay on Population*, London: J.M. Dent.
Manning, Patrick, Yun Zhang, and Bowen Yi (2015), "Volume and Direction of the Atlantic Slave Trade, 1650–1870: Estimates by Markov Chain Carlo Analysis," *Journal of World-Historical Information*, 2/3 (2), https://jwhi.pitt.edu/ojs/index.php/jwhi/article/view/31, accessed July 8, 2017.
Mapping the Republic of Letters, Stanford University, http://republicofletters.stanford.edu/, accessed July 8, 2017.
Marks, Robert (2006), *Tigers, Rice, Silk, and Silt: Environment and Economy in Late Imperial South China*, New York: Cambridge University Press.
Marks, Robert (2012), "The (Modern World) Since 1500," In *A Companion to Global Environmental History*, ed. John Robert McNeill and Erin Stewart Mauldin, 57–78, Hoboken, NJ: Wiley.
Marks, Robert (2017), "Explanations of Species Extinction in Nineteenth Century China and Europe," In *Encounters Old and New in World History: Essays Inspired by Jerry H. Bentley*, ed. Alan Karras and Laura J. Mitchell, 121–35, Honolulu, HI: University of Hawai'i Press.
Martin, Janet (1986), *Treasure of the Land of Darkness: The Fur Trade and Its Significance for Medieval Russia*, New York: Cambridge University Press.
Marzagalli, Silvia (1999), "The French Atlantic," *Itinerario*, 23 (2): 70–83, https://doi.org/10.1017/S0165115300024773.
Mason, Haydn T. (1999), "Voltaire, la guerre et le patriotisme," in *L'Armée au XVIIIe siècle (1715–1789)*, ed. Geneviève Goubier-Robert, 311–19, Aix-en-Provence: Publications de l'Université de Provence.

Matteson, Kieko (2012), "The Revival of Tradition in France's Forests," *Solutions Journal*, 3 (6): 69–75.
Matteson, Kieko (2015), *Forests in Revolutionary France: Conservation, Community, and Conflict 1669–1848*, New York: Cambridge University Press.
Mavidal, Jérôme, ed. (1890), *Archives parlementaires de 1787 à 1860. Première série, 1787 à 1799*, Paris: Dupont.
Maxwell, Kenneth (2004), *Conflicts and Conspiracies: Brazil and Portugal, 1750–1808*, London: Routledge.
Mazzaoui, Maureen Fennell (2009), "The First European Cotton Industry: Italy and Germany, 1100–1800," in *The Spinning World: A Global History of Cotton Textiles, 1200–1850*, ed. Giorgio Riello and Prasannan Parthasarathi, 63–87, Oxford: Oxford University Press.
McCabe, Ina Baghdiantz (1999), *The Shah's Silk for Europe's Silver: The Eurasian Trade of the Julfa Armenians in Safavid Iran and India, 1530–1750*, Philadelphia, PA: University of Pennsylvania Press.
McCann, James (2005), *Maize and Grace: Africa's Encounter with a New World Crop, 1500–2000*, Cambridge, MA: Harvard University Press.
McCusker, John J. (1989), *Rum and the American Revolution: The Rum Trade and the Balance of Payments of the Thirteen Continental Colonies*, Vol. 1, New York: Garland Publishing.
McDonnell, Michael (2012), "Facing Empire: Indigenous Histories in Comparative Perspective," in *The Atlantic World in the Antipodes: Effects and Transformations since the Eighteenth Century*, ed. Kate Fullager, 220–36, Newcastle upon Tyne: Cambridge Scholars Publishing.
McMahon, Darrin M. (2001), *Enemies of the Enlightenment: The French Counter-Enlightenment and the Making of Modernity*, New York: Oxford University Press.
McNeill, J.R. (1992), *The Mountains of the Mediterranean World*, New York: Cambridge University Press.
McNeill, J.R. (2010), "The State of the Field of Environmental History," *Annual Review of Environment and Resources*, 35 (1): 345–74.
McPhee, Peter (1999), *Revolution and Environment in Southern France, 1780–1830: Peasants, Lords, and Murder in the Corbières*, New York: Oxford University Press.
Melish, Joanne Pope (2001) "Emancipation and the Embodiment of 'Race'," in *A Centre of Wonders*, ed. Janet Moore Lindman and Michele Lise Tartar, 223–36, Ithaca, NY: Cornell University Press.
Mémoires secrets pour servir à l'histoire de la république des lettres en France depuis 1762 jusqu'à nos jours (1780–6), London: John Adamson.
Meuwese, Mark (2012), *Brothers in Arms, Partners in Trade: Dutch-Indigenous Alliances in the Atlantic World, 1595–1674*, Leiden: Brill.
Mikhail, Alan (2011), *Nature and Empire in Ottoman Egypt: An Environmental History*, New York: Cambridge University Press.
Miller, Christopher L. (2008), *The French Atlantic Triangle: Literature and Culture of the Slave Trade*, Durham, NC: Duke University Press.
Mirabeau, Honoré Gabriel Riqueti, comte de (1784), *Doutes sur la liberté de l'Escaut*, G. Faden.
Mirabeau, Honoré Gabriel Riqueti, comte de (1788), *Aux Bataves sur le Stathoudérat*.
Mitchell, Laura J. (2009), *Belongings: Property, Family, and Identity in Colonial South Africa. An Exploration of Frontiers c. 1725–1840*, New York: Columbia University Press.

Mitchell, Laura J. (2012), "Appraising Nature: Pastoralist Practice, Hunting Logics, and Landscape Ideology in Colonial Southern Africa," in *Landscape, Environment and Technology in Colonial and Post-Colonial Africa*, ed. Toyin Falola and Emily Brownell, 42–61, London: Routledge.

Mokyr, Joel (1981), "Irish History with the Potato," *Irish Economic and Social History*, 8: 8–29.

Montesquieu, Charles-Louis de Secondat, Baron de La Brède et de ([1748] 1900), *The Spirit of the Laws*, New York: Colonial Press.

Morgan, Edmund S. (2003), *American Slavery, American Freedom*, New York: W.W. Norton.

Morgan, Jennifer (2004), *Laboring Women: Reproduction and Gender in New World Slavery*, Philadelphia, PA: University of Pennsylvania Press.

Morgan, Philip D. (1991), "British Encounters with Africans and African-Americans, Circa 1600–1780," in *Strangers Within the Realm*, ed. Bernard Bailyn and Philip D. Morgan, 157–219, Chapel Hill, NC: University of North Carolina Press.

Morgan, Philip D.(2004), "The Poor: Slaves in Early America," in *Slavery in the Development of the Americas*, ed. David Eltis, Frank D. Lewis, and Kenneth L. Sokoloff, 288–323, Cambridge: Cambridge University Press.

Mowry, Melissa M. (2004), *The Bawdy Politic in Stuart England, 1660–1714: Political Pornography and Prostitution*, Aldershot: Ashgate.

Muldrew, Craig (2013), "Afterword: Mercantilism to Macroeconomics," in *Mercantilism Reimagined: Political Economy in Early Modern England and its Colonies*, ed. Philip J. Stern and Carl Wennerlind, 371–84, Oxford: Oxford University Press.

Muthu, Sankar (2003), *Enlightenment against Empire*, Princeton, NJ: Princeton University Press.

Mulryne, J.R., Helen Watanabe-O'Kelly, Margaret Shewring, Elizabeth Goldring, and Sarah Knight, eds (2004), *Europa Triumphans: Court and Civic Festivals in Early Modern Europe*, 2 vols, Aldershot: Ashgate.

Neal, Larry (1993), "The Dutch and English East India Companies Compared," in *The Rise of Merchant Empires: Long Distance Trade in the Early Modern World 1350–1750*, ed. James D. Tracy, 195–223, Cambridge: Cambridge University Press.

Nechtman, Tillman W. (2010), *Nabobs: Empire and Identity in Eighteenth-Century Britain*, Cambridge: Cambridge University Press.

Nolan, Cathal J. (2008), *Wars of the Age of Louis XIV, 1650–1715: An Encyclopedia of Global Warfare*, Westport, CT: Greenwood Press.

Nunn, Nathan and Nancy Qian (2011), "The Potato's Contribution to Population and Urbanization: Evidence from a Historical Experiment," *Quarterly Journal of Economics*, 126 (2): 593–650.

O'Neill, Daniel (2016), *Edmund Burke and the Conservative Logic of Empire*, Oakland, CA: University of California Press.

Ordonnance du roi, portant règlement pour le payement des troupes de Sa Majesté, pendant l'hiver. Du 20 Février 1757 (1757), Paris: L'Imprimerie Royale.

Outram, Dorinda (1995), *The Enlightenment*, Cambridge: Cambridge University Press.

Outram, Dorinda (2004), "Cross Cultural Encounters," in *The Enlightenment World*, ed. Martin Fitzpatrick, Peter Jones, Christa Knellwolf, and Iain McCalman, 551–67, London: Routledge.

Paesie, Ruud (2016), *Slavenopstand op de Neptunus: kroniek van een wanhoopsdaad*, Zutphen: Walburg Pers.

Pagden, Anthony (1995), *Lords of All the World: Ideologies of Empire in Spain, Britain and France c. 1500–c. 1800*, New Haven, CT: Yale University Press.

Palos, Joan Lluís and Magdalena S. Sánchez, eds (2016), *Early Modern Dynastic Marriages and Cultural Transfer*, London: Routledge.
Parker, Geoffrey (2008), "Crisis and Catastrophe: The Global Crisis of the Seventeenth Century Reconsidered," *American Historical Review*, 113 (4): 1053–79.
Parker, Geoffrey and Lesley M. Smith, eds (1997), *The General Crisis of the Seventeenth Century*, London: Routledge.
Parry, John Horace (1974), *Trade and Dominion: The European Overseas Empires in the Eighteenth Century*, London: Sphere Books.
Parthasarathi, Prasannan and Giorgio Riello, eds (2009), "Introduction: Cotton Textiles and Global History," in *The Spinning World: A Global History of Cotton Textiles, 1200–1850*, ed. Giorgio Riello and Prasannan Parthasarathi, 1–13, Oxford: Oxford University Press.
Peirce, Leslie (1993), *The Imperial Harem: Women and Sovereignty in the Ottoman Empire*, Berkeley, CA: University of California Press.
Perkins, Franklin (2004), *Leibniz and China: A Commerce of Light*, Cambridge: Cambridge University Press.
Phillips, Carla Rahn (2004), "Hard Times for the Tuna King: The Fisheries of the Duke of Medina Sidonia in 1728," *Mediterranean Studies*, 13: 121–45.
Phillips, Carla Rahn (2017), "Who Owns the Fish in the Sea? The Dukes of Medina Sidona and Spain's Tuna Fisheries," in *Encounters Old and New in World History: Essays Inspired by Jerry H. Bentley*, ed. Alan Karras and Laura J. Mitchell, 78–90, Honolulu, HI: University of Hawai'i Press.
Pocock, J.G.A. (1999), *Barbarism and Religion, Vol. 1: The Enlightenments of Edward Gibbon, 1737–64*, Cambridge: Cambridge University Press.
Polasky, Janet (2015), *Revolutions without Borders: The Call to Liberty in the Atlantic World*, New Haven, CT: Yale University Press.
Pomeranz, Kenneth (2000), *The Great Divergence: China, Europe, and the Making of the Modern World Economy*, Princeton, NJ: Princeton University Press.
Poska, Allyson (2016), *Gendered Crossings: Women and Migration in the Spanish Empire*, Albuquerque, NM: University of New Mexico Press.
Prakash, Om (2009), "The Dutch and the Indian Ocean Textile Trade," in *The Spinning World: A Global History of Cotton Textiles, 1200–1850*, ed. Giorgio Riello and Prasannan Parthasarathi, 145–60, Oxford: Oxford University Press.
Pratt, Mary Louise (1992), *Imperial Eyes: Travel Writing and Transculturation*, London: Routledge.
Rajan, S. Ravi (2006), *Modernizing Nature: Forestry and Imperial Eco-Development 1800–1950*, London: Clarendon Press.
Ramos, Donald (1976), "Social Revolution Frustrated: The Conspiracy of the Tailors in Bahia, 1798," *Luso-Brazilian Review*, 13 (1): 74–90.
Rapport, Michael (2000), *Nationality and Citizenship in Revolutionary France*, Oxford: Oxford University Press.
Raveux, Olivier (2009), "The Birth of a New European Industry: L'Indiennage in Seventeenth-Century Marseille," in *The Spinning World: A Global History of Cotton Textiles, 1200–1850*, ed. Giorgio Riello and Prasannan Parthasarathi, 291–306, Oxford: Oxford University Press.
Reitsma, Ella (2008), *Maria Sibylla Merian & Daughters: Women of Art and Science*, Amsterdam: Rembrandt House Museum.
Richards, John. F. (2003), *The Unending Frontier: An Environmental History of the Early Modern World*, Berkeley, CA: University of California Press.

Richardson, Brian W. (2010), *Longitude and Empire: How Captain Cook's Voyages Changed the World*, Vancouver, BC: UBC Press.
Roberts, Michael (1995), "The Military Revolution, 1560–1660," in *The Military Revolution Debate: Readings on the Military Transformation of Early Modern Europe*, ed. Clifford Rogers, 13–35, Boulder, CO: Westview Press.
Robertson, John (2005), *The Case for The Enlightenment: Scotland and Naples 1680–1760*, Cambridge: Cambridge University Press.
Roche, Daniel (1998), *France in the Enlightenment*, trans. Arthur Goldhammer, Cambridge, MA: Harvard University Press.
Roger, Jacques (1997), *Buffon*, trans. Sarah Bonnefoi, Ithaca, NY: Cornell University Press.
Romney, Susanah Shaw (2015), *New Netherland Connections: Intimate Networks and Atlantic Ties in Seventeenth Century America*, Chapel Hill, NC: University of North Carolina Press.
Rood, Daniel B. (2017), *The Reinvention of Atlantic Slavery: Technology, Labor, Race, and Capitalism in the Greater Caribbean*, New York: Oxford University Press.
Rossum, Matthias van and Jeannette Kamp (2016), "Leaving Work across the World: An Introduction," in *Desertion in the Early Modern World: A Comparative History*, ed. M. van Rossum and J. Kamp, 3–14, London: Bloomsbury.
Rothschild, Emma (2011), *The Inner Life of Empires: An Eighteenth-Century History*, Princeton, NJ: Princeton University Press.
Rousseau, Jean-Jacques ([1755] 1917), *A Lasting Peace through the Federation of Europe and The State of War*, trans. Charles Edwyn Vaughan, London: Constable.
Rupert, Linda Marguerite (2012), *Creolization and Contraband: Curaçao in the Early Modern Atlantic World*, Athens, GA: University of Georgia Press.
Ryan, Michael T. (1981), "Assimilating New Worlds in the Sixteenth and Seventeenth Centuries," *Comparative Studies in Society and History*, 23: 518–38.
Safier, Neil (2008), *Measuring the New World, Enlightenment Science and South America*, Chicago, IL: University of Chicago Press.
Sahlins, Peter (1994), "Fictions of a Catholic France: The Naturalization of Foreigners, 1685–1787," *Representations*, 47: 85–110.
Saint-Pierre, Charles-Irénée Castel de (1713), *Projet pour rendre la paix perpétuelle en Europe*, Utrecht: Schouten.
Savary, Jacques (1675), *Parfait négociant, ou Instuction generale pour ce qui regarde le commerce*, Paris: Louis Billaine.
Schama, Simon (1977), *Patriots and Liberators: Revolution in the Netherlands, 1780–1813*, New York: Knopf.
Schiebinger, Londa (2007), *Plants and Empire: Colonial Bioprospecting in the Atlantic World*, Cambridge, MA: Harvard University Press.
Schmidt, James (2003), "Inventing the Enlightenment: Anti-Jacobins, British Hegelians, and the Oxford English Dictionary," *Journal of the History of Ideas*, 64 (3): 421–43.
Schulze, Reinhard (1996), "Was ist die islamische Aufklärung?," *Die Welt des Islams*, New Series, 36 (3): 276–325.
Scott, J.S. (1996), "Crisscrossing Empire: Ships, Sailors, and Resistance in the Lesser Antilles in the Eighteenth Century," In *The Lesser Antilles in the Age of European Expansion*, ed. Stanley L. Engerman and Robert L. Paquette, 128–43, Gainesville, FL: University Press of Florida.
Semerdijan, Elyse (2016), *"Off the Straight Path": Illicit Sex, Law, and Community in Ottoman Aleppo*, Syracuse, NY: Syracuse University Press.

Sen, Sudipta (2002), *Distant Sovereignty: National Imperialism and the Origins of British India*, New York: Routledge.
Seth, Suman (forthcoming), *Difference and Disease*, Cambridge: Cambridge University Press.
Seth, Vanita (2010), *Europe's Indians*, Durham, NC: Duke University Press.
Sidbury, James (1997), "Saint Domingue in Virginia: Ideology, Local Meanings, and Resistance to Slavery, 1790–1800," *Journal of Southern History*, 63 (3): 531–52.
Sigal, Pete (2000), *From Moon Goddesses to Virgins: The Colonization of Yucatecan Maya Sexual Desire*, Austin, TX: University of Texas Press.
Skocpol, Theda and Meyer Kestnbaum (1990), "Mars Unshackled: The French Revolution in World-Historical Perspective," in *The French Revolution and the Birth of Modernity*, ed. Ferenc Fehér, 13–29, Berkeley, CA: University of California Press.
Sleeper-Smith, Susan (2001), *Indian Women and French Men: Rethinking Cultural Encounter in the Western Great Lakes*, Amherst, MA: University of Massachusetts Press.
Slezkine, Yuri (1994), *Arctic Mirrors: Russia and the Small Peoples of the North*, Ithaca, NY: Cornell University Press.
Smith, Adam (1776), *An Inquiry into the Nature and Causes of the Wealth of Nations*, London: T. Nelson & Sons.
Smith, S.D. (2003), "Gedney Clarke of Salem and Barbados: Transatlantic Super-Merchant," *New England Quarterly*, 76 (4): 499–549.
Smithies, Michael, ed. (1997), *The Siamese Memoirs of Count Claude de Forbin, 1685–1688*, Chiang Mai: Silkworm Books.
Snowman, Daniel (2010), *The Gilded Stage: A Social History of Opera*, New York: Atlantic Books.
Sobel, Dava (1998), *Longitude: The True Story of a Lone Genius Who Solved the Greatest Scientific Problem of His Time*, New York: Walker.
Somerset, Anne (2013), *Queen Anne: The Politics of Passion*, London: Knopf.
Sorkin, David (2011), *The Religious Enlightenment: Protestants, Jews, and Catholics from London to Vienna*, Princeton, NJ: Princeton University Press.
Spear, Jennifer M. (2003), "Colonial Intimacies: Legislating Sex in French Louisiana," *William and Mary Quarterly*, 60 (1): 75–98.
Stern, Philip (2012), *The Company-State: Corporate Sovereignty and the Early Modern Foundations of the British Empire in India*, Oxford: Oxford University Press.
Stern, Philip and Carl Wennerlind, eds (2013), *Mercantilism Reimagined: Political Economy in Early Modern England and Its Colonies*, Oxford: Oxford University Press.
Stevenson, John (2014), *Popular Disturbances in England, 1700–1832*, London: Routledge.
Stoler, Ann Laura (1995), *Race and the Education of Desire*, Durham, NC: Duke University Press.
Stone, Bailey (1994), *The Genesis of the French Revolution: A Global Historical Interpretation*, Cambridge: Cambridge University Press.
Subrahmanyam, Sanjay (1993), *The Portuguese Empire in Asia, 1500–1700: A Political and Economic History*, London: Longman.
Sunderland, Willard (2007), "Imperial Space: Territorial Thought and Practice in the Eighteenth Century," in *Russian Empire: Space, People, Power, 1700–1930*, ed. Jane Burbank, Mark Von Hagen, and A.V. Remnev, 33–66, Bloomington, IN: Indiana University Press.
Sutcliffe, Adam (2003), *Judaism and Enlightenment*, Cambridge: Cambridge University Press.

Sweet, Jeremy (1997), "The Iberian Roots of American Racist Thought," *William and Mary Quarterly*, 54 (1): 143–66.
Swingen, Abigail (2013), "Labor: Employment, Colonial Servitude, and Slavery in the Seventeenth-Century Atlantic," in *Mercantilism Reimagined: Political Economy in Early Modern England and its Colonies*, ed. Philip J. Stern and Carl Wennerlind, 46–73, Oxford: Oxford University Press.
Takeda, Junko (2011), *Between Crown and Commerce: Marseille and the Early Modern Mediterranean*, Baltimore, MD: Johns Hopkins University Press.
Takeda, Junko (2014), "Silk, Calico and Immigration in Marseille: French Mercantilism and the Early Modern Mediterranean," in Special Issue: *Merkantilismus: Wiederaufnahme einer Debatte*, ed. Moritz Isenmann, *Vierteljahrschrift für Sozial- und Wirtschaftsgeschichte*, 228 (3): 241–63.
Takeda, Junko (2015), "French Mercantilism and the Early Modern Mediterranean: A Case Study of Marseille's Silk Industry," in Special Issue: France and the Early Modern Mediterranean, *French History*, 29 (1): 12–17.
Takeda, Junko (2017), "'The Princesses' Representative' or Renegade Entrepreneur? Marie Petit, the Silk Trade, and Franco-Persian Diplomacy," in *Colonization, Piracy, and Trade in Early Modern Europe: The Roles of Powerful Women and Queens*, ed. Estelle Paranque, Nate Pobrasco, and Claire Jowitt, 141–66, Basingstoke: Palgrave Macmillan.
Taylor, Jean Gelman (2009), *The Social World of Batavia: European and Eurasian in Dutch Asia*, 2nd edn, Madison, WI: University of Wisconsin Press.
Te Brake, Wayne P. (1985), "Popular Politics and the Dutch Patriot Revolution," *Theory and Society*, 14: 199–222.
Thion, Stéphane (2008), *French Armies of the Thirty Years' War*, Auzille: LRT.
Thornton, John (2012), *A Cultural History of the Atlantic World, 1250–1820*, Cambridge: Cambridge University Press.
Thys-Senocak, Lucienne (2008), *Ottoman Women Builders*, Burlington, VT: Ashgate.
Todd, Denis (1995), *Imagining Monsters*, Chicago, IL: University of Chicago Press.
Tomlins, Christopher (2001), "Reconsidering Indentured Servitude: European Migration and the Early American Labor Force, 1600–1775," *Labor History*, 42 (1): 5–43.
Tozzi, Christopher (2016), *Nationalizing France's Army: Foreign, Black, and Jewish Troops in the French Military, 1715–1831*, Charlottesville, VA: University of Virginia Press.
Trivellato, Francesca (2009), *The Familiarity of Strangers: The Sephardic Diaspora, Livorno, and Cross-Cultural Trade in the Early Modern Period*, New Haven, CT: Yale University Press.
Trumbach, Randolph (1998), *Sex and the Gender Revolution, Vol. 1: Heterosexuality and the Third Gender in Enlightenment London*, Chicago, IL: University of Chicago Press.
Tucker, Judith (2000), *In the House of the Law: Gender and Islamic Law in Ottoman Syria and Palestine*, revised edn, Berkeley, CA: University of California Press.
Twinam, Ann (1999), *Public Lives, Private Secrets: Gender, Honor, Sexuality, and Illegitimacy in Colonial Spanish America*, Stanford, CA: Stanford University Press.
Usselinx, Willem (1622), *Anderde discours. By forma van messieve. Daer in kortelijck ende grondich verthoondt wort, de nootwendicheyt der Oost ende West Indische navigatie*.
Van Campen, Jan (2015), "The Hybrid World of Batavia," in *Asia in Amsterdam: The Culture of Luxury in the Golden Age*, ed. Karina Corrigan, Jan van Campen, and Femke Diercks, 40–122, New Haven, CT: Yale University Press.

Vaughan, Alden T. (1995), *Roots of American Racism*, New York: Oxford University Press.
Vink, Markus P.M. (2003), "'The World's Oldest Trade': Dutch Slavery and Slave Trade in the Indian Ocean in the Seventeenth Century," *Journal of World History*, 14 (2): 131–77.
Vink, Markus P.M. (2007), "Indian Ocean Studies and the 'New Thalassology'," *Journal of Global History*, 2 (1): 41–62.
Vitkus, Daniel J. (1997), "Turning Turk in Othello: The Conversion and Damnation of the Moor," *Shakespeare Quarterly*, 48 (2): 145–76.
Voltaire, François Marie Arouet de ([1759] 1969), *Candide and Other Tales*, trans. Tobias Smollett, Geneva: Heron Books.
Voltaire (1877–85), *Oeuvres complètes de Voltaire*, Paris: Garnier.
Voyages: The Transatlantic Slave Trade Database (n.d.), http://www.slavevoyages.org/assessment/estimates.
Wahrman, Dror (2004), *The Making of the Modern Self*, New Haven, CT: Yale University Press.
Walshaw, Jill (2012), "Counterfeiting in 18th-Century France: Political Rhetoric and Social Realities," in *Proceedings of the Western Society for French History*, Vol. 40, http://quod.lib.umich.edu/w/wsfh/0642292.0040.005?view=text;rgn=main.
Walthall, Anne, ed. (2008), *Servants of the Dynasty: Palace Women in World History*, Berkeley, CA: University of California Press.
Ward, Kerry (2009), *Networks of Empire: Forced Migration in the Dutch East India Company*, Cambridge: Cambridge University Press.
Weststeijn, Arthur (2012), "Republican Empire: Colonialism, Commerce and Corruption in the Dutch Golden Age," *Renaissance Studies*, 26 (4): 491–509.
Wheeler, Roxann (2000), *The Complexion of Race*, Philadelphia, PA: University of Philadelphia Press.
White, Sam (2011), *The Climate of Rebellion in the Early Modern Ottoman Empire*, New York: Cambridge University Press.
White, Sophie (2012), *Wild Frenchmen and Frenchified Indians: Material Culture and Race in Colonial Louisiana*, Philadelphia, PA: University of Pennsylvania Press.
Wiesner-Hanks, Merry E. (2010), *Christianity and Sexuality in the Early Modern World: Regulating Desire, Reforming Practice*, 2nd edn, London: Routledge.
Williams, Eric (1944), *Capitalism and Slavery*, Chapel Hill, NC: University of North Carolina Press.
Williams, Eric (1980), *Capitalism and Slavery*, New York: Pedigree.
Winn, Phillip (2010), "Slavery and Cultural Creativity in the Banda Islands," *Journal of Southeast Asian Studies*, 41 (3): 365–89.
Withers, Charles W.J. (2007), *Placing the Enlightenment: Thinking Geographically about the Age of Reason*, Chicago, IL: University of Chicago Press.
Wolf, John (1968), *Louis XIV*, New York: Norton.
Wrigley, R. (1997), "Transformations of a Revolutionary Emblem: The Liberty Cap in the French Revolution," *French History*, 11 (2): 131–69.
Ze'evi, Dror (2006), *Producing Desire: Changing Sexual Discourse in the Ottoman Middle East*, Berkeley, CA: University of California Press.

NOTES ON CONTRIBUTORS

Ian Coller is Associate Professor of History at the University of California, Irvine. His first book, *Arab France: Islam and the Making of Modern Europe, 1798–1831* (University of California Press, 2010), was the winner of the W.H. Hancock award of the Australian Historical Association. He is currently completing a new monograph on the French Revolution and Islam.

Karwan Fatah-Black is an Assistant Professor at the Institute for History, Leiden University. He is author of *White Lies and Black Markets: Evading Metropolitan Control in Colonial Suriname, 1650–1800* (Brill, 2015) and co-editor (with Catia Antunes) of *Explorations in History and Globalization* (Routledge, 2016).

Michael H. Fisher is the Emeritus Danforth Professor of History at Oberlin College, Oberlin, Ohio. He has published extensively about interactions between people from India and from Europe as they occurred in both India and Europe. His most recent books are *Short History of the Mughal Empire* (Tauris, 2015); *Migration: A World History* (Oxford University Press, 2013); and *The Inordinately Strange Life of Dyce Sombre: Victorian Anglo Indian M.P. and Chancery "Lunatic"* (Hurst and Oxford University Press, 2013).

Laura J. Mitchell teaches African and world history at the University of California, Irvine, where she strives to make sense of the early modern world in the digital age. Her book *Belongings: Property, Family and Identity in Colonial South Africa* (Columbia University Press, 2009) won the American Historical Association's Gutenberg-e Prize. She is co-author (with Ross E. Dunn) of *Panorama: A World History* (McGraw-Hill, 2014) and co-editor of a global primary source collection, an anthology of world historiography, and (with

Alan Karras) *Encounters Old and New in World History: Essays Inspired by Jerry H. Bentley* (University of Hawaii Press, 2017).

Vanita Seth is Associate Professor of Politics at the University of California, Santa Cruz. She is the author of *Europe's Indians: Producing Racial Difference, 1500–1900* (Duke University Press, 2010). Vanita is a co-editor of the *Journal of Postcolonial Studies* (2005–15), and now sits on its editorial board.

Abigail Swingen is Associate Professor of History at Texas Tech University. She is the author of *Competing Visions of Empire: Labor, Slavery, and the Origins of the British Atlantic Empire* (Yale University Press, 2015) and has published articles and book chapters on the role of unfree labor in forging the early British Empire. She has received external support from the Huntington Library, the Beinecke Library at Yale, and the NEH. Her latest project focuses on the politics of Britain's Financial Revolution and its implications in terms of empire and state formation.

Junko Takeda is Associate Professor of French History at Syracuse University. Her first book, *Between Crown and Commerce: Marseille and the Early Modern Mediterranean* (Johns Hopkins University Press, 2011), explores the political tradition of civic republicanism in the context of French international trade with the Ottoman empire. She is currently working on her second monograph, *The Other Persian Letters: France and Economic Globalization in the Age of Enlightenment*.

Christopher Tozzi is senior lecturer at Rensselaer Polytechnic Institute, Troy, New York. He is the author of *Nationalizing France's Army: Foreign, Black, and Jewish Troops in the French Military, 1715–1831* (University of Virginia Press, 2016). He is currently completing a manuscript titled "'Revolutionary until the Peace': War and Political Culture in Revolutionary France," which examines the relationship between war and political change during the French Revolution.

Merry E. Wiesner-Hanks is Distinguished Professor of History and Women's and Gender Studies at the University of Wisconsin–Milwaukee. She is the longtime senior editor of the *Sixteenth Century Journal*, editor of the *Journal of Global History*, and editor-in-chief of the nine-volume *Cambridge World History* (Cambridge University Press, 2015). She is an author or editor of more than thirty books and more than one hundred articles that have appeared in English, German, French, Italian, Spanish, Portuguese, Greek, Chinese, Turkish, and Korean. Her books include scholarly monographs, translations, thematic overviews, edited collections, textbooks, and source readers for the college classroom, and books for young adult and general readers. Her research has been supported by grants from the Fulbright and Guggenheim Foundations, among others.

INDEX

Abbas I, Shah (r.1587–1629) 53–4
abolition, of slavery 18, 20–1, 141, 180
absolute monarchs 30, 31, 33–4, 40–1
absolute power 7
Act of Abjuration (1581) 171
Adelman, Jeremy 18
Adolf Frederick of Sweden (r.1751–71) 125
Adolphus, Gustavus 26
African Company, British 106, 107, 108–9
African slave trade. *See* slavery
Age of Absolutism 25, 33–4
Age of Enlightenment 1, 8–12
Age of Exploration 45
Age of Revolution 5, 41–3, 170, 179–80, 181–2
agents, inciting rebellions 181
agricultural production
    Asia 74–5
    cultivation of new foods 77–8
    France 57–8
    plantation agriculture 16, 84–6
    potato cultivation 77–8
    rice cultivation 74–5
Alembert, Jean le Rond d' 36, 57
Alexei I of Russia (r.1645–76) 146
American Revolutionary War (1775–83) 8, 19–20, 28, 32, 59, 115, 133, 179, 181, 183
ancien régime 11
Angel, Philippe 52

Anne of Great Britain and Ireland (r.1702–14) 111, **146**
anti-imperialism 171
Antwerp, fall of 172
Apologie 171
Arbuthnot, John 191
Arcadio, Lionne 134–5
Armenians, New Julfan 52–5
armies
    aggregate contract armies 25
    of France 31–2, 34
    indigenous/native peoples in 176
    in inter-imperial conflicts 176
    Prussian army 38
    race, religion, culture in 30–3
    revolutionary 42–3
    slave 174
    Swedish 26
artisan production 120
artists 52
Asia, agricultural production 74–5
asiento de negros 18, 94, 95–8, 102, 106–7, 108–16
astrology, and difference 192
Aubert, Guillaume 193
Australia, transportation of criminals to 133
Austro-Turkish War (1788–91) 39

Bacon Rebellion (1676) 205
Bahia Conspiracy (1798) 183

Ballantyne, Tony 4
ballet 149–50, 151
Banda islands 85
Banks, Joseph 89
Barbados 104, 205
Bastille, fall of 11
Batavia 48–9
Bell, David 42
Belle, Dido 17
Bengal 76
Berbice slave revolt (1763) 169, 177, 183
Bermuda 205
Bernier, François 9
Bertin, Rose 151
bigamous unions 160
biological determinism 187
black free labor 199
black poor people, migrating to Africa 140
black soldiers, in France's army 32
Blackburn, Robin 203
blackness 190, 202
Blakely, Allison 189
bluefin tuna 81–3
Bonaparte, Napoleon 21, 116, 127
Boogaart, Ernst van den 190, 192
borderlands, and resistance 170, 174
Boston Massacre (1770) 58
Boston Tea Party (1773) 59
botanical gardens 88–9
Bougainville, Louis Antoine de 89
Braude, Benjamin 193–4
Brazil 96–7, 173–4, 175–6, 204
Breda, surrender of 27
Breen, T.H. 205
Britain and the British Empire
  African Company 106, 107, 108–9
  American colonization 99–102
  American Revolutionary War. See American Revolutionary War (1775–83)
  and corporate sovereignty 15–16
  East India Company 15–16, 21, 29, 58–9, 66–7, 161
  economic acceleration 78
  English Civil War (1642–51) 72
  food riots 72
  fossil fuel revolution 70
  and France 109, 111, 114–15
  Glorious Revolution (1688) 72, 146
  imperial policy of 104
  indentured servitude 103–4
  and intermarriage 163–4
  large-scale trade and the colonies 87
  London, black people in 189
  and the Netherlands 171–2
  political instability 72
  resistance against the empire 183
  Royal African Company 106, 107, 108, 111
  and slavery 103, 114–16, 202
  South Sea Company 109, 111, 113, 114
  and Spain 111–13, 171
  trade 58–60
  Virginia Company 103
Brouwer, Hendrik 176
Brown, Christopher 115
Buffon, Comte de. *See* Leclerc, Georges-Louis
Burbank, Jane 3, 143
Burke, Edmund 169, 180
Burke, Peter 153

cahiers de doléances 39–41
Calico Act (1700) 58, 60
canals 122
Candide 12–13, 14, 195
Capellen tot den Pol, Joan Derk van der 38
capital, trading of shares 15
capitalism, and slavery 18, 203, 205
Capitalism and Slavery 203
Caribbean islands 16, 83, 183 (*see also* names of individual islands)
Carlos II of Spain (1665–1700) 102
Cary, John 108
castas 158–9
Catherine I of Russia (r.1725–27) 146
Catherine II of Russia (The Great) (r.1762–96) 16, 125–7, 146, 156, 166
Catherine of Braganza 133
Chakrabarty, Dipesh 11
Chaplin, Joyce E. 193
Charles I of England (r.1625–49) 121
Charles II of England (r.1660–1685) 105–6, 121, 133
Charles II of Spain (r.1665–1700) 145
Charles V (r.1519–56) (Charles I in Spain), Emperor 14, 144–5
Charles VI (r.1711–40), Emperor 145

chattel slavery 16, 135 (*see also* slavery)
children
    child labor 62
    of slaves 165
    trafficking of 103
China
    Chinese Catholic converts 134–5
    and European scientific development 63–4
    extinction of animals 89–90
    and intermarriage 161–2
    Qing dynasty 4, 64
Christian discipline 164
Christianity, and whiteness 196
cities, and colonialism 129
civilizing process 11, 152–3
Clarke, Gedney 169, 177
class
    and the civilizing process 153
    disparities 205–6
    and luxury goods 16
    and mobility 119–20
    and race 192–3
    and self-restraint 152
    and sexuality 156
climate change
    Little Ice Age (LIA) 6, 71, 76, 86
    and long-distance trade 15, 71–2
    and Ottoman empire 76
Clive, Robert 67
Clusius 88
Code Marchand (1673) 56
Code Noir (1724) 18, 102, 206
coffeehouses 62–3
Colbert, Jean-Baptiste 37, 51, 56, 66, 81, 101, 121
colonialism/colonization (*see also* empire(s); imperialism)
    of Britain 99–102, 103
    and cities 129
    European 46
    of France 99–102
    and knowledge 87–8, 91
    social discipline/the sexual mixture in colonies 157–66
    social structure of colonies 158–9, 206
    transportation overseas 66
    and travel narratives 138
Columbian Exchange, and aftermaths 77–80, 88, 128–9

Committee for the Relief of the Black Poor 140
Compagnie des Indes 15, 57
Compagnie des Indes Occidentales 101
Compagnie des Indes Orientales 50
Compagnie du Cap Vert et du Sénégal 100
Compagnie du Guinée 102, 109
competition, between empires 174–9
conquistadors 83
consumer revolution 62–3
consumer society 151
consumerism 63–4, 120
convicts 85, 133, 204
Cook, James 9, 11, 89
Cooper, Frederick 3, 143
cooperation, inter-imperial 177–8
corn cultivation 78
corporate sovereignty 15–16
Corvisier, André 28
cosmopolitanism 49, 63
Costa, Emilia da 191–2
cotton manufacturing 60–1
crimes
    sexual 155
    and sin 153
criminal justice system 65–6
criminals, transportation of 66, 133, 204
"crisis of the European mind" 14
Crisis of the European Mind, The 9
Cromwell, Oliver 104
Crosby, Alfred 70, 79, 128
Crouch, Christian 29
Cuba 181
cultural history 2
culture(s)
    cultural identity of African slaves 136–7
    cultural power 147–52
    and Enlightenment warfare 43
    of mobility 46, 141
    and warfare 29, 30–3
Cumming, Thomas 84
Curaçao 97, 98, 114, 175, 180, 181
Cuvier, Georges 90

dance 149–50
Davis, David 192, 202
Declarations du Roy portant l'établissement d'une Compagnie pour le Commerce des Indes Orientales 56
Defoe, Daniel 111

deforestation 80, 84
Degler, Carl 202
Deng Qi'nan 89–90
deportations, forced 204 (*see also* transportation of criminals)
Dessalines, Jean-Jacques 116
Detaille, Edouard 24
Deverite, Louis-Alexandre 192
Dictionnaire de l'Académie française 57
Dictionnaire françois 36
Diderot, Denis 9, 36, 57, 192, 197
difference
    and astrology 192
    representation of 189–99
    and sexuality 143
diplomacy 50–1, 121
Diplomatic Revolution (1756) 147
Discours sur les révolutions de la surface du globe 90
diseases, and indigenous populations 79
diversity
    of the colonies 169–70
    demographic in armies 30, 31–2
    in Europe 189
    racial 18
Drake, Francis 171
Drescher, Seymour 203
dress, proper 151
Dutch empire (*see also* Netherlands)
    Dutch East India Company (VOC) 14–15, 48–50, 60, 85, 96, 122–3, 160, 176
    traders 16
    West India Company (WIC) 96–8, 114
Dutch Republic (*see also* Netherlands)
    Dutch Patriots' Revolt (1781–7) 37–9
    Dutch Revolt (1568–1648) 96, 171
    land reclamation 72
    political instability 72
    and water-borne transportation 122–3

Earle, Rebecca 190, 191, 192, 193
East India Company, English 15–16, 21, 29, 58–9, 66–7, 161
economic globalization 67
economic liberalism 57
economic power 46
economies, plantation 16
Edict of Nantes 121
Egypt 20–1, 76

Eighty Years' War (1568–1648) 72
Elias, Norbert 152–3, 192
elites
    colonial 183
    consumerism of 63–4
    from minority populations 53–4, 175
    and mobility 124–5
    and novels 138
    Russian 124–5
    and trade 56
    and warfare 36–7
    white European 159
Elizabeth I of England (r.1558–1603) 171
Elizabeth of Russia (r.1741–62) 146
Elliot, Henry 187
Eltis, David 96, 107
empire(s) (*see also* colonialism/colonization; imperialism; names of individual empires)
    defining 5–6
    and the Enlightenment 11, 12–16
    and the environment 69–70, 74, 80, 83, 90
    first and second 5
    and indigenous peoples 3–4
    informal 131
    inter-imperial cooperation 177–8
    maritime 167–8, 174
    merchant 14–15 (*see also* Dutch East India Company (VOC))
    and mobility 17, 117–19, 127–37
    and race 185
    and resistance 167–70, 184
    resistance in the competition between empires 174–9
    resistance in the origins of 170–4
    resistance in the transformation of 179–84
    rethinking 3–8
    and ships 129, 130–1, 139
    and smuggling 181–3
    territorial expansion 16
Enclosure movement 72
Encyclopédie, ou dictionnaire raisonné des sciences, des arts et des métiers 9, 36, 57, 192
engagés 99–100
English Civil War (1642–51) 72
Enlightenment
    Age of 1, 8–12

and empire 11, 12–16
geographical distinctiveness of 12
entrepreneurs 56–60
environment (*see also* natural worlds)
    changes to and slavery 83–4
    and the Columbian Exchange 78, 128–9
    deforestation 80, 84
    and empires 69–70, 74, 80, 83, 90
    environmentalism 89
    European environmental history 80–1
    extinction of animals 89–90
    overfishing 72, 82
    and record-keeping 90–1
Equiano, Olaudah 140–1
Esguerra, Jorge 191–2
Estado da India 47–8
Estates-General, France 39–41
ethnic identity 121
Europe, diversity in 189
Europeans, superiority of 153, 194–5
Exercitiegenootschap Sneek 29
Exploration, Age of 45

family, and reproduction of empires 17
famine, and climate change 71
Fan Shouyi, Louis/Luigi 135
farmer-citizens 60
Fénélon, François 36
Ferdinand, Charles William 38
Ferdinand III (r.1637–57), Emperor 121
Fields, Barbara 206
Finucane, Adrian 113
fiscales 160
fish resources/fishing 72, 81–3, 123
Fontenoy, battle of (1745) 23, *24*
food riots, England 72
forests 80, 81, 84
Fort Caroline massacre 34–5
Fort William Henry, siege of 29
fossil fuels 70, 73
Foucault, Michel 12, 152–3, 155
France and the French empire
    agricultural production 57–8
    American colonization 99–102
    army of 31–2, 34
    and Britain 109, 111, 114–15
    Compagnie des Indes 15, 57
    Compagnie des Indes Occidentales 101
    Compagnie des Indes Orientales 50
    Compagnie du Cap Vert et du Sénégal 100
    Compagnie du Guinée 102, 109
    and the Dutch Patriots' Revolt (1781–7) 37–9
    Estates-General 39–41
    fall of the Bastille 11
    Franco-Ottoman trade 51
    French Revolution 19–21, 37, 42–3, 116, 127–8, 180
    and intermarriage 162–3
    invasion of Egypt 20–1
    Marseille 16, 51, 53, 55, *61*, *64*
    navy of 32, 180
    Paris and fashion 151–2
    resource management 81
    and slavery 100–2, 114–15, 116, 180
    and Spain 102
    and trade 50–1, 56–8
France in the Enlightenment (*La France des lumières*) 9
Francisation 162–3
Frederick II of Prussia (the Great) (r.1740–86) 127
Frederick William I of Prussia (r.1713–40) 127
French Revolution 19–21, 37, 42–3, 116, 127–8, 180
Fronde rebellion (1648–53) 7
fur trade 86–7
Fyodor III of Russia (r.1676–82) 146

gender
    and mixed-race people **161**
    patterns of labor 62
    and travel narratives 138
George I of Great Britain and Ireland (r.1714–27) 146
Gilroy, Paul 199
Glacken, Clarence 190
global economy, premodern 54–5
globalization
    economic 67
    of politics and war 133
Glorious Revolution (1688) 72, **146**
Goens, Rijkloff von 161
Gordon, Robert Jacob 90
Graeff, Nicolaus de 49
Great Bengal Famine (1769–1773) 67
Great Confinement 153, 155

great divergence 3
Great Dying 79
Grillo, Domingo 106
Grove, Richard 70, 89
Guadeloupe 174, 180, 183
Guasco, Michael 204
Guiana coast 176
guilds, trade and craft 120
Guimard, Mademoiselle *149*
Guiomar, Jean-Yves 42

Habsburg, House of 14, 144–5
Haiti (Saint Domingue) 114, 169, 174, 180, 181–2, 205
    Haitian Revolution 21, 42, 116
Hannaford, Ivan 187
Harley, Robert 109–10
Harlot's Progress, A 154
Harrison, John 88
Hazard, Paul 9
Hellie, Richard 94
Henri IV of France (r.1589–1610) 25
hereditary dynasties, and sexuality 144–7
High Enlightenment 33
highwaymen 121
Histoire Naturelle 89
Hobbes, Thomas 7, 198
Hobsbawm, Eric 6
Hogarth, William 154
Hu Ruowang, John/Giovanni 135
Hugues, Victor 180
Hume, David 195
Hunter, G.K. 190, 196
hunting, commercial 86

Iberia, decline of 45
identity(ies)
    of African slaves 136–7
    ethnic identity 121
imperialism (*see also* colonialism/ colonization; empire(s))
    in the Americas 78–9
    anti-imperialism 171
    conquest and extraction 80–3
    European 47, 65, 131
    imperial policies 87, 104
    imperial power 14, 143
    and mobility 118
    and science 88–9
    state-led 56

imperium, western 4
indentured laborers 103–4, 133, 204–5
India
    and the East India Company 67
    India Act (1858) 67
    Indian cotton 58, 60–1, 131
    and intermarriage 161
Indian Ocean, trade 48
indigenous/native peoples
    in armies 176
    Australian aboriginal peoples 133
    and diseases 79
    elites and resistance 175
    and empires 3–4
    and intermarriage 162–3
    and the moral reformation 157
    noble savages 197
    and plantation agriculture 86
    and religious missions 160
    resistance of 175, 176–7
    and slavery 94, 100, 103, 204
    and warfare 29
industrial revolution, and slavery 18
industrialization 69, 70
industrious revolution 15
infanticide 154
information, codification of 91
Innes, Stephen 205
Inquisition 159
Interesting Narrative of the Life of Olaudah Equiano, or Gustavus Vassa, The African, Written by Himself, The 141
Invalides 27
Iran 53–4
Irish people 133, 192, 204, 205
Isaac, Benjamin 187
Islamic slave trade 203

Jamaica 105, 106, *107*, 113, 183
James II of England (r.1685–88) 105, 108, 146, 150–1
Jamestown colony 103
Janissaries 124
Japanese empire under the Shogunate (1600–1867) 131
Java 48
Jefferson, Thomas 60
Jewish people, Russia 126–7
joint-stock companies 15
Jordan, Winthrop 202

Kant, Immanuel 8, 33, 195
Karlowitz, treaty of (1699) 7
Kestnbaum, Meyer 39
Kidd, Colin 192, 194, 198
knowledge
    and colonization 87–8, 91
    European advantage in 139
Kowner, Rotem 196
Kwass, Michael 58

labor (*see also* slavery)
    child labor 62
    engagés 99–100
    entrepreneurs 56–60
    free and unfree labor 18, 93–4, 99–102, 199, 204
    free blacks 199
    gender patterns of 62
    indentured laborers 103–4, 133, 204–5
    labor shortages 100, 103–4, 119–20
    non-European servants 134
    poverty of laborers 66
    reproduction of 165
    serfdom 94, 120, 125
    servitude 66
    from servitude to slavery 103–8
    slave labour in plantations 84
    transportation of criminals 66, 133, 204
    of women 62
laissez-faire trade 57
land reclamation projects 72
land rights and uses 83
language
    control of 154–5
    and difference 195–6
    linguistic diversity 32
Latin America, births out of wedlock 160
Lauffer, Johan Rudolph 181
law(s) and legislation
    Act of Abjuration (1581) 171
    Calico Act (1700) 58, 60
    Code Marchand (1673) 56
    Code Noir (1724) 18, 102, 206
    environmental 81
    India Act (1858) 67
    Maryland law (1664) 206
    Navigation Acts (1651–1663) 58, 60
    and sexuality 156–7, 165
    Sharia law 165
    and slavery 18, 206

Tea Act (1773) 58–9
Townshend Acts (1767–8) 58–9
trade protectionism 58, 60
Leclerc, Georges-Louis 89, 191, 197, 198
Leibniz, Gottfried von 12–13, 14
Lemire, Beverly 52
Leopold I (r.1658–1705), Emperor 7
Levée en Masse 42, 127
Leviathan 7
Lieberman, Victor 74
Lindsay, John 17
Linnaeus, Carl 88–9
literacy, and race 139
literature
    autobiography 138
    novels 138–9
    travel narratives 137–8
Little Ice Age (LIA) 6, 71, 76, 86
Locke, John 198
London, black people in 189
Louis XIV of France (r.1643–1715) 7, 26, 37–9, 81, 101, 121, *144*, 148
Louis XVI of France (r.1774–91) 127
L'Overture, Toussaint 116, *178*
luxury goods 16, 61
Lynch, Thomas 106

maize cultivation 78
Malthus, Thomas 73
manners, reformations of 152–7
Maria Theresa of Austria (r.1740–80) 145
Marie-Antoinette 151
maritime activity, European 46
maritime mobility 122
maritime technology 88
Marks, Robert 74
marriage(s)
    bigamous unions 160
    intermarriage 145, 147, 159, 160–4
    marital strategies 144–7
    marriage market 151
    and mobility 125
    and power 155–6
    and religion 156, 159–60, 166
    and sexuality 154
    and status 166
    temporary 161–2
Marseille 16, 51, 53, 55, 61, 64
Martinique 99
Mary II of England (r.1689–94) 146

Maryland law (1664) 206
Maurice of Nassau (1585–1625) 25
Maurits, Johan 97
McDonnell, Michael 4
Medina Sidonia, dukes of 81–3
Mediterranean trade 51–2
menageries 89
merchants
    Armenian 52–5
    boutiques of 151
    Dutch East India Company (VOC)
        49–50
    and entrepreneurs and new vocabularies
        of political economy 55–60
    French 51–2
    Portuguese 47–8
Merian, Maria Sybilla 88
Michael I of Russia (r.1613–45) 146
migration
    European 131–3
    forced 127, 135–7
    Iberian to the Americas 129–30
    rural–urban 120
    women migrants 130, 161
Mikhail, Alain 76–7
military entrepreneurs 25
military expansionism 65
military revolution 8, 25–8
Minas Conspiracy (1788–9) 183
minority populations, and non-state trade
    networks 52–5
Mirabeau, Count of 38–9
missionaries, and morality 157
Mississippi Bubble 57
Mitchell, Laura 6
mobility
    and the accumulation of knowledge 139
    and class 119–20
    cultures of 46, 141
    and elites 124–5
    and empires 17, 117–19, 127–37
    intercontinental in overseas european
        empires 128–37
    intracontinental among empires within
        Europe 119–28
    and marriage 125
    and morality 164
    and politics 120–1
    and religion 131
    of slaves 124, 140

state-forced migrations 127
transportation of criminals 66, 133, 204
and warfare 120–1, 133
water-borne transportation 122
written expressions of cultures of
    mobility 137–41
modernity 137
modernization 69, 87
Mokyr, Joel 78
Molesworth, Hender 106
monarchy
    absolute monarchs 31, 33–4, 40–1
    the breakdown of universal 14
money, counterfeit 65–6
Monsiau, Nicolas 20
Montcalm, Marquis de 28
Montesquieu, baron of 36, 139, 190
Monteverdi, Claudio 149
Moors/Turks 189–90, 196
morality 152–7, 164
Morgan, Edmund 203
Morgan, Philip 189, 205
Moucheron, Balthazar de 173
Mughal empire (1526–1858) 76, 131
Murray, Elizabeth 17
Murray, William 17
music 150
Muslims 4–5, 127

nabobs 15
Narai, King of Siam 50
nation, concept of 56
nation-states 118
nationalism 37
natural history 88
natural worlds (*see also* environment)
    the biological old regime 71–7
    Columbian Exchanges and aftermaths
        77–80, 88, 128–9
    global redistribution of plants 78
    imperial heartlands transformed 80–3
    transformations abroad 83–7
navies, French 32, 180
Navigation Acts (1651–1663) 58, 60
navigational science 45–6
Neptunus 178
Netherlands (*see also* Dutch empire; Dutch
    Republic)
    and Brazil 175–6
    and Britain 171–2

Dutch Revolt 96, 171
and intermarriage 160-1, 163
and Portugal 96-8, 175-6
Prussian influence over 38
and slavery 96-8, 114
and Spain 171
networks
of early modern oceanic exchange 55-6
imperial 32
kinship 164
trading 8, 15, 16, 50, 52-5, 71
New Julfa 54
noble savages 197
North America, and intermarriage 163-4
Northern War (1700-21) 125

"Of national characters" 195
opera 148-9, 151
Orangists 38
Others
Africans as 96
dressing as 64
non-White subjects as 138
Ottoman empire 4-5, 50-1, 76, 93-4, 123-4, 129, 146-7, 165
Outram, Dorinda 8-9

Pale, the 126
paramilitary forces 65
Paris, and fashion 151-2
Paris, Treaty of (1763) 115, 133
Partenope 151
Pastorius, Francis Daniel 132
Pauw, Cornelius de 197, 198
Peace of Utrecht (1714) 168
Peace of Westphalia (1648) 74
peasants
and forest restrictions 81
peasant revolts 71
Penn, William 131, *132*
Pennsylvania 131
people trafficking 103, 204-5 (*see also* slavery)
Pernambuco 96-7
Persian Letters 9, 139
Peter III (1728-62, r.1762), Russian Emperor 125
Peter the Great (r.1682-1725), Russian Emperor 124-5
petite guerre 30

Philip V of Spain (r.1700-24 and 1724-46) 7, 102
Phillips, Carla 82
Philosophical Dictionary 34, 36
Philosophical Transactions 191
Phrygian (liberty) cap 180-1
Picart, Bernard 9-10
Pietersz, Jan 48
pieza de indias 111
piracy 65
Pitt, William 38
plantation agriculture 84-6
plantation economies 16
Plassey, battle of (1757) 67
Pocock, J.G.A 8
Poisson, Jeanne-Antoinette 148
Poivre, Pierre 90
policies, imperial 87, 104
politics
globalization of 133
of mercantilism 60
and mobility 120-1
political change and warfare 39-41
political economy, new vocabularies of 55-60
political instability 71-2
political power 46
political revolutions 63
sexual 144, 147-52
polygenesis 198
Pomeranz, Kenneth 3, 87
Pompadour, Madame de 148
poor people, deportation of 204
population decline 71, 79
population growth 62, 73-4, 78
Portugal 94, 96-8, 129, 160, 175-6, 202, 203
Postlethwayt, Malachy 15
Postma, Johannes 114
potato cultivation 77-8
power
absolute 7
cultural 147-52
of the Dutch East India Company (VOC) 14-15
economic 46
imperial 14, 143
and marriage 155-6
political 46
royal patronage 49

Russian imperial 4
and technical rationality 12
Pragmatic Sanction 145
printing presses 139
production
    agricultural. *See* agricultural production
    artisan 120
productivity, western 64
Proposals for Raising a New Company for Carrying on the Trades of Africa and the Spanish West-Indies 109
prostitution 155, 163
protectionism, trade 51, 56, 57, 58–9, 60, 61
Protestant reformation 14
Prussian army 38

Qianlong, Emperor 64
Qing dynasty 4

Race 187
race
    blackness 190, 202
    categorization of 158
    and the civilizing process 153
    and class 192–4
    and cultural signifiers 191
    and empire 185
    environmental explanations 190–1
    Iberian racism 203
    and literacy 139
    noble savages 197
    origins of 185–9
    and purity of blood 157, 165, 193
    racial diversity 18
    racial diversity in armies 31–2
    racial physiognomy 189, 191
    racial science 187, 207
    racism and capitalism 18
    racism and travel narratives 138
    racism defined 187
    and religion 192–4, 197–8
    representing difference 189–99
    skin color 158–9, 164, 192, 196
    and slavery 189, 199–207
    and wars and expulsions 121
record-keeping
    and the environment 90–1
    and reformations of manners and morals 153

reformation, Protestant 14
reformations of manners and morals 152–7
refugees, and resistance 173
regulation, of sexuality 206
religion
    and armies 30
    Chinese Catholic converts 134–5
    Christian discipline 164
    Christianity and whiteness 196
    and the Enlightenment 11
    and marriage 156, 159–60, 166
    and migration 130
    and mobility 131
    and morality 153
    Protestant reformation 14
    and race 192–4, 197–8
    religious persecution 189
    and resistance 173–4, 177
    and sexuality 164
    and wars and expulsions 121
"Religious Ceremonies and Customs of the World" 9
republican civic virtue 60
resistance
    and borderlands 170, 174
    in the competition between empires 174–9
    and empire 167–70
    history of 169
    of indigenous/native peoples 175, 176–7
    in the origins of empire 170–4
    and religion 173–4, 177
    by slaves 84, 116, 137, 205
    smuggling as 172–3, 184
    and social hierarchies 170
    to the Spanish empire 171, 179, 184
    in the transformation of empires 179–84
    to Western empires 184
resources
    contested 80–1
    natural 90
revolts 6, 71
    Dutch Patriots' Revolt (1781–7) 37–9
    Dutch Revolt (1568–1648) 96, 171
    slave revolts 84, 116, 169, 174, 177, 180–1, 183
Revolution, Age of 5, 170, 179–80, 181–2

revolutionaries, and republican civic
    virtue 60
revolutionary age
    the dawn of 19–21
    warfare in 41–3
revolutions, political 120–1
rice cultivation 74–5
Richards, John 70, 74, 86, 88
Richelet, César-Pierre 36
rights
    land rights and uses 83
    of people of color 18
rivers, and mobility 122
road building, and mobility 121
Roche, Daniel 2, 9
Roman *imperium* 4–5
Romanov dynasty (1613–1917) 124, 146
Rossetti, Joseph Gabriel 55
Rothschild, Emma 2
Rousseau, Isaac 52
Rousseau, Jean-Jacques 35, 197, 198
Royal African Company, British 106, 107, 108, 111
royal courts, cultural power and sexual politics in 147–52
royal patronage, and trade 49
Rushforth, Brett 100
Russian empire 4, 86–7, 94, 124–7

Saint Domingue (Haiti) 21, 42, 114, 116, 169, 174, 180, 181–2, 205
Saint-Pierre, Charles-Irénée Castel de 33, 35
Saratoga, battle of (1777) 28
Sasportas, Isaac 181
Savary, Jacques 57
Saxe, Maurice de 30
Schmidt, Benjamin 96
science
    European scientific development 63–4
    and imperialism 88–9
    navigational 45–6
    racial science 187, 207
seamen, mobility of 134
self-governance 63
self-representation, using print 137
self-restraint, and class 152
Selim III (r.1789–1807), Emperor 25
serfdom 94, 120, 125
servants, non-European 134

servitude 66, 103–8
Seth, Vanita 96
Seven Years War (1756–63) 8, 19–20, 28, 115, 133, 145
sexuality
    and class 156
    and control 143, 166
    extramarital sex 163
    hereditary dynasties 144–7
    and imperial power 143
    and marriage 154
    modern 166
    reformations of manners and morals 152–7
    regulation of 206
    and religion 164
    same-sex relations 155
    sexual politics 144, 147–52
    and slavery 164–5
    social discipline/the sexual mixture in colonies 157–66
shares, trading of 15
ships
    and empires 129, 130–1, 139
    and mobility 122
    and trade 46
Siberian peoples 87
Sierra Leone 140
silk trade 54–5, 61
silver, and slavery 94
sin, criminalization of 153
Skocpol, Theda 39
slavery
    abolition of 18, 20–1, 141, 180
    in the Americas 94
    asiento de negros 18, 94, 95–8, 102, 106–7, 108–16
    Atlantic slave trade 16, 65, 94, 96–8, 102, 104, 107, 108–9, 114–15, 135–6, 199–200
    and Bonaparte 21
    and Britain 103, 114–16, 202
    and capitalism 18, 203, 205
    and Caribbean islands 16, 183
    chattel slavery 16, 135
    and the Enlightenment 17–19
    and environmental changes 83–4
    and France 100–2, 114–15, 116, 180
    illegal slave trade 106, 107, 113
    increasing levels of 183

and indigenous/native peoples 94, 100, 103, 204
and inter-imperial cooperation 177–8
and intermarriage 163–4
Islamic slave trade 203
justifications for 195
mobility of slaves 124, 140
and the Netherlands 96–8, 114
people trafficking 103, 204–5
pieza de indias 111
and Portugal 94, 202, 203
and race/racism 189, 199–207
resistance of slaves 84, 116, 137, 205
and sexuality 164–5
slave revolts 84, 116, 169, 174, 177, 180–1, 183
and Spain 94, 95–8, 202
and United States 115
and violence 95–6
Slezkine, Yuri 86
Smith, Adam 59, 77
smuggling 65, 106, 170, 172–3, 181–3, 184
social discipline 153–5, 156, 157–66
social hierarchies, and resistance 170
social status 159 (*see also* class; elites)
social structure, of colonies 158–9, 206
Society for the Reformation of Manners, London 155
sodomy 155, 160
Sorkin, David 11
South Sea Company, British 109, 111, 113, 114
sovereignty, corporate 15–16
Spain
  and Britain 111–13, 171
  control of domestic resources 81–3
  and France 102
  and intermarriage 160
  and the Netherlands 171
  resistance to the Spanish empire 171, 179, 184
  and shipping 129
  and slavery 94, 95–8, 202
Spear, Jennifer 206
spice trade 15, 85
statecraft, and European oceanic trade 52
states, emergence of strong 7
Stern, Philip 15
Stoler, Ann 207

sugar production 16, 83–4, 100–2, 104, 115
Sultanate of Women, Ottoman empire 146
superiority, of Europeans 153, 194–5
Suriname 176
Swedish armies 26
Sweet, James 203
Swingen, Abigail 16

Tavernier, Jean-Baptiste 52
taxation, and warfare 26, 36–7, 40
Tea Act (1773) 58–9
technical rationality, and power 12
technologies
  Asian 46, 62
  maritime technology 88
  and mobility 122
  technological innovation 73
territorial disputes, and mobility 123–4
textile industries 55, 60–1, 62
theater 150, 151
Thirty Years' War (1618–48) 14, 26, 120
To the Netherlands People 38
tobacco trade 103
Toft, Mary 198–9
Townshend Acts (1767–8) 58–9
trade
  the Atlantic trade zone 62
  and Britain 58–60
  chartered companies 99
  in colonial goods 61–2
  the commercial revolution 151
  dark side of 65–7
  and elites 56
  European private overseas activity 52
  and France 50–1, 56–8
  free trade 56, 60, 114
  fur trade 86–7
  Indian Ocean 48
  and Japan 131
  laissez-faire trade 57
  long-distance trade and climate change 15, 71–2
  long-distance trans-oceanic 45–6, 52
  Mediterranean 51–2
  merchants, entrepreneurs, new vocabularies of political economy 55–60
  monopoly 108–9

non-state trade networks and minority populations 52–5
protectionism 51, 56, 57, 58–9, 60, 61
raw materials, commodities, the consumer revolution 60–5
and royal patronage 49
silk trade 54–5, 61
smuggling 65, 106, 170, 172–3, 181–3, 184
spice trade 15, 85
tobacco trade 103
trade and craft guilds 120
trade environments, diplomacy, politics of global exchange 47–52
trading companies 47–8, 105–7, 108–13, 130–1 (*see also* names of individual companies)
trading networks 8, 15, 16, 50, 52–5, 71
trans-imperial trade 45, 47, 52
and violence 47, 66
and water-borne transportation 122–3
transportation of criminals 66, 133, 204
travel narratives 137–8
Treaty of Karlowitz (1699) 7
Treaty of Paris (1763) 115, 133
Treaty of Utrecht (1713) 7, 111
Treaty of Westphalia (1648) 7, 121
Turhan Hatice Sultan (r.1651–1683) 146
Turks/Moors 189–90

unfree labor 18, 93–4, 204
Union of Utrecht (1579) 171
United States, and slavery 115
universal monarchy, breakdown of 14
universities 120
urbanization 69, 120, 129
Usselinx, Willem 173
Utrecht, Peace of (1714) 168
Utrecht, Treaty of (1713) 7, 111
Utrecht, Union of (1579) 171

Vaillant, François le 89
Vauban, Sébastien Le Prestre de 26–7
Velasquez, Diego 27
Velde, Hermanus van der 29
Venice, and the Ottoman empire 50–1
Versailles 7, 148
Vienna, Ottoman siege of 5, 7, 124

violence
  and slavery 95–6
  and trade 47, 66
Virginia 205
Virginia Company, British 103
Vitkus, Daniel 196
Volontaires de Saxe 31–2
Voltaire 12–13, 34, 35–6, 195

War of Jenkins' Ear (1739–48) 113
War of the Austrian Succession (1740–48) 113, 145
War of the Bavarian Succession (1778–9) 35, 145
War of the Spanish Succession (1701–14) 7, 102, 109, 145
Ward, Kerry 15
warfare (*see also* names of individual wars)
  in the age of revolutions 41–3
  aggregate contract armies 25
  colonial 28–9
  on colonial frontiers 28–30, 34–5
  conscription 42
  during the Enlightenment 23, 24–8
  Enlightenment attitudes towards 35–7
  existential 34, 42
  financing of 34
  France and the Dutch Patriots' Revolt (1781–7) 37–9
  globalization of 133
  and indigenous/native peoples 29
  military reform and the colonial frontier 28–30
  the military revolution 24–8
  and mobility 120–1, 133
  paramilitary forces 65
  and political change 39–41
  race, religion, culture in armies 30–3
  reasons for in the age of reason 33–5
  and taxation 26, 36–7, 40
  total war 42–3
  wars of independence 179
wealth, and marriage 151
West India Company (WIC), Dutch 96–8, 114
"Western Design" 105
Westphalia, Peace of (1648) 74
Westphalia, Treaty of (1648) 7, 121
Wetter, Rodolphe 55
"What is Enlightenment?" 12

Wheeler, Roxann 190, 191
White Over Black 202
White, Sam 76
whiteness 159, 196
Wiesner-Hanks, Merry 18
William III of England (William of Orange) (r.1689–1702) 146, 171
William V, Prince of Orange (r.1751–1806) 37–8
Williams, Eric 18, 115, 203
Winckelmann, Johann Joachim 191
Wolfe, James 28
women
    authors 139
    counterfeiting monies 66
    and the Enlightenment 11
    labor of 62
    migrants 130, 161
    non-European and European men 134
    prostitution 155, 163
    and sexuality 155
    and Sharia law 165
    slaves 124, 165
    traders 161
writers, non-European 139–40 (*see also* literature)
written expressions of cultures of mobility 137–41

Yorktown, battle of (1781) 28

Zahedieh, Nuala 106
Zong 17
Zumaya, Manuel de 151